FISH, CHIPS & FOOTBALL

FISH, CHIPS & FOOTBALL

A Season by the Seaside

Daniel Ford

First published in 2024 in the UK by Chase My Snail
www.chasemysnail.com
info@chasemysnail.com

Copyright © Daniel Ford 2024
Cover illustration: copyright © Abby Morrice 2024

The right of Daniel Ford to be identified as the Author of the Work has been asserted in accordance with the Copyright, Designs and Patents Act 1988

All rights reserved. No part of this book may be reproduced, stored in retrieval systems or transmitted in any form by any means without the written permission of the publisher

Editor: Anthony Ernest
Proofreader: Richard Nye
Cover illustrator: Abby Morrice
Cover designer: Darren Exell
Typesetting: Chase My Snail

A CIP catalogue of this book is available from the British Library

ISBN: 978-1-0685180-0-3

Printed and bound in Great Britain by Cloc Book Print, London

Contents

Acknowledgments 6
Introduction 7

1. Summertime and the Playin' is Easy 11
2. Dead Leaves and the Football Ground 47
3. When the Watchin' Gets Tough 107
4. We've (still) Got a Good Game Going 155
We've Got that Winning (and Losing) Feeling 207

Notes 221

Acknowledgments

To the team that helped me put this book together, my thanks to editor Anthony Ernest, cover illustrator Abby Morrice, cover designer Darren Exell, proofreader Richard Nye, Andrew Morris for IT support, and Euan Brindley for the 'next match' idea. For information included in this book, my thanks to football historian and photographer David Bauckham, Chris Berezai (GroundhopUK), Mike Brown (Mid Sussex Football League), Brian Chambers, Bill Norton, and Adam Smith (Parkfield), all the staff at Eastbourne Library, Stephen Edwards and James Reynolds (Men United East Sussex), Russell Eldridge (Little Common), Paul Garnell (Sovereign Saints), Simon Jasinski (Liss Athletic), veteran photographer Joe Knight (who sadly passed away as this book was being written), Richard Marsh (Eastbourne FA and Eastbourne Town), Karen Parsons (Eastbourne United Women's Recreational Team), Adam Smith (Hastings United), Brian Shacklock and Elliot Davey (Sussex County FA), Dave Shearing and Mackenzie Whitehouse (Eastbourne Town), Nick Stevenson (Eastbourne Rangers), Anthony Storey, Emma Storey, and Matt Thompson (Eastbourne United), and Barry Winter for tracking down a copy of his book, *Inside United* (2021), for me.

Although this book is a snapshot of a season and was never intended to be a definitive guide to the history of the clubs, any angry letters, e-mails, and thrown milkshakes (I like strawberry) concerning mistakes or omissions should be directed to me.

• *This book is dedicated to my mum, who always encouraged me to follow my passion and become a writer, and without whom I might still be carrying tiles up the scaffolding in the frost.*

Introduction

Just over a year ago I moved to a part of Eastbourne called the Lower Meads. The Meads is home, apparently, to a population that is the oldest in Britain, at an average of 71.1 years old.[1] I'm pleased to say that my arrival brought that average down a bit, although the lady I see on most days pushing her walker-cum-shopping trolley along the pavements bursting with tree roots that push through the block paving and tarmac, is certainly countering my attempts at demographic change.

Apart from seagulls, ice creams, and of course, fish and chips, Eastbourne — together with many of the surrounding towns and villages in the area — is known as a place where people go to retire. Do they even play football in a town full of pensioners?

Well, it turns out they do. In fact, it has a thriving football scene — and a rather good one. The area, as history reveals, actually has a tradition in the game that stretches back a fair way. More than 600 years in fact. Author Morris Marples[2] notes that, as early as the 15th century, the Sussex village of Selmeston was partial to a bit of medieval football. That's the version of the game where hordes of neighbouring villagers would gather to beat seven bells out of each other as they chased a pig's bladder. Lancing College, in the town where Sussex County FA is based, apparently devised its own code of football in 1856, while its Sussex-born former student, Jarvis Kenrick, knocked in the first ever goal in the FA Cup when he scored for Clapham Rovers against Upton Park on 11 November 1871. He went on to win three consecutive finals with Wanderers, scoring in two of them, and turned out for an England representative side against Scotland.[3] Not bad for a county that is rarely mentioned when it comes to football.

And things are still holding up rather well for the game in Eastbourne today. It has three senior clubs (a rarity for a town of this size): Eastbourne Borough in the National Conference South (tier six in the football pyramid), Eastbourne Town, now in the

Isthmian League South East (tier eight), and Eastbourne United in the Southern Combination Premier League (tier nine). Then, further down the ladder there is Eastbourne Athletic, Eastbourne Rangers, and Sovereign Saints in the Mid Sussex League, while two other Eastbourne-based sides, Jesters Town and Parkfield, play in the East Sussex League. There is also Men United East Sussex, as well as a string of other teams that turn out on Sunday mornings. That's the men's first teams. Add to these a good number of women's teams, and a fair mix of reserves, U23, U19, and U18 teams, as well, plus plenty of junior sides.

Spurred on by my discovery, I set out to chart a season by the seaside and to uncover the stories, the history, and the drama that unfolds at these clubs. This book is the story of 103 games along the coast — from Dover to Havant. It covers teams at all levels — from the shiny professionals in their stadiums to those who play on forgotten, muddy fields.

As you will discover, the lady I see battling the pavements of Eastbourne to get her bread each day clearly has lots of much younger great-grandchildren — and so do her friends. Always assuming, of course, she has time for friends after her tortuous journey to get her daily bread.

Daniel Ford, Eastbourne, England, September 2024.

Notes: *Fish, Chips & Football* has been written 'as live', so facts, figures, and observations relate to the time the matches were watched. I have not changed how I viewed things in hindsight, except to add in facts and correct the spelling of players' names etc. In cases where I could not confirm a player's name (sometimes spectators and even their own teammates did not know it), you will see 'the no. 6', 'the left midfielder', or similar. I have checked facts for anything I have been told, but in instances where confirmation wasn't possible, it should be clear that it's 'terrace gossip'. The Man of the Match (MOM) and Woman of the Match (WOM) choices are my own, although sometimes they are the same as the 'official' (ie, someone else's) choice.

Fish, Chips & Football

1
Summertime and the Playin' is Easy

Game 1: Saturday 8 July (3pm) at Priory Lane, Eastbourne
Eastbourne Borough 1 Aldershot Town 0 (Friendly)
Weather: warm and sunny
MOM: Triallist F (or was it G?)[1]

By a stroke of luck, my first outing of the new football season is a visit to Eastbourne by my own team, Aldershot Town. Although this doesn't really feel like the football season, to be honest. I am wearing shorts and flip-flops and the sun is shining (intermittently, this being the English summer). There are lots of Italian and Spanish students along the beachfront, each group seemingly unable to move forward unless they do so in a clump (a lesser-known collective noun for foreign-language students). It makes it very difficult to walk along the seafront in a straight line, although the mobility scooters, which are increasing in number as the summer takes hold, seem oblivious to the existence of the students, their drivers speeding through the clumps as fast as their little scooter batteries will allow. The seagulls take no notice of nationality or age and just circle endlessly waiting for the idiot who holds out an ice cream for a split second.

It's early July and the Champions League Final was played only 27 days ago. But football is now a year-round sport, and although its coverage in the media is squeezing my other love, cricket, out of the limelight, I decide to embrace this footballing moment in early July.

I have watched football in the sun many times — it was certainly shining bright during the games I saw in South Africa, Malawi, Zanzibar, Mauritius, Cyprus, Spain, and Argentina — but it always feels decidedly odd in England. I grew up watching matches where I could barely feel my feet and hands after ten minutes, or where I would get home drenched, only to be told by my mum to "get out of those wet clothes". That's how English football should be in the minds of older fans: a cup of Bovril at half-time, a burger of a quality you'd never contemplate eating anywhere else — and getting wet and cold. Psychologists might say the fans enjoy feeling this way, as though they are part of the action, sharing the pain and the joy with the players. Somehow, we reason, it was us standing in the cold and catching the flu that salvaged a point for our team last weekend. It's rubbish, of course, but at least believing we are helping our team makes us feel better about wasting another Saturday afternoon.

Priory Lane doesn't have any Bovril on sale as far as I can see, but it does have a hut selling beer. The solitary bar lady (there's not enough room for anyone else in the hut) smiles quizzically when I ask if I can take a photo. Then she smiles happily when I say it's the best bar I've ever seen. All bars are good, but the ones by the side of a football pitch are the best. Fans of the top teams can only dream of drinking beer while watching a match, while followers of non-league football know that this is the way it should be and happily sup their Long Man Helles Lager in plastic cups as errant shots whistle past their ears.

Aldershot are pretty dominant in the first half on the 3G pitch,[2] creating a lot of chances with no end result, only to find themselves 1–0 down after a goal by, er, "1–0 to Borough, but I'm not sure who got that one,"* the announcer rather honestly declares. The goal is a good one. After an excellent move up the wing, the overlap opens up some space for the pull back from out wide and it is finished nicely.

---

* The goal was scored by Borough's Triallist B.[3]

I've got my 1990s Aldershot shirt on (original, not retro, of course) and midway through the second half an Eastbourne fan standing next to me asks if many of the first team are playing.

"A few were in the first half but I don't recognise any of this lot," I tell him. "But then the team changes every year."

"Didn't think so," he replies, pointing to the team sheet, which just reads Triallist A, Triallist B, Triallist C, and so on.

One or two of the triallists might have come from the junior sections of Football League clubs, having failed to make the grade, but the bulk of them will be non-league hopefuls from clubs such as Braintree Town and Chelmsford City. At all but a few clubs, the majority of players at this level are given nine- to ten-month contracts so that the clubs don't have to pay them over the summer when they have little income coming in. The downside is that all of those players are out of contract at the end of the season. And so, for most non-league clubs, the pre-season becomes an annual merry-go-round of search-and-replace, as they try to find enough decent players to add to the assortment of youths already on their books. Triallist A, Triallist B, Triallist C, and so on. Occasionally, among the players that fans joke are being "signed on the bus" en route to the game, a club will stumble across a gem, as Aldershot did one year when they signed 18-year-old Adam Webster on loan from Portsmouth. Webster shone on his debut in the 1–1 draw at Grimsby in 2013 and went on to play for Brighton. Sadly, clubs like Aldershot will never hang on to players this good for very long.

Eastbourne Borough, however, are looking to get off the merry-go-round. They have a new owner and nearly everyone I meet in Eastbourne who likes football has heard that the club "has money and ambition". Optimism abounds that Borough may become the next Salford (without the ex-Manchester United players as owners). They may, of course, soar to similar heights. But don't hold your breath, because lower league football is now awash with clubs with money and ambition. The Vanarama National League, which Borough need to reach first before the giant step to League Two, is packed with former clubs from the Football League. This season, the National League includes Oldham Athletic (once of the Premier League), Chesterfield (FA Cup semi-finalists in 1997), as well as Football League stalwarts such as Southend United, Rochdale, and Hartlepool. Luton Town, now freshly back in the top tier of English football, wallowed in this league for five years before finding their way into League Two in 2014. Wrexham, now rejuvenated by Hollywood money, only returned to the Football League after a long 15-year absence. It's not an easy league to get out of; with only one automatic promotion place and another available through the play-offs.

The attendance today is a healthy 1,165, which perhaps shows that the attractions of the beach and pier are not for everyone. A lot of the spectators exit through the gate at half-time but there are no chants of "We can see you sneaking out". The clubhouse is outside the ground, so the gates are opened at the break and raffle-type tickets are handed to exiting supporters so they can re-enter later without being asked to pay again. Let the half-time beer drinking commence.

The second half passes with little action apart from a string of substitutions and a blond triallist from Aldershot eventually having a shot on target after much huffing and puffing upfront. The half is enlivened, for me, by meeting a couple of young lads from Pevensey Bay. One of them tells me he will be the referee for the upcoming Eastbourne Town friendly and suggests I come along and give him some friendly stick. That's a first.

• *For Eastbourne Borough's next match see Game 18 on page 50.*

Game 2: Tuesday 18 July (7.30pm) at the Saffrons, Eastbourne
Eastbourne Town 2 Hastings United 4 (Friendly)
Weather: dry and warmish
MOM: Delwin Duah. Displays composure under pressure and delivers some beautifully measured passes from the back

The game has already started when I arrive at the Saffrons, home ground of Eastbourne Town, even though I'm on time for the 7.30 kick-off.

"Oh, I think they decided to kick off early," I'm told by one of the other spectators as if this is a perfectly normal thing to happen.

There are a few people in replica football shirts and they are all Hastings United fans, a team that plays in the Isthmian League Premier, a couple of notches higher up the pyramid than Town. It's no surprise that United dominate the early proceedings and go 1–0 up with an early strike (scored by a triallist), then add another before conceding through an own goal. Some of the fans sporting the replica shirts are singing songs (of a sort). The Hastings ultras move down the other end of the ground in the second half so they can continue singing their songs from behind the goal their team is now attacking. They are improvising a lot, seemingly making up random chants as they pop into their heads.

It's not as difficult as it sounds. Most football chants are based on a few verses of well-known songs and tunes. Di-di-di-di-der-der etc (remember that one?). You can replace the original words from a song with any of your own as long as the syllables and cadence are roughly right and it (vaguely) sounds like it fits. If it doesn't quite work, just force a couple of syllables together or add in an "ooh" here and an "ah" there. Try it, it's fun.

One of the favourite tunes used by football fans is *Seven Nations Army* by the White Stripes. Di-di-di-di-der-der etc (now do you get it?). Nice and easy that one. Steady, melodic drumbeat, then just as the guitar kicks in… "We're the red and blue army, we're the red and blue army" (insert other colours to suit your chosen team). Other football chants are based on musicals (*You'll Never Walk Alone* is a tune from the Rodgers and Hammerstein musical *Carousel*); pop favourites (*Sailing*, made famous by Rod Stewart but first recorded by the Sutherland Brothers, is the basis for the Millwall fans' chant of "No one likes us and we don't care"); and even East End pub songs like *Knees up Mother Brown* ("You're no good, and you know you're not…").[4] Basically, any tune will do as long as it's easy enough to follow and you can replace the original words with your own.

I chat to Steve in the second half, the gateman who asked me if

I should pay full price (£5 tonight) or if I qualify for a concession (£3 for the oldies). I forgive him because he's a nice guy, although I was briefly tempted to lie and save a couple of quid by saying I was a few years older than I actually am. He fills me in on some of the players at Town — who have tried their luck at a higher level but have now returned. He also tells me that if I'm watching a lot of football at this level this season, then I am bound to hear rumours that some clubs pay players £500 a week thanks to the generosity of sponsors. Not bad for a part-time job.

He articulates what most fans at this level fear, as Hastings score another goal: getting promoted up the leagues too quickly can be a double-edged sword. The pyramid is wonderful because it allows clubs to move upwards, providing a route to the very top — at least in theory. But the reality is, clubs like Eastbourne Town and Hastings United aren't really going to storm through the divisions to the Premier League and win the Champions League unless something really remarkable happens. A miracle, perhaps. Going up rapidly, however, can kill clubs off completely. A brief moment of glory after a lucky play-off win means that ground improvements are needed, and new players (on higher wages) required — yet the crowds won't grow enough to sustain it all in the higher league. Things can quickly go wrong when this happens. Because while the pyramid system means clubs can move swiftly upwards it also means they can move swiftly downwards as well. The history of football is littered with tales of teams who have flown too close to the sun before their wings are ready.

Maidstone United are a case in point. The club spent their early years in the Kent League before joining the Southern League and rising to the top tier of non-league football (then called the Alliance League) in the 1970s, before finally reaching the Football League in 1989. But by then, they had sold their ground to a furniture retailer and were sharing with Dartford. Attendances fell by a thousand. By 1992 the club were in liquidation.[5]

In Scotland, the town of Gretna (close to the village of Gretna Green, where young lovers from England traditionally eloped to get married) had a club that reached the Scottish Cup Final in 2006, qualified for the UEFA Cup, and very briefly played in the Scottish Premier League. The rise and demise of Gretna FC was rapid. As a border club, they had been playing lower down the English pyramid, but in 2002 they were admitted to the Scottish League. After a couple of seasons in the Third Division, they shot upwards with three successive promotions and started the 2007–08 season in the top tier. But debts were mounting, and their owner fell ill, meaning he could no longer support them. They received a ten-point deduction for entering administration, finished bottom, and due to their financial problems were kicked back down to the Third Division. They swiftly resigned from the Scottish League altogether.[6]

How about that for a nice cheery topic to start the season? Meanwhile, Nathan Hover gets a second for Town, but tonight's game finishes in a 4-2 win for Hastings, which is not a bad result for Town considering how much their seaside neighbours have dominated the game. A chatty spectator tells me that a large chunk of the Hastings team is from London and that training sessions alternate between Hastings and London to accommodate this. As it happens, the Isthmian League club did indeed try this system of training a while back, but don't use it now.[7]

• *For Eastbourne Town's next match see Game 5 on page 22.*

Game 3: Thursday 27 July (7.30pm) at the Saffrons, Eastbourne
Eastbourne Town Women 2 Eastbourne United Women 4 (Friendly)
Weather: drizzly and a bit chilly for the summer
WOM: The Eastbourne United left winger. She shows off some classy dribbling skills. But best of all, she says sorry to an injured opponent who is lying on the floor before twisting around her and crossing the ball. Professional but polite

It's a bit of a miserable night in Eastbourne, with lots of wind and rain about. My sister is visiting, so I decide to treat her by taking her to watch football in the rain. She's wearing one of those long coats that are essentially duvets with a zip. I should remind you that it's July.

My sister likes football — not that she had much choice. Growing up with a football-loving brother, marrying a Manchester City fan and having three footballing sons has put paid to her own opinion on the matter. And as an inveterate organiser, she has thrown herself fully into the sport. Her house is littered with football kits from various teams; her number is on Amazon's speed dial for deliveries of football posts, nets, and corner posts; she has even been manager of a couple of junior teams in her village when no one else came forward to do the job.

Tonight, she is most impressed by the Eastbourne United winger, a slim and tricky operator. United are clearly the better team and the Town defenders are struggling early on. The winger is pretty good, gliding around the right full-back with ease and setting up chance after chance. It's no surprise when United take the lead with a header from her, although she had inexplicably passed it earlier on in the move when she was in on goal. Maybe she's just teasing the Town defence or tiring them out? The crowd of about 30 seems happy enough but the rain is getting me down, so I suggest a pint in the nearby clubhouse long before half-time.

At that moment, the tricky winger clashes with the Town right back and the defender goes down, writhing around and holding her leg. As she fires off some expletives aimed at her aggressor (although it is clearly an accident), the winger inexplicably stops on ball. "I'm sorry," she says. "Are you alright?" I look at my sister open-mouthed, but she just shrugs. "It's a girl thing." The winger, satisfied that her opponent is fine, dribbles around her and puts in a cross. I look at my sister again. I'm told to shut up, so I do.

Town's goalkeeper has been replaced by a smaller keeper because of an injury. The replacement is a good shot-stopper but her kicks are not going very far. It's putting even more pressure on the already stressed Town defence. I fear the score could mount. But at least the full-back who received the apology from the tricky winger has recovered and is running around again.

My sister's fledgling football career was cut short by some untoward advances in the showers after her first training session at a club near to where we grew up. I remember asking her how it went when she came home that night. "Alright", she replied. "But I'm not going again." She never did.

I'm a bit taken aback at learning the details of her experience for the first time tonight, so many years later, and start expressing some frank opinions. Once again, I'm told to shut up. Luckily the half-time goes as the rain gets heavier and we head for the clubhouse.

There are more people in the bar than watching the game, even though it costs nothing to get in to the football. Town somehow fight back a bit in the second half and overcome their replacement keeper's lack of kicking skills to avoid getting overrun, but United still win 4–2.
• *For Eastbourne Town Women's next match see Game 19 on page 51.*
• *For Eastbourne United Women's next match see Game 31 on page 70.*

Game 4: Saturday 29 July (3pm) at the Oval, Eastbourne
Eastbourne United 1 Haywards Heath 1 (Southern Combination Premier)
Weather: very windy
MOM: Callum Barlow. The big striker shows determination, a big voice, and (according to the dubious goals' panel) scores

I get off the Loop bus and ask a couple of locals if they know where Eastbourne United's ground is. They've just got off with full shopping bags, so I assume they are locals anyway.

"No idea," they say, shaking their heads.

It turns out that the ground, known as the Oval, is about 200 yards down the next road from the bus stop, albeit a bit hidden in a small side road between a row of houses. Each to their own, I suppose. Not everyone likes football. But it does seem strange that people who live so close to a senior football club don't know where the ground is. I'm not massively into opera, but I'm pretty sure I'd know if there was an opera house in the street next to mine.

It's eight quid to get in and I also buy a couple of strips of raffle tickets, even though the lady selling them has no idea what the prizes are. I never do hear the numbers read out, so I've probably got a bottle of wine sitting around waiting for me somewhere. Still, I do get a decent programme for free (nominally priced at two pounds) as part of the entrance charge, which is a bonus.

As the game's about to kick off, I ask a United fan how good Haywards Heath are.

"We'll find out in a minute," he answers philosophically. He hasn't got a clue, just like me, in other words.

The only guideline is what has gone before. Haywards Heath have just come down from the Isthmian League South East Division after being relegated via the inter-step play-offs.[8] United finished fourth in the Southern Combination Premier last season[9] so it should be an even game I reckon.

After the relatively relaxed pace of the friendlies I've watched so far, this game is frenetic, with players from both sides hustling and bustling as if it's a cup final. It only takes ten minutes for the first scuffle to break out. This is more like it; the lads have obviously been missing the action over the very short summer (the previous season only ended in April). The pitch is in good condition and is bevelled from the centre lengthways towards the touchlines, presumably to aid drainage (or maybe just by luck). But it's clear from pitchside that it's far from flat. The undulations, but more significantly the swirling wind, make the game appear even faster and more furious, and when shots are fired in, they seem to be sucked over the bar by the wind.

Inside the toilet there is a first for me. A brasslike plaque reads: 'The Richie Gunter Memorial Urinal'. It's hard to laugh when you are peeing but I still manage it. In the bar I'm told that it was put up as a bit of a joke and Gunter loves it (he's still very much alive and regularly comes to games I'm assured). Apparently he donated some money to renovate the urinals. How much, I wonder, do you need to contribute to have a urinal dedicated to you? I have always thought the Laurie Cunningham snack bar at Leyton Orient was the strangest footballing eponym I'd ever come across, but that dubious honour now passes to Richie Gunter. As it happens, the man himself walks in. Or at least I think it's him, judging from the reaction of the bar staff. As it turns out it is his brother-in-law. He runs me through some more details of the story. It's all true, he tells me, Gunter loves it.

Over on the far side of the bar, a group of people are enjoying sandwiches, cakes, and hot tea from a large metal teapot that looks as if it is ex-Army issue. I can't work out if they are the corporate hospitality group, the directors, or just some people who decided to bring their own snacks. I conclude that they are the match day sponsor enjoying the fruits of their donation to the club.

The first half was a stalemate, but I suspect that's only because Heath, who look the better side, were pegged back by the wind. And so it proves. With the gust behind them they are in full flow at the start of the second half, and it only takes a few minutes for the visitors to go 1-0 up with a headed goal from Max Blencowe.

"We are the Heath, we are the Heath, we… are the Heath!" their ultras behind the goal chant. These seem to be the only lyrics they have mastered. The group of ten — eight middle-aged men, a young one, and his girlfriend, who looks decidedly uncomfortable — occasionally try to sing something else, but it never takes hold. So they revert to what works.

"We are the Heath, we are the Heath, we… are the Heath!"

But the most interesting thing about the second half is a man in a blue sweatshirt who is standing about midway between the halfway line and the goal line. He is clearly a self-appointed assistant to the assistant referee and, by luck, there is a spell when the ball keeps going out near to where he is standing. Each time it goes out he points to the spot from where the throw should be taken (according to him), getting irate if the thrower creeps forward, and berating the assistant referee if he allows the player to steal a few inches. Strangely, when a throw is awarded to United he seems a bit less precise with his pointing. Luckily for all concerned, the ball moves away from his sphere of influence and he shows no interest in moving from his spot. Come the return fixture in November, the Heath ultras may have worked out a song for him.

Although I've now lost the entertainment of watching the self-appointed assistant to the assistant referee, the game has picked up and United are beginning to apply some pressure. The archetypal BMU (big man upfront) for United, Callum Barlow, has started dropping deeper, which is pulling some Heath players out of position and opening up spaces elsewhere. Then, from a corner, United equalise. There are so many bodies flying about in the box that nobody seems to know who has scored. The fans in my vicinity have various suggestions, but the most popular of them seems to be that the keeper punched it into his own net, so for now I'm going with that.

After the game I chat to some Carshalton fans who are down here on holiday. "We always come and watch a game when we are down here," they tell me, clearly lovers of Eastbourne holidays and lower league football. They follow Carshalton home and away and once travelled four and half hours to Lowestoft for an FA Cup match, they proudly tell me.

When they've gone, a young man in a tracksuit asks me if the other seats on my table are free. I recognise him as a United player, so I question him about who actually scored the equaliser.

"Callum Barlow," he tells me, and although the young boy with him agrees with my theory that the keeper punched it into his own net, I accept his explanation. "Callum Barlow headed it before the keeper's punch," he insists. So know you know. Maybe.

Later, on X, United announce that according to "the dubious goals' committee, the goal is Callum Barlow's".[10] So now you know for sure. Maybe.

That's one thing sort of settled at least. I never do meet Richie Gunter, legend of the urinal sign though.

• *For Eastbourne United's next match see Game 7 on page 28.*

Game 5: Tuesday 1 August (7.30pm) at the Saffrons, Eastbourne
Eastbourne Town 1 Crowborough Athletic 2 (Southern Combination Premier)
Weather: warmish with a bit of rain
MOM: Tom Boddy. The Crowborough captain's solid throughout and helps them grind out a well-deserved win

I arrive at the game thinking of Doctor Who. The real one: Tom

Baker. He lives/lived in Crowborough apparently.[11] The real Doctor Who is the one you grow up with as child; the others are mere pretenders. It's not even their Tardis, for goodness' sake. I watched in amazement as a child that the good Doctor had the skill to dodge those dastardly Daleks as they inched their way towards him at two miles per hour. Then I'd hide behind the sofa in case they shot out of the screen and got me instead. "They can't see you through the TV screen," my mum would reassure me. Little did she know that technology would change all of that in a few years. Anyway, at that age, all I knew was that those Daleks were out to get us all. Even at two miles per hour.

Crowborough, it seems, is a bit of a celebrity hangout, the nearby Ashdown Forest — where Winnie the Pooh and Christopher Robin roamed in AA Milne's imagination — clearly an attraction. As well as the good Doctor, Sir Arthur Conan Doyle, Dirk Bogarde, David Jason, and Cate Blanchett have also called Crowborough home at some time or another. The infamous KGB agent Kim Philby had a house there too. He would have been excellent at spying on the footballing opposition no doubt, but I suppose you'd constantly be worried that he'd go and sell your secrets to someone else.[12]

Despite all this celebrity stuff, however, I don't even know where Crowborough is. So I look it up on a map. It's Town's first home game of the season in the league and I feel as if I should do some proper research. It's a town of just over 20,000 people apparently, and the photos I see online make it look quite nice. I text my friend Peter, who once ran a pub there. "It has the highest pub in the South of England," he tells me. I look up the Blue Anchor pub, which at 790 feet above sea level is indeed fairly high for this part of the world, but maybe not the sort of place where you are likely to get snowed in for a week with only pub grub and cask ale for company — something which must be on the bucket list of many pub lovers.

On the pitch, Crowborough are looking good but it's raining again. I can't wait for the winter when it's cold as well. Eastbourne

Town are under pressure. The visitors should score early on, but the header is glanced wide from a neat pull back. Crowborough are playing it long and pressuring the full-backs but the Town defence holds firm, especially the long-legged Delwin Duah, who looks like a player that refuses to be rushed. It feels as if it only a matter of time before Crowborough will go ahead, but the closest they come is when the Town keeper, Chris Winterton, is forced to save low on the 40-minute mark.

There's plenty of scoring going on in the bar at half-time though, because the Hundred is on the TV. Southern Brave have just started their innings. The bar, which caters for the various sports teams that use the Saffrons, is quite rightly sticking to the correct sporting seasons when it comes to what they decide should be screened. And it's still cricket season, even if football is muscling in on its summer territory. Cricket is in full flow at the Saffrons tonight: players are practising in the nets behind the football pitch, the cricket committee are having a meeting, and as well as the Hundred on the TV, I spot an iPad showing the West Indies v India game.

Cricket has deep roots at the Saffrons. The first game was played here in 1884[13] (before the footballers arrived) and Sussex regularly used the ground until 2000 — playing a total of 226 first-class matches here. They returned to Eastbourne in 2017 for a one-day match.[14]

First-class cricket arrived at the ground in 1896 when South of England took on Australia here in a touring match, and six years later the Australians visited to play an England XI, with Hugh Trumble taking 14-84 for the visitors as they won by 131 runs. In 1928 the West Indians made a visit, with Kent player John Knott scoring 261 not out for Harlequins (Oxford),[15] while in 1973 Eastbourne hosted a Women's World Cup match between Young England and New Zealand. But the most famous match at the Saffrons came on 27 August 1921, when, according to *Wisden*, the Australians "narrowly missed setting a record that might have stood for all time". He may have been an ex-England captain, but Archie MacLaren was nearly 50 when he led his England XI out at Eastbourne. The amateur side, which included a string of Cambridge University players and only one current Test cricketer, hardly looked a threat to the all-conquering visitors. But despite being skittled out for a paltry 43 when they batted first, it was this team that ended Australia's dream of going unbeaten through their 38-game tour. England restricted Australia's first innings lead to 131 and bounced back with 326 in their second innings thanks to 153 from South African Aubrey Faulkner, who came in at number six with his side still trailing by 71. Clement Gibson (born in Argentina) then took six wickets as Australia crashed to an unlikely 28-run defeat.[16]

Back at the football, the second half starts in hurry, with Town scoring through Ollie Davies, the home side's George Cook getting sent off, Crowborough equalising through Harry Forster, and Town's Leon Greig getting sin binned.

The concept of a sin bin — a sort of 'naughty step' for a player who has done something wrong, according to sports writer Adam Hathaway[17] — comes from ice hockey, and dates back to at least the 1930s (it was mentioned in Canada's *Windsor Daily Star* in 1939).[18] Rugby league introduced the idea in Australia in 1981 and the first rugby union player to be binned was in 1997.[19] Football, ever fashionably late to the party, started trialling it in the lower leagues in the 2019–20 season. The Southern Combination is one of 31 leagues that are part of the experiment and early indications are that dissent towards referees has declined.[20] The threat of the sin bin clearly doesn't work with Greig, however, and he gets ten minutes to 'cool down'.

Despite the extra players, Crowborough only ram home the advantage fully with 15 minutes left, when Rory Slater strikes following a long ball forward. Exterminate. The renewed use of the long-ball tactic in the second half is a surprise after a prolonged spell of measured passing to create space by the visitors. Doctor Who's team celebrate their second win of the season, while Town still await their first point.

• *For Eastbourne Town's next match see Game 6 on page 26.*

Game 6: Saturday 5 August (3pm) at the Saffrons, Eastbourne
Eastbourne Town 1 Faversham Town 3 (FA Cup Extra-Preliminary Round)
Weather: raining with intermittent sunny spells
MOM: Warren Mfula. The Faversham winger is a class above everyone else and scores two goals

The FA Cup in August. Now that's a novelty for me. The FA rule is that beer is not allowed in the ground today. It all seems a bit silly and the spectators seem to agree, so the bar only empties at the very last minute before kick-off. When I head out for the start myself, I meet a small group gathered on the steps of the clubhouse. "The view's better here mate and you can watch with a beer," they say. I feel guilty about not putting £7 into the coffers of the lower league clubs (the gate money is split between the two clubs in the FA Cup less expenses) but I decide they have a good point and get another beer. I vow to blame the FA for my bad form.

I ask a Faversham fan which league they play in. "No idea," he replies wearily. "Some long name with lots of words in it. I watch them every week but I can't get the hang of the league names these days. Too long to remember." For the record, Faversham Town play in the Southern Counties East Football League Premier Division, which I must admit is a bit long-winded — especially compared to its previous name, the Kent League, which it was called until 2013.[21] The league is also ranked as tier nine on the football ladder, supposedly the same level as Eastbourne Town, but Faversham look more than a fair bit better than Town judging by the early exchanges I watch from the steps. Which are not really exchanges at all, but rather their no. 24 Warren Mfula ghosting past the Town defence at will.

"He's their record signing," I'm informed, and it's no surprise that Mfula scores the first and adds a second before half-time. Faversham have just got relegated from the Pitching In Isthmian South East Division (no wonder that fan gets confused about league names) and seem destined to get back into that six-worded league with players like him raging upfront.

But apart from Mfula, who really is a class act, the most dramatic thing about the first half is an injury to the linesman. The group on the steps had pointed him out to me earlier for the speed of his running. Or lack of it. Let's call it jogging. Maybe ambling. But eventually he does break into a run. It's the worst thing he could do because he's soon bent over double, not moving for a number of minutes. The laughter stops when everyone realises he's actually very ill. Talk starts to ripple around the ground about an ambulance being called. But luckily, he is able to walk off with some assistance, and thoughts on the steps turn back to the game.

The FA, in their wisdom, have decided that the world's oldest football tournament doesn't need fourth officials at this early stage. After all, what chance is there of an official getting injured in one of the 208 Extra-Preliminary Round games? You can imagine it now:

"We've got the FA Cup coming up chaps, what shall we do?"

"The FA Cup? That only starts in January."

"The early rounds. The little clubs who have absolutely no chance of getting anywhere. They've sent us their entrance fees (£75 this year).[22] Are we going to appoint fourth officials? This did used to be the jewel in our crown remember. Before we got involved with the Premier League." Choruses of Amen.

"Fourth officials? We can't afford that. Let's ban beer instead. We must be seen to be doing something."

"Agreed. Next issue on the agenda…"

So here we are. A crowd of over a hundred (plus a lot of us on the steps of the clubhouse), now wondering what will happen. Then a young man is plucked reluctantly from the crowd. He runs off to his car to get his boots and returns wearing an Eastbourne Town tracksuit to take charge of the flag. It turns out that he's the Town U18 manager, Ryan Reid, although the club's X account ignores this and calls him a 'replacement'. He does a fine job. Probably not paid either. Certainly not by the FA.

The clubs that win the FA Cup's Extra-Preliminary Round ties earn £1,125 in prize money, which I calculate is enough to pay Jordan Henderson's wages following his move to Al Ettifaq in Saudi Arabia, for 16 minutes. The losers' £375 would secure five minutes of sideways passing. Today, that'll be Town, by the look of things.[23]

Town do push a bit in the second half, but a long ball sees Josh Vincent get the ball in space and shoot off on a long run before setting up a third for Faversham. It's all over. Or so they think. Faversham ease up and the home side take advantage with Harvey Greig lashing one into the net for the goal of the match, albeit only a consolation. Concentrate on the league, anyone?
• *For Eastbourne Town's next match see Game 9 on page 32.*

Game 7: Saturday 12 August (3pm) at the Oval, Eastbourne
Eastbourne United 1 Shoreham 1 (Southern Combination Premier)
Weather: sunny(ish) but with a bit of wind and the threat of rain
MOM: Mason Creese. Plenty of threatening mazy dribbles

The cheeseburger from the United hot food bar is very good, with just the right amount of fried onions. I decide that I will hold a burger play-off involving burgers from the three senior Eastbourne clubs later in the year and appoint myself head judge. The burger must be the type that can only be bought at football grounds (where do they get them and why can't these burgers be found anywhere else?). My only complaint today is that the bottle of burger sauce is a bit low and it takes ages and multiple puffs and spurts to get enough out. This, of course, will be a key consideration when it comes to the burger play-offs. Football burgers need plenty of sauce, we all know that. But that's for later in the season. For now, it's hats off to the ladies who made this burger, and the bar staff for the excellent pint of Eastbourne United Pilsner which completes my culinary extravaganza.

Shoreham haven't got a point from their first couple of games, but they are causing United some trouble early on. United's number 10, is pushing back with his probing runs, however, so it's a big loss when he has to go off injured. "Who is he?" I ask a man with an official looking United top. "Gary Ingram," I am informed. "He can play in the nine or ten, but looks like he was playing off the nine today. Actually, more like the eight role." I must admit, I'm a bit lost. I blame Football Manager, the rather addictive game that football lovers immerse themselves in for hours and its endless positional permutations. What's wrong with centre forward, winger, and attacking midfielder?

I am, of course, being simplistic, but I do like the traditional positions. There are quite a few books on football tactics but the best of them all is Jonathan Wilson's iconic *Inverting the Pyramid*. Formations are, in fact, so important that Wilson says: "Football is not about players, or at least not just about players; it is about shape and about space, about the intelligent deployment of players, and their movement within that deployment."[24]

It could quite reasonably be referred to as the 'nerd's handbook' of tactics, it is that good. The author looks at formations used in key matches and their influence, but the best bit for me is seeing how formations have evolved. When football started, I think we can conclude that it was pretty attacking, with a lot of teams lining up in a 1-1-8 formation. You've got to feel sorry for the lonely chap at the back facing eight forwards. Remarkably the scores weren't too silly in those days because players would generally just dribble the ball until they lost it.[25] In fact, the first ever international match, played at Hamilton Crescent — a cricket ground in Partick, Glasgow — between England and Scotland in 1872, finished 0-0 despite the attacking intent. The dribblers (passing was considered unmanly) of England were in a 1-2-7 that day but Scotland were leading the way with tactics at the time and used 2-2-6 for their passing game. I'm not sure if the England players actually told their counterparts that passing was unmanly. Probably not.

The Scottish system developed into one of the longest-running formations ever used: the pyramid. The 2-3-5 line-up was being used as early as 1878[26] and it remained popular for nearly 50 years. At least now the lonely defender had a mate to chat to while the glory hunters were chasing the goals. Then the Italians and Hungarians started tinkering with this formation by using some players in more withdrawn roles, and by the time the glorious Hungarian teams had emerged in the 1950s — famously shocking England with a 6-3 win at Wembley in 1953, and following up with a 7-1 thrashing a year later — the formation had become a 3-2-1-4 (morphing into 3-2-3-2 when chasing possession). But what made the Hungarians so effective was their fluidity within the formation, as made clear by the notebook of their coach Gusztáv Sebes, in Wilson's book. The author concludes that their "system was a hair's-breadth from a 4-2-4".

The pyramid was followed by what most older football fans would probably consider to be the 'classic' formations: the 4-2-4 of Pele's Brazil, the 4-4-2 of England's 'wingless wonders' that secured the World Cup in 1966 (it was actually a 4-1-3-2 because Nobby Stiles played in a withdrawn role behind Bobby Charlton), and the 4-3-3 that catapulted Johan Cruyff and Ajax to the top of European football in the 1970s.

These, and variations of them with silly names like the Christmas Tree, the Diamond, and the Magic Rectangle, lasted for years. Then along came Football Manager. This remarkably popular game (FM24 has more than seven million players) is, of course, just reflecting what is happening on the pitch with its various permutations, but it's opened up the eyes of many fans to just what can be achieved with ten outfield players.[27]

Joshua Gould scores for Shoreham on the stroke of half-time, but the tide of the game turns in the second half. Callum Barlow is hustling upfront, George Olulode is solid as always, and the impressive youngster Mason Creese is embarking on some threatening mazy dribbles. It's one of his dribbles that creates the equaliser. And it is goal machine Barlow who whacks it home. Shoreham are all at sea for the rest of the game. Panicky sliced clearances, shirt pulling, and long balls are all called into action as they scrap for their first point. They get it. And I doubt if they care what formation they are using at the end.

• *For Eastbourne United next match see Game 11 on page 36.*

Game 8: Monday 14 August (7.30pm) at the Saffrons, Eastbourne
Eastbourne Town U18 2 Peacehaven & Telscombe U18 1 (FA Youth Cup Extra-Preliminary Round)
Weather: chilly but clear
MOM: Sonny Walsh. Numerous threatening runs and two goals

There are refs and there are, er, refs. Tonight there is an er, ref. Quite what he sees in a decent match that involves some exuberance and a few sliding tackles, but little else in terms of aggression, to dish out a string of yellow cards and two reds is a mystery. "Someone at the FA will be kept busy collecting fines this week," someone jokes on the terraces. Town players collect six yellows (a second yellow leads to a red for Ralf Burke), while Peacehaven notch four (they also get a red later). Cards are flashing up and down like a (fill in your favourite analogy) and even the usually rather genteel Eastbourne crowd — mostly mums, dads, little brothers and sisters, and friends — are shouting abuse at the referee after a while.

For a game that emerged from a 'sport' in which medieval villagers would beat each other up as they chased a ball, it's not surprising that rules were brought in to punish unruly players. And what worse punishment could there be than to deprive a footballer of playing football by sending him off while the other players continue to enjoy themselves?

Peru's Plácido Galindo has the dubious distinction of being the first player to be sent off in a World Cup finals match, when his country played Romania in a group match in 1930 in Uruguay.[28] Not many people saw it happen, mind you, because the match had the smallest attendance of any in finals history, officially 2,459 (although football historian Cris Freddi believes it was just 300).[29]

But it was an incident in a World Cup quarter-final 36 years later that would eventually lead to the idea of red and yellow cards. Ken Ashton, who was in charge of the referees during the 1966 finals, had to enter the field himself to try and sort out the chaos that followed the sending off of Argentina's Antonio Rattín against England. Language barriers between the South American, the German referee and Ashton only added to the confusion on the pitch.[30] Frustration for today's fans over VAR decisions has nothing on what the fans at Wembley would have been going through that day.

Some time later, while stopped at some traffic lights on Kensington High Street according to the BBC,[31] Ashton had the idea of using coloured cards in line with the traffic light system. Red was for 'off you go sonny' and yellow (presumably amber was a bit too similar to red) was for 'don't be a naughty boy again'. But it was Ashton's wife, Hilda, who brought the idea to life. Upon hearing of her husband's brainwave, she headed off and cut up two pieces of coloured card — one red and one yellow — that fitted into the pocket of his kit.[32] Thanks Hilda.

The cards (presumably not the actual ones Hilda cut up) were duly introduced for the World Cup finals in 1970. Although several yellow cards were shown (Francis Lee picked up two for England) a red was not flashed in the finals until 1974.[33] English domestic football only started using them in 1976, with Dave Wagstaffe receiving the first ever red card for Blackburn Rovers in the 36th minute of their match against Leyton Orient on 2 October. Thirty-one minutes later that afternoon, George Best also saw red for Fulham. The FA decided to discontinue the use of cards in 1981 because they feared that they were winding up fans at a time when the terraces already had their fair share of trouble. They were re-introduced for the 1987–88 season. Which at least is keeping one person happy tonight.

Town are clearly the better side and despite being a player down for a large chunk of the second half (P&T's sending off comes too late to make much difference), the two well-finished goals from Sonny Walsh are enough to see them to victory, despite an excellent late goal for the visitors, lashed home from inside the box by Kamron Edwards.

I spot the linesman who was running the line at Eastbourne United on Saturday and say hello. "I'm back here tomorrow for Varndeanians," he tells me. Funny that, so am I.

• *For Eastbourne Town U18's next match see Game 21 on page 54.*

Game 9: Tuesday 15 August (7.30pm) at the Saffrons, Eastbourne
Eastbourne Town 2 Varndeanians 1 (Southern Combination Premier)
Weather: warm
MOM: Evan Archibald. A striker who just runs and runs

Dave Shearing, the Eastbourne chairman, says "hello" and questions his keeper's new brown kit. "What happened to the Day-Glo one?" I ask. "I'm not sure brown will put off the strikers like the bright kit." I receive a nod of agreement. I was chatting to Shearing last night and he's obviously delighted to see someone who has returned after the evening's cardgate. The always nattily dressed Shearing has been chairman at Town since 2022–23 but he has a long history in local football, having managed Shinewater Association, Eastbourne United, Langney Wanderers, Rye Town, Hailsham Town, Bexhill United, St Francis, Worthing United, Steyning, Seaford Town, Wealden, and AFC Uckfield, as well as being Director of Football at Town, and chairman at both Bexhill United and AFC Uckfield.[34] His aim is for the club to get promoted to the Isthmian League this season and in the longer term to ensure they remain firmly established at that higher level.[35]

Varndeanians get a goal after ten minutes and the Eastbourne Town chairman groans. Tonight is supposed to be the night that Town pick up their first victory after four games without a win. The Isthmian League is looking a long way off at the moment.

The Corner Flag, the ground's burger and snack place, can be found, yes, you've guessed it, in a corner of the ground (between Eastbourne Bowls Club and the Sid Myall and Taffy Jones stand). Just outside it I meet a friendly Varndeanians fan who fills me in on the comings and goings of the local football scene. "Josh Gould who scored that free kick for Shoreham against United on Saturday played for Littlehampton in the Isthmian League the next day.[36] Different league, dual signing, so it's allowed. There was a lower-ranking cup final once when six players had played in the Isthmian League the day before. Although I still call that league the Ryman League," he tells me.

"So do I," I nod. The stationers (run by Theo Paphitis, formerly of *Dragons' Den*) sponsored the Isthmian League for 20 years from 1997[37] so it is difficult to shake such a long association from your head. "I'm new to the area so don't know much about the local scene yet," I tell the fan, hoping he'll give me a quick overview. He's a nice guy and fills me in a bit about various local clubs.

But it's the mention of Farnham Town that really perks up my ears. I trained with them as a 14 year old and although I made the bench for the reserves, I never got on because the manager said my dad would kill him if he sent me out "against those big lumps". When he left the club, I lost my lift to training, so my hopes of playing for them were thwarted. Farnham play in the Combined Counties League which, like the Southern Combination, is a feeder league to the Isthmian, but they made the national news earlier this year because, of all things, they decided to sell a particular soft drink at their matches for just £2.

Prime Hydration is a drink owned by Logan Paul and KSI, both of whom are in the fight game and social media influencers, and at the time the drink was hard to come by, with many supermarkets sold out of it. So, when the Surrey team declared they would sell it at their matches for its normal price — a corner shop in Wakefield claimed to be selling it for £100 a can — *The Sun* lauded Farnham Town for "some incredibly smart marketing". Which it was. The guests at one game were the Sidemen, who produce content for YouTube and have more than 138 million subscribers across their various channels.[38] The video of their visit to Farnham Town received 8.7 million hits.[39] Clever lads, clever club.

Varndeanians are apparently the only club that don't pay their players in this league.[40] And after a while it begins to show as Town start to get on top. In the 60th minute Ollie Davies comes on, and despite the enthusiasm of the announcer on the PA system, only a couple of people clap. I think it's a good substitution myself.

Evan Archibald, the veteran striker who is starting to cause the Varndeanians defence trouble with his runs, politely tells the linesman (the same one as yesterday) that "level is onside", in case he hasn't read up on the rule change. The linesman just smiles.

But Archibald's hard work and the realisation by the wingers that the keeper is looking a bit shaky against hard, whipped crosses, eventually leads to an equaliser. Fortunate is not the word, as a shot-cum-cross eventually makes its way, ever so slowly, across the line. The keeper is distraught and his confidence in tatters. In injury time, another mistake from the goalkeeper leads to a winner

being bundled in from Nathan Hover. A few spectators behind the goal begin to heckle the Brighton keeper as he holds his head in his hands and wishes it had been the ball. Who'd be a keeper?
• *For Eastbourne Town's next match see Game 12 on page 38.*

Game 10: Thursday 17 August (7.30pm) at the Saffrons, Eastbourne
Eastbourne Town U23 2 Bexhill United U23 0 (Southern Combination U23 East)
Weather: warm and clear
MOM: Tyler Pearson. Two well-taken goals

I'm sitting on the bus and waiting for it to leave so I can watch Eastbourne United U23 and decide to check X to kill time. United youngsters have already won apparently. That's a surprise because I haven't even seen the game yet. I've got the time wrong. By 24 hours. A victim of trying to follow multiple social media feeds and not paying enough attention.

Luckily, I see that Eastbourne Town U23 are at home tonight and not yesterday, so I jump off the bus having donated £2 to Stagecoach for a two-minute sit-down and walk up to the Saffrons instead.

This will be my third game in four days at the ground and I must admit I'm feeling a bit claustro-football-phobic being here again. The barman suggests I join the club. "You get a discount on drinks. You'll get the membership back in a week." Whatever could he mean? (If my mum is reading this, the membership is only £10, so it's not as bad as it sounds.)

Under-23 football has always baffled me since it became a thing. People of that age should be playing senior football. They are men already. When I finished school the only option was to join a men's team if I wanted to keep playing. As I was born in July, and thus a bit of a youngster for my year, it was only a few days after my 16th birthday when training for my 'men's' team began. Sink or swim. Granted, it might seem a bit severe in this day and age. But isn't it stretching it for the age groups to run up to under 23?

Competition rules generally state that a player must be under the age stipulated before the season or tournament starts to be eligible. This means players can turn 23 (or whatever the age group is), a couple of days after the competition starts but still be able to play. I saw James Milner play in the UEFA U21 Championships in Sweden in 2009 when he was 23 years and six months old. The rules stated that all players had to under 21 on 1 January 2008 (the year the qualifying rounds started). He was born on the 4th of that month. He wasn't even under 21 when England played their first qualifying match.[41] Not his fault, of course, and pretty handy for England in that tournament.

Milner made his debut for Leeds United in the Premier League when he was just 16 years ten months and six days old (in 2002). He'd made more than 200 top-flight appearances by the summer of 2009,[42] and just weeks after England U21 lost the final to Germany U21 in Sweden that year, he made his full debut for his country, so it would take some stretch of the imagination to consider him an up-and-coming young player.

Of course, anyone who is any good will be called up to the senior team regardless of age (Wayne Rooney and Michael Owen anyone?) while turning 35 hardly means an instant move to veterans' football, as Dino Zoff showed when he lifted the World Cup for Italy, aged 40, in 1982.[43]

Tonight, Bexhill initially look more composed on the ball, but Eastbourne are more threatening. Such is the paradox of football; looking good on the ball means nothing without goals. And so it proves. The home side score in the 66th minute when Tyler Pearson, the big striker, who is proving a handful, slots home after a great bit of skill on the right wing and a low, hard cross. He adds a second not long afterwards, also from up close.

• *For Eastbourne Town U23's next match see Game 27 on page 63.*

Game 11: Saturday 19 August (3pm) at the Oval, Eastbourne
Eastbourne United 3 Sheerwater United 0 (FA Cup Preliminary Round)
Weather: sunny
MOM: Hayden Beaconsfield. The lad can certainly cross a ball

There is thunder in the air, though the sun is shining bright and the weather is clear. Airbourne, the Eastbourne air show, is in town, so the sky is filled with planes twisting, turning, and making loud rumbling noises. It's been going on for days. The buses can't get down Marine Parade, the beachfront road, so I decide to walk to the United ground.

The road is particularly busy. Campervans are parked along the side and have set up for the weekend by the look of it, with food, deck chairs, and drinks to keep their owners in comfort as they watch the trails from the planes in the sky. Eastbourne's pebble beach is full of families watching from the seashore, many of them with tents to store their food and drink, and to provide some shade from the sun. The rest of the plane lovers clog the streets and stare upwards with mouths open, slowing my progress to the game. Don't they know that the FA Cup is in town?

After a quick pint in the Fishermens (a club that was formed in 1930), where the weekly meat raffle is delighting winning punters with legs of lamb and bags of sausages, I go to see what Sheerwater are like these days. I used to play against them many moons ago, but they have clearly progressed upwards since then. The FA Cup Preliminary Round may mean nothing to fans of Premier League clubs, but for the average park footballer it would be a dream to play in it.

It reminds me of the comment from Dutch coach Thomas Rongen in the highly acclaimed *Next Goal Wins*, a documentary which charted American Samoa's attempt to qualify for the 2014 World Cup. Hopes were not high; their 12 previous World Cup qualification matches resulted in 12 defeats, with just two goals scored and 129 conceded, including a 31–0 defeat to Australia in 2001. Undeterred, Rongen tells his team: "This is the World Cup. Do you know what that means? I would cut off a testicle to play in the World Cup."

The threat of losing a testicle must have motivated his team because under his guidance they beat Tonga 2–1 to end a run of 37 consecutive defeats spanning 28 years.[44] Still, Airbourne is nice too, I suppose.

United are too good for Sheerwater and Hayden Beaconsfield's crosses in particular are causing them problems. United's big defender, Alfie Headland, nods the home side ahead from one of Beaconsfield's crosses just before the break. And the youngster scores himself, direct from a corner, soon after the restart. Sheerwater threaten little but do have a penalty shout, which causes one of their fans with a notebook to go into meltdown when it's turned down.

"Disgrace, an absolute disgrace," he screams, as the referee books the player from Sheerwater for diving instead. Perhaps he is writing the match report because he at least walks down the touchline to ask people who had a better view what actually happened (he was about 60 yards away) before coming back to declare: "It was blatant dive apparently, so he deserved the booking." Shame and contrition? No. Not in the least.

Ed Ratcliffe's long-range effort which clips the post on its way into the net completes the victory. The dizzy heights of the 1st Qualifying Round for United it is then, and just one more win for them to be in the pot with their more illustrious neighbours Eastbourne Borough.

• *For Eastbourne United's next match see Game 16 on page 48.*

Game 12: Tuesday 22 August (7.30pm) at the Saffrons, Eastbourne
Eastbourne Town 3 Shoreham 0 (Sussex Royal Ulster Rifles Charity Cup 1st Round)
Weather: a clear and cool summer evening
MOM: Leon Greig. A constant menace down the right that Shoreham just can't deal with

Shoreham have just been promoted to the Southern Combination Premier and are looking to re-establish themselves there after three seasons in Division One. So far, they have only one point from four games in the league (against Eastbourne United), and defeat tonight would see them knocked out of the RUR Cup, so things aren't looking positive at the moment.

The RUR Cup (now known as the Sussex Principal Royal Ulster Rifles Charity Cup for sponsorship reason) certainly has history. The 1st Battalion of the Royal Irish Rifles (as they were called then) swept aside the other sides in the county in 1885–6 to win four trophies and be dubbed the 'Sussex champions'. The next year, the officers and men of the regiment presented a new cup to the Sussex FA as a memento of their achievement and that is what is played for today. It's a famous story and historic cup to win.

Eastbourne Town have lifted the RUR Cup six times, the first time in 1932–33, and most recently in 2014–15. They have also been runners-up five times. It's no more than you'd expect from a club that is 'the oldest senior football club in Sussex'.[45] And old they certainly are.

Under the headline of 'United Football Club', the *Eastbourne Chronicle* of 13 November 1880 reports: "This new club, which is the amalgamation of the Eastbourne Club and the Rovers, promises to have a prosperous season." You'll also be pleased to know that on the Wednesday prior (this would have been 10 November 1880) "…there was a goodly muster of members at the Gildridge Manor Ground, where a 'pick-up' match was engaged" as a trial. Even more promising was that (with a liberal use of commas) "…proceedings were, throughout, very enjoyable, the play, as a whole, being excellent".[46]

It's nice to know that some people were enjoying themselves back then because elsewhere things were grim. The newspaper reports "…that in one case a boy eight years old and in another, one of seven years old, were sent to gaol".[47] (For those whose archaic English is a bit rusty, the old word for jail[48] should not be confused with the idea that the youngsters were given gloves and asked to play between the posts at Gildridge Manor Ground.) Meanwhile, the newspaper reports that nearly 200 people attended the Eastbourne Total Abstinence Society meeting[49] (I bet they would be fun at an end-of-season party), and that the examiner at the children's workhouse "found no improvement from year to year in the efficiency of the school".[50] Note the euphemistic use of the word 'school'. It's a newspaper that almost makes the *Daily Mail* seem jolly.

But lest (sorry, this archaic language is addictive) I leave you with the impression that things were all doom and gloom back then, you'll be pleased to hear that fishermen Ball and Webster, who'd be presumed drowned while out fishing, had turned up safe and sound along the coast near Rye Harbour.[51] Hopefully with plenty of time to get back to Eastbourne for the abstinence meeting.

But back to the newly merged football club. The first fixture, announces the newspaper, would be played against Hastings and St Leonards at Eastbourne Cricket Club, followed by fixtures against Scarlet Runners, St Leonards Spartans, and St John's College, Hurst. Quite what sport they'd be playing, though, is a different matter because the next week the same newspaper reports that Eastbourne United FC beat the visitors "by two goals, four tries and two rouges to one goal three tries and two rouges"[52] and there were 15 players on each side.[53] Sounds remarkably like the version of football where players can pick the ball up to me.

But by time the Hurst game had come around it looks like they'd changed their minds about what sport they wanted to play (people were changing the rules of sports an awful lot in those days) because the United team won by "five goals to nil"[54] and the teams had 11 players each. They lined up in what would be considered at that time a 'Scotland-style' 2-2-6 formation,[55] with six United players from the Hastings and St Leonards game (which I think we can safely assume was a rugby match) also playing the game against Hurst (which, I think we can safely assume was a football match).

The United tag (nothing to do with the Eastbourne United we know today if you were wondering) lasted less than a year, before the name was changed to Eastbourne FC. This lasted two weeks before it was changed again — to Devonshire Park FC — in what must be one of the earliest instances of a sponsorship deal when a club that weren't a firm side were named after their sponsors. In return for the club using that name, the football club received match supplies and expenses for away games from the park company running the site which today hosts the Eastbourne International tennis tournament.[56] Red Bull Salzburg eat your heart out.

The football club's name was back to Eastbourne FC after a few years and they moved a few hundred yards up the road to the Saffrons. Although they were known as the 'Town club' for many years, they didn't actually take on the name of Eastbourne Town officially until the early 1970s.[57]

Leon Greig, as has been the case throughout the season so far, is Town's main threat. Just before the 20-minute mark, after a good run up the right, he sets up Evan Archibald who guides the ball home without breaking stride. The only other incident in the first half is a bit of a melee and some finger pointing. The new signing from Bexhill United, Tom Vickers, pulls up his shirt to show the referee some marks from a challenge he's just been on the end of, and a couple of bookings follow. Then everybody heads to the clubhouse to check out the TV and catch the latest score in the Hundred.

In the second half, another goal, a header by Nathan Hover, and then a third by Ollie Davies complete a fairly easy win for Town. It's their second victory on the trot, and after a rocky start, manager Jude McDonald has got their season well and truly underway. Welsh Fire win the Hundred match by the way.

• *For Eastbourne Town's next match see Game 13 on page 41.*

Game 13: Monday 28 August (11am) at the Little Common Recreation Ground
Little Common 1 Eastbourne Town 2 (Southern Combination Premier)
Weather: hot and sunny
MOM: Ollie Davies. Causes doubt in the defence from the very start of the game

As the train from Eastbourne approaches Cooden Beach, it passes some enviable properties overlooking the sea. It's a lovely place, although apart from the train station, it seems to consist of little more than a nice hotel, a golf club displaying 'private' signs, and a beauty parlour.

Sadly the Little Common ground is a 20-minute walk from here, mostly uphill. After passing through the pleasant village, I find Green Lane. The Common club are nicknamed the Green Lane Boys, which throws up all sorts of images — thanks to *Green Street*, the 2005 film about football hooligans who follow West Ham United.[58] The only person I come across in the lane is a lady pruning her rose bushes. She's dressed more for a wedding than gardening but politely points me in the direction of the 'Recreation Ground' with a wave of her secateurs. I don't mention the film for fear it will make her roses wilt.

Little Common is a great club with an excellent clubhouse (built in 2002)[59] and I am delighted to see a Common flag draped across the fence behind the goal. The flag features the badges of Chelsea and Glasgow Rangers, but it's in the blue and maroon colours of Little Common (which are also the colours of West Ham). The Little Common club were formed in 1966 by Ken Cherry, a keen advocate of youth football, as Albion United.[60] They initially ran U14 and U16 sides, but a senior side was born a few years later. They entered the Hastings League before moving to the East Sussex League and climbing to the Sussex County League. The club were renamed Little Common Albion in 1986.[61]

The manager of the first team is Russell Eldridge, the grandson of Ken and his wife Margaret. Eldridge, who had been playing Isthmian League football with Hastings United and Horsham, was in his late 20s when the opportunity to get involved with the club formed by his grandparents came along. He couldn't resist it. He took over as player-manager in November 2011,[62] so has been in charge for nearly 12 years — about 20 per cent of the club's existence. It's certainly dedication. Other family members, Daniel (chairman and secretary), Kim (treasurer), and Chris (committee member) are also involved, so it's obviously a club close to their hearts.[63] And for good reason. In 2013, Ken and Margaret Cherry were presented with commemorative medals for their dedication to Little Common by Prince William at Buckingham Palace as part of the FA's 150th anniversary celebrations.[64]

The Recreation Ground is a neat facility, with green fencing enclosing it, and two modular stands behind the goal at the clubhouse end, each seating 50 spectators. There are a few people sitting down today but it's way too nice to be in the shade, so most of us are lined up around the pitch enjoying the football and the sun. The club moved to the ground in 1974 and prior to the permanent fencing being erected, temporary fencing had to be put up to enclose the ground before every match. Then dismantled. It gives a new meaning to pop-up sports arenas.

Little Common gained promotion to the Southern Combination Premier at the end of 2016–17 but ground regulations meant they had to groundshare with Eastbourne United at the Oval for three and a bit seasons. However, the club were working hard to return home and a Football Foundation grant of £72,000 enabled them to erect the fencing, purchase the stands, and add paving to the southern part of the ground. They were able to return to at the Recreation Ground by the end of 2021.[65] The club had been supposed to play neighbours Bexhill United at home on 27 December, but the game was called off due to bad weather, so the next fixture was ironically an away match at the Oval against Eastbourne United, which they drew 1-1. The homecoming was finally sealed on 11 January 2022, when they lost 3-0 to Three Bridges in the Sussex Senior Challenge Cup in front of a crowd of over 200. Little Common finished tenth that season, their highest finish to date.

Bank Holiday football is always a treat, especially when there is a morning kick-off, although the Common left back probably wouldn't agree with me. He's having a torrid time facing winger Ollie Davies, who is patrolling the bottom end of the side-to-side sloping pitch. Davies is temporarily put out of action when a burly central defender blasts the ball into his face from close range with the most accurately placed ball of the game so far. But the winger has already done the damage and punctured the home side's belief, even if his own powers have been dimmed by a dose of concussion (he returns after a few minutes by the way). It's often said that one key moment in sport can determine a result. If so, today's moment is a protracted one: Davies's performance in the first 20 minutes.

Not long after the restart Town find themselves two up, thanks to goals from Tom Vickers and Evan Archibald (a penalty). The after-effects of being blasted in the face and the fact that he is now operating on the less used top part of the slope, mean Davies is not the main man in proceedings for either goal.

But Little Common are a tough and robust side and pull one back through Freddie Warren in a late onslaught. Town are having to battle hard to hang on, especially when they lose a defender to the sin bin. Only remarkable leg-stinging blocks and late tackles keep the score at 2–1, as the home side fall to their first defeat of the season after an impressive start of three wins and a draw in their first four games.

• *For Eastbourne Town's next match see Game 15 on page 47.*

Game 14: Tuesday 29 August (7.45pm) at Priory Lane, Eastbourne
Eastbourne Borough U18 1 Burgess Hill U18 3 (Isthmian Youth League Cup 2nd Round)
Weather: drizzly and none too pleasant
MOM: Damien Theodore. Hits Hill's equaliser with a nice strike and leads the comeback

I chat to a man in a bright yellow top about becoming a steward at Borough. The idea of getting paid to watch football and tell paying spectators to move back from the painted area in a loud voice has always appealed to me. But it's raining, so before learning more about the job, I go and sit in the stand where most of the other spectators are already huddled. Some of them are clasping cups of tea in both hands to warm up, which really is a bit odd at the end of August.

The rain on the 3G pitch is glistening thanks to the power of the floodlights and the surface is playing very fast, with the ball zipping around. Add to this 22 young players with boundless amounts of energy and you get a match on turbo speed. Up down, up down; it's a game that is hard to keep up with. Borough score the first, somewhat against the run of play when Tyler Wood blasts the ball home after 25 minutes. The crowd of 86 — mums, dads, sisters, brothers, and friends — leap from their seats, dreaming of an exciting Isthmian League Cup run.

But the Burgess Hill players have clearly not heard that Borough are now a club going places and by half-time the score is 2-1 to the visitors. The first goal from Damien Theodore goes in via a deflection but it's a cracking shot nonetheless, and this is quickly followed by another goal from Joseph George Overy. After a late third goal by substitute Daniel Burbulis to wrap up things for Burgess Hill in the second half, not even the most hard-nosed Borough fans (or mums and dads) would claim that the scoreline is an unfair reflection of the game.

I have to leave a few minutes early to get the bus (or hang around for two hours), but as it's still raining I don't feel so bad. In any case, the Borough fans have already postponed their League Cup dreams for another season.

• *For Eastbourne Borough U18's season summary see page 209.*

2
Dead Leaves and the Football Ground

Game 15: Friday 1 September (7.30pm) at the Saffrons, Eastbourne
Eastbourne Town 2 Bexhill United 0 (Southern Combination Premier)
Weather: a pleasant summer(ish) evening
MOM: Evan Archibald. Two good finishes to seal a routine victory

Eastbourne Town have had what managers would call "a difficult start to the season". A draw and two defeats in the league, with an early exit from the FA Cup wedged in between can certainly be described as 'difficult'. But since then there have been two league wins on the bounce plus a victory in the RUR Cup. Tonight makes it four wins in a row, with both goals from Evan Archibald, the first after great work from Ollie Davies out wide on the stroke of half-time and the second a looping header just after the break. The Pirates are well and truly sunk and never really look like getting back into the game.

Tonight is #FloodlightFriday and social media is all abuzz with people announcing which games they are off to. I meet an Indian student who is studying in Eastbourne and he tells me he has been training with the U23 side. He's come to watch the game, though I'm not sure he has heard of the hashtag buzz. He just wants to watch a match. As it seems, do a lot of other people. The crowd is considerably larger than usual — the local derby, nice weather, and the Friday evening kick-off all contributing no doubt.

It's normally fairly easy to work out (roughly) how many people are watching a match at Town because spectators usually stand in little groups of four to six with a nice space between each group.

But tonight the clusters have merged into each other and it's difficult to count. I discover later that the attendance is a healthy 305, about double the usual turnout. "Can we play you every week? And preferably on a warm, Friday night", the chairman is sure to be singing when he checks the takings later.

• *For Eastbourne Town's next match, see Game 17 on page 49.*

Game 16: Saturday 2 September (3pm) at the Oval, Eastbourne
Eastbourne United 2 Epsom & Ewell 1 (FA Cup 1st Qualifying Round)
Weather: hot
MOM: Callum Barlow. A cracking goal (so I'm told) and a huge determination to win the ball and set up the winner

I miss the opening goal after taking too long to finish my half-time pint, so I ask a couple I am sitting next to in the main stand who has scored. "Was it Callum Barlow by any chance?" It's a fair guess as he's Eastbourne United's leading scorer and seems to be on target every game

"It was," they tell me. "He's our grandson." Luckily, I have also remarked that he is very good player. It's never nice to upset a grandmother. And he *is* a good player: strong, battling for every ball, not greedy if others are on for a chance at goal, but a player who knows how to find the back of the net if an opportunity comes his way. He's scored six — seven if you believe the dubious goals' panel in the first game — already this season.

We swap stories about how nice it is to live in Eastbourne and where we lived before. Everyone I meet seems to have a story about where they are from. Is anyone actually from Eastbourne originally? But just as we are looking forward to a cup victory, Epsom & Ewell equalise. They've been clawing their way back into the game with sheer guts and effort and it eventually pays off. I exchange disappointed glances with the grandparents. Maybe it's not meant to be.

United have got close to making the 1st Round proper of the FA Cup on two occasions: in 1966–67 and 1978–79, when they lost to Sutton United and Gravesend & Northfleet respectively.

They also reached the 3rd Qualifying Round in 1958–59, 1961–62, and 1968–69 (when they lost to Eastbourne Town).[1] However, in their current incarnation (after merging with Shinewater Association in 2003),[2] the club have never reached the 2nd Qualifying Round, so it would be some achievement to go into the hat with the National League North and South clubs, including their neighbours Eastbourne Borough.

As the game ticks towards extra time, United launch a ball towards the burger van corner (that's almost certainly not its official name). It looks like an easy win for the Epsom & Ewell defender. But Barlow has other ideas and his grandparents urge him on with the rest of us. Somehow, he wriggles the ball free from the defenders and sets up an opening. In a crowded box Hayden Beaconsfield is able to slam it home. Maybe it *is* meant to be, after all.

• *For Eastbourne United's next match, see Game 25 on page 60.*

Game 17: Tuesday 5 September (7.30pm) at the Saffrons, Eastbourne
Eastbourne Town 3 Saltdean United 0 (Southern Combination Premier)
Weather: sunny (early on), warm and dry
MOM: Ollie Davies. Owns the right side of the field tonight and is having a great season

At the game I meet Joe and John, who run Students of the Game, probably the best football shop I have ever visited. The shop is in a rather smart part of town near the Saffrons, where Eastbourne Town play, and has an amazing selection of framed programmes and football shirts. Have you ever come across a Sierra Leone shirt for sale in England?

But it is the genius idea of setting Subbuteo men in a box frame (choose your team's colours) that does it for me. Everyone of a certain age knows Subbuteo is the greatest football game ever invented. Probably better than the real thing sometimes. So, while I no longer 'flick to kick' (although I'm up for a game if anyone has a set), merely seeing the little painted players is enough to let the nostalgia from my childhood run free. The village I grew up in even had a Subbuteo league, modelled on the story of Mike's Mini Men — a cartoon strip from the *Roy of the Rovers* comic, of course — and we took it all a bit too seriously. But that's enough about my 40s.

Unfortunately for the Saltdean fans it's *their* players who are wobbling around on their bases tonight, and the Town players stroll around them all too easily during the match. Saltdean are struggling this year and have yet to get a point after the first four games. They show little signs of doing so here. Tom Vickers, who has recently joined Town, is particularly fired up, and he competes for every challenge within striking distance in an attempt to show the local fans why he has been signed. The game ends 3–0 to Town, with goals from Frankie Chappell, Tom Vickers, and Ollie Davies. Along with Joe and John, I head off to Bibendum, the nearby pub, to discuss the finer tactics involved in flicking little plastic men around a green baize pitch over a couple of post-match pints.

• *For Eastbourne Town's next match, see Game 20 on page 52.*

Game 18: Wednesday 6 September (7.45pm) at Westleigh Park, Havant
Havant & Waterlooville 1 Eastbourne Borough 2 (National League South)
Weather: balmy
MOM: Leone Gravata. Too good and too quick for Havant, despite the attempts to keep him quiet

I've never had egg tikka rice before, but it's on the menu at the Havant Tandoori, which is just outside Havant station. I've got some time to kill because my nephews, who I am meeting for the game, are running late after finishing work. They tell me to meet them at the Heron pub near the ground, and despite the 20-minute walk from the town, I still beat them to the beer garden.

Havant's coastal area is the renowned Hayling Island, a summer haunt of mine on weekends in my younger days. Oh, how we loved to queue on the one bridge to the island for two hours, just to sit on the beach for a similar amount of time before spending another two hours getting back over the bridge for the return journey. It's what was considered a fun Sunday when I was younger.

Havant & Waterlooville's decent ground is in Leigh Park — which is most definitely not by the sea. But it is at least in a more accessible part of Havant. I'm after a programme, so a helpful steward locates the club shop man who is watching the game by the corner flag, and getting some fresh air. I soon realise why he stands outside on warm nights like tonight: the tiny room he works in is like a sweatbox.

The pace on the 3G pitch is electric and it's not hard to see that the home side are targeting the Borough danger man Leone Gravata, judging by the number of robust challenges being dished out by the Havant players. One of the home players winks at his bench after getting booked for one such challenge. Gravata is a handful to say the least.

All the goals in the game come in rapid fire towards the end. Fletcher Holman slides in a potential winner for Borough in the 80th minute, but just when the away side are counting the three points, Havant get a penalty, and it is slotted home calmly by Callum Kealy on the stroke of 90 minutes. But 90 minutes is far from the end of the game these days and, after a chaotic attempt at defending a late free kick, Havant concede another well into added time.

The Havant manager is sacked in the morning.
• *For Eastbourne Borough's next match, see Game 22 on page 55.*

Game 19: Sunday 10 September (2pm) at the Saffrons, Eastbourne
Eastbourne Town Women 7 Horsham Sparrows Women 2 (SCWGFL Premier)
Weather: balmy
WOM: Dani Parfitt. Causes trouble throughout the game and claims a hat-trick to boot

I've certainly seen faster paced matches this season, but not many that are as entertaining as this one. There are some cracking goals as well. After just a couple of minutes it's pretty clear that Town are the better side, and so it proves, although Sparrows do set up a good chance that is well blocked by the keeper Sarah Walshaw before the onslaught begins. Dani Parfitt, the best player on the pitch this afternoon by a country mile, loops in the first from a corner, probably fortuitously by the look on her face when it goes in. The second is a more conventional lob, when the Horsham defence falls asleep from a long ball, and then Parfitt adds another after rounding the goalkeeper after a punt forward. Barely 20 minutes have elapsed and things are already looking bleak for the visitors.

I chat to a couple who tell me they are hardcore fans of Town's women's side, and they reel off some players' names — Lucia Law, Melissa Orme, Ali Das — as if they are longtime buddies. The attendance is small. The queue for the bouncy castle, set up for a company party on the cricket outfield, probably boasts more people. I must add at this point that, while passing through the company fair/fete/whatever it is, I chip a ball through the small target hole in one of the inflatable plastic goals these fair/fete/whatever it is, has set up as part of the entertainment so that football lovers can show off their skills. Through the hole it went. With my flip-flops on. The kids were impressed anyway.

The Sparrows decide to stay on the pitch at half-time, and who can blame them in this near 80-degree heat? It's a rare day of actual warmth this summer. Naturally we all complain nonetheless. About the heat, that is, not the visiting team staying on the pitch.

But if staying on the pitch — as manager Phil Brown infamously made his Hull City side do when they trailed 4–0 to Manchester City at half-time in 2008 (on Boxing Day, so probably not so warm) — is supposed to inspire the Sparrows, it doesn't. It's soon seven to Town courtesy of a brace each from Geri Burt and Diane Vilciu, although the Sparrows do grab a late goal from Thea Ryder — her second and probably the best goal of the game — from a shot that is lashed in with perfect timing to make it 7-2. Pow.

Sweet Caroline rings out from the DJ's speakers in the fair/fete/whatever it is just over the fence. And I head off for another go at chipping the ball through the target with my flip-flops.

• *For Eastbourne Town Women's next match, see Game 26 on page 62.*

Game 20: Tuesday 12 September (7.30pm) at the Saffrons, Eastbourne
Eastbourne Town 2 Horsham YMCA 3 (Sussex Senior Challenge Cup 1st Round)
Weather: still weather for shorts but starting to get a tad chilly
MOM: the stadium announcer. Delivers a classic remark after a goal goes in — "And the goal…" he says, with a breathless, rising voice, "er, who was it now? Hang on, oh yes…"

The Sussex Senior Cup — officially the Sussex Transport Senior

Challenge Cup for sponsorship reasons — has been going for a fair while now. In fact, it is 141 years old, started at a time when the game was essentially an upper-class sport dominated by public schools. The first competition took place in 1882–83 and was won by Brighton Rangers.[3]

Recently a rather better-known club from that town, Brighton & Hove Albion, formed in 1901, have dominated — they've won the cup ten times since 2000, even though they enter an U21 side these days. This year's final will be played at their ground, and apart from a few notable exceptions — Lewes' Dripping Pan early on and Eastbourne Borough's Priory Lane between 2000 and 2010 — Brighton's stadium has been the main venue for the Sussex FA's premier competition. First it was the Goldstone Ground, now it is the Amex Stadium.

Naturally, the smaller local clubs love to get drawn against Brighton & Hove Albion in the county cup because a fixture against a Premier League side inevitably attracts a decent crowd. But it's fair to say that the enthusiasm is hardly likely to be mutual from a club who have just qualified for Europe for the first time in their history.

The same might be said of Eastbourne Town tonight. The not being too concerned about the county cup bit rather than European competition being their main priority, of course. They are 3–0 down entering the last few minutes. They've not put out a completely full-strength team — a few youngsters are playing — but there are still plenty of hardened regulars on the pitch, so the score is still a surprise for a team that has been on a good run recently.

It is at this point, however, that Town decide to turn up the tempo against YMCA (I'm not the only one humming *that* song, am I?). Tyler Pearson drills one in from distance and then the stadium announcer, who is fast becoming my favourite announcer of all time for his enthusiasm, tells the 87-strong crowd: "There is a minimum of five added minutes to be played."

Town burst into action and Horsham go all ultra-defensive. The bar is rattled from a dipping shot, then shortly afterwards Frankie Chappell powers a header in. They've left it too late though and

it's the visitors who will be finding many ways to be having a good time tonight. Sorry.
• *For Eastbourne Town's next match, see Game 30 on page 69.*

Game 21: Thursday 14 September (7.30pm) at the Saffrons, Eastbourne
Eastbourne Town U18 6 Bexhill United U18 0 (Southern Combination U18 East)
Weather: bit chilly for my shorts and flip-flops (bad decision)
MOM: Flynn Sweeting. Hat-trick

The historic turnstile block at the Meads Road End — one person I know refers to it as the, er, Bell End, because it is close to the Town Hall's clock tower, or probably just to get an easy laugh — is still not operational.

The original structure was donated by Mr Alderman and JC Towner way back in November 1914, just as young men across the continent were settling down for their all-too short stays in the mud and guts of the Western Front. A fire in 2004 destroyed the block but it was rebuilt that year.[4] It seems a real shame that the turnstiles are not ticking over these days.

But the gate right next to the block is open (it's free entry tonight) and I find a nice spot on the terrace behind the goal. I can, in fact, choose from a multitude of nice spots on the three-tiered terracing because I am the only one using it. A whole end of a ground to myself. That's a first.

Getting all possessive of my place behind the goal, I jokingly tell a young man who arrives a few minutes after kick-off "not to use up any of the space on 'my' terrace". He reminds me of my comment when I see him later along the side of the pitch after I get bored of standing on my own. It's not all it's cracked up to having a whole end to yourself.

The Bexhill keeper is in fine form — as he needs to be, because Town are dominant. The goals fly in regularly — Leo Groombridge, Spencer Morley, and Calum Pollitt topping up Flynn Sweeting's hat-trick — and Town's youngsters wrap up another victory in what is fast becoming a very nice start to the season.
• *For Eastbourne Town U18's next match, see Game 23 on page 57.*

Game 22: Saturday 16 September (3pm) at Priory Lane, Eastbourne
Eastbourne Borough 0 Worthing 1 (FA Cup 2nd Qualifying Round)
Weather: sunny and warm
MOM: Rocco Rees. Outstanding saves from the Worthing goalkeeper

It's FA Cup day and we're back to that old, confusing chestnut about no beer pitchside again. Doesn't the FA know that I need some lubrication because today is round one of my Eastbourne Football Cheeseburger Challenge? Borough's burger is first to be tried in this competition between the burgers of the town's three senior clubs — Borough, Town, and United. The winner will announced on the @FishChipsFooty X account. I tuck into a decent enough burger, although it loses marks for being pre-cooked and left in the warmer a bit too long.

Near the burger kiosk there is a small group of hardcore Borough fans. The words they are using in their chants are of the type that would have led my grandmother to approach them and ask politely (with a smile, of course): "Would you young men mind your grammar please?" The young enthusiasts grin from ear to ear as their chants, urged on by the thump-thump of a large drum, heckle the fans at the other end of the ground, who support a side just a few miles down the road in West Sussex. The East-West Sussex rivalry, which I never knew existed, means the supporters are segregated today, unlike most matches at Borough, so this end of the ground is strictly for home fans.

I shift to the side terrace, slightly out of earshot of this dozen or so 'singers', when they start running through their repertoire of songs for a third time. It's all becoming a bit monotonous. Here, I start chatting to a fan wearing a fez. Sadly, the fez wearer is not a distant relation of the popular entertainer Tommy Cooper (he was Welsh and this man is from Eastbourne). He tells me the hats were being handed out to fans at away game some time ago (why, oh why, I should have asked) and he has held on to it. Unfortunately, although the fez looks moderately amusing on this fan, he doesn't have the aura of Cooper, a man who could make people burst into fits of laughter just by walking onto the stage. Just like that. Sorry.

Cooper, however, does have links to Eastbourne. His niece owned a magic shop in Cornfield Road until 2017[5] and a metal silhouette of the entertainer can still be found outside the former holiday home he owned in Motcombe Lane, in Old Town.[6] So I suppose this fan has a vaguely good reason to be sporting a fez today. Sort of.

Borough are on top and Rocco Rees in the West Sussex goal is called into action on the half-hour mark, first with a point-blank save after they carve an excellent opening up the right, then shortly afterwards with an acrobatic tip over the bar.

Sadly for the segregated East Sussex home fans, Ben Dudzinski in the Borough goal can't replicate his opposite number's performance, and a few minutes later, after an aerial clash with striker Jake Robinson following a cross, the ball trickles over the line. Dudzinski is not given the usual protection afforded by referees (ie, touch a keeper and it's a free kick) and to the dismay of the fans at this end, the goal stands. As it turns out, that slightly fortuitous strike is all it takes to settle the game, and apart from endless updates about the Brighton match from spectators staring at their phone screens and two men discussing whether to throw their plastic cups in the gutter or walk a few steps to the bin, the rest of the game passes fairly rapidly.

But it's the first-goal-wins rule that applies today thanks to more great goalkeeping from Rocco. Zak Emmerson, who has just joined Borough on loan from Blackpool, became the second youngest player to play in the Football League when he came on as a substitute for Oldham Athletic against Walsall in 2019, aged 15 years and 73 days.[7] He has two caps for England U18 and has just turned 19. But he has not found the easiest keeper to face on his full debut for Borough and the home fans (between more updates about Brighton) are already questioning "how the hell he plays in League One". By the end, Emmerson is so bamboozled by Rocco's performance that he freezes in indecision in a one-on-one chance and runs straight into his splayed body.

But the Worthing keeper is keeping his best till the dying

moments. He saves well to a great low shot from substitute Decarrey Sheriff, then somehow finds his feet in time to get a hand to the follow-up header from, you've guessed it, Emmerson. Even the drummer has stopped thumping now.
• *For Eastbourne Borough's next match, see Game 32 on page 72.*

Game 23: Monday 18 September (7.45pm) at the Saffrons, Eastbourne
Eastbourne Town U18 2 Cobham 4 (FA Youth Cup 1st Qualifying Round)
Weather: mild and dry
MOM: Subby Noiki. Nippy and dangerous, the wide man creates problems for Town from the outset

The different competitions are coming thick and fast (I've seen 11 already this season) but it's a pleasure to be watching my second FA Youth Cup game. Town youngsters are on a bit of a roll after getting through a couple of preliminary rounds (one of them up at Westside in Wandsworth) and hopes are high tonight.

But it doesn't look good early on; Cobham are fast and energetic while Town are unusually subdued. There is an early Cobham goal from up close and then another shortly after. The cup hopes are evaporating for Town and the mostly youthful crowd, no doubt cheering on their friends, look dispirited. Star striker Leo Groombridge (who scored off the bench for the first team on Saturday) is looking frustrated along with the other front men, as Town battle to get enough of the ball to create something.

A total of 630 teams were accepted as entrants into the cup this year,[8] and although teams like Eastbourne Town and Cobham know they are not going to get close to playing in the final at a stadium like the Emirates, Old Trafford, or Villa Park, it would be nice to get a bit further than this.

The FA Youth Cup is often dragged out as 'proof', when a player makes the first team, to show that the youth system in football is working. The most quoted instance relates to the Manchester United team between 1992 and 1995 which won the FA Youth Cup twice and were losing finalists in between. David Beckham, Gary Neville, Phil Neville, Ryan Giggs, Paul Scholes, Nicky Butt — the commentators drool at the sheer talent churned out through the FA's youth version of its famous competition. But what about those who don't go on to glory such as the other players from that famous United youth set-up? Dessie Baker, David Hilton, or Richard Irving anyone? For the record, Irishman Baker headed home to play in the League of Ireland and picked up three national U23 caps, Hilton played one professional match for Darlington, while Irving turned out nine times for Macclesfield Town after a solitary appearance for Nottingham Forest. At least they can say they once played with Gary or Phil Neville.[9]

The reality is, playing in the FA Youth Cup final doesn't guarantee a player will reach the highest level in football. A few do have decent enough careers lower down the leagues but many of the youngsters disappear from the game altogether, without so much as a Wikipedia entry to their name. Take a look through the teams from past finals and you'll spot the odd big name but shrug unknowingly at most. The reason the Manchester United example is quoted so often is because it's a rarity. The first teams of big clubs just aren't filled with players who have progressed through their youth system. One of them breaking through is seen as a success these days. Maybe it's a case of why bother when we can buy someone ready-made from another club with our TV money?

Cobham ease through tonight's tie 4–2 thanks to the buffer of their early goals, despite a spirited effort from Town and replies from Joseph Hill and Fletcher Sheppard.

• *For Eastbourne Town U18's next match, see Game 55 on page 111.*

Game 24: Wednesday 20 September (2pm) at Priory Lane, Eastbourne
Eastbourne Borough Academy U19 5 Charlton Athletic Trust 1 (National League U19 Alliance Division B)
Weather: autumn is coming and there a chill in the air
MOM: Stanley Ketchell. A commanding display and a blasted goal from inside the penalty area

Mid-afternoon football on a weekday is a bit of a treat. It's like something you really shouldn't be doing. Like when I used to climb over the fence at school to avoid the next lesson. But unlike those days, when I'd sit on the bridge by the stream in the woods, more bored than I would have been in maths, this game is pretty entertaining.

Both teams proudly wear the kit and display the logos on their chests of their respective senior clubs. But both sides are also linked to colleges — in Borough Academy's case the link is with Bexhill College. All the players go there, apparently, so sport and education are interconnected. There are few faces I recognise in the Borough Academy squad: Tyler Wood from Borough U18, Delwin Duah, Calum Pollitt, and Shay Hollobone from Town, and Koby Farrell from United. These are decent players, so Borough Academy team are certainly no mugs and, even though they are wearing the famous red of Charlton Athletic, the visitors are no match for them.

The Robins' youngsters go bob-bob-bobbin from bad to worse during the first period and are 4–1 down at half-time, the one away goal only thanks to a dodgy call by the linesman who rules that the ball has crossed the line following a corner. The attendance is sparse to say the least, but I spot a couple of faces that I've seen at other local games. Nigel and Ian, like myself, move around the local clubs in this area and are happy that there is a game on a Wednesday afternoon.

Ian is a hardcore Borough fan and fondly remembers the days when they were a park side, playing on the grass area that is now beyond the stadium when the club had to hang netting along the fence by the road to stop people watching matches for free. Thirty-seven years ago, I'm told, he helped move rubble behind the goal at the far end to the clubhouse and was often hard at work with a cement mixer as the stadium took shape.

Grandparents watching their grandsons play are becoming a current theme at matches on my journey around the grounds, and in the second half I chat to a man who is here to see his grandson play for Borough. He goes home happy as Borough Academy run out 5–1 winners, with goals from Arthur Karapetyan (2), Stanley Ketchell, Charlie Gibson, and Tyler Wood, despite the manager making a string of changes to give the rest of the squad a runout.

• *For Eastbourne Borough Academy U19's next match, see Game 65 on page 130.*

Game 25: Saturday 23 September (3pm) at the Oval, Eastbourne
Eastbourne United 1 VCD Athletic 0 (FA Vase 2nd Round Qualifying)
Weather: sunny and warm
MOM: James Broadbent. Anyone who can score from a free kick taken from inside his own half, especially when he slips while kicking it, gets my vote

> *I will remember*
> *The fourteenth day of September*
> *A freak goal was changin' the minds of the Vickers*
> *While chasin' the doubts away*
> (With apologies to Earth, Wind and Fire)

It's a glorious day to be watching my first FA Vase match and the early exchanges are fairly even. Gary Ingram is his usual busy self in midfield, but despite his efforts this continues to be the most evenly matched game I've seen all season. It's not surprising that it takes a remarkably freakish goal to separate the two teams.

VCD Athletic are from Kent and their badge displays a cannon to mark their roots as a football club. The letters stand for Vickers, Crayford & Dartford, an armaments company which closed in 1999. The club were formed during World War I by new employees at the factory, and although they could only play inter-departmental games during the war, they joined the Kent League in 1919. Their largest attendance was recorded that year when 13,500 watched them play Maidstone United, thanks no doubt to the seven Arsenal players who were still finishing their military service and playing for Vickers (Erith) FC, as they were known initially.[10]

Eastbourne United reached the semi-final of the FA Vase in 2013–14, while the visitors have reached the 5th Round twice since the turn of the century, so both clubs have come agonisingly close to playing at Wembley in the final. The prize money is fairly low in the Vase (£725 for the winners of today's match), but the chance of stepping out at the national stadium is some carrot.

The FA Vase was started in 1974–75, replacing the old FA

Amateur Cup, and notable previous winners include Forest Green Rovers, who reached League One in 2022, and Guiseley, who played in the National League for a few seasons. West Country clubs Taunton Town and Truro City, who have also lifted the FA Vase, line up against Eastbourne Borough in the National League South this year.[11]

The cup is open to teams playing in tier nine or ten in the football pyramid, and although it's probably a bit early in the competition to start checking out hotels in North London, teams flying high in their respective divisions will already be eyeing a chance of Wembley glory.

England are playing in the Rugby World Cup later today and at half-time a few of the bar regulars, who like a drink but never seem to watch the United matches, are warming up for the rugby by watching *Tipping Point*. It's a strangely addictive quiz show. Mesmerised by the movement of little discs, we all sit glued to the 'action'. The show is, of course, based on the arcade games you often find in seaside towns and I vow to head down to the pier at some stage to find one of these games to try to win a big pile of two pence pieces. Once I've worked out how they manage to hang onto the edge without tipping over, I will enter the TV show. There might even be a question on Eastbourne United, who are rapidly turning out to be the most entertaining team I have watched this season.

The question would go something like this: "Which goalkeeper took a free kick in his own half, slipped as he kicked it, then leapt in the air in delight as his opposite number made a hash of defending it and let it in for the winner in an FA Vase match?"

"That'd be James Broadbent. That's my answer Ben."

To be honest, a freak goal like that is the only way a game like this could ever have been decided without the need for penalties. There are just a few minutes remaining when the goal goes in. Another FA Vase match for United it is then. But what odds on another winner from their keeper?

• *For Eastbourne United's next match, see Game 28 on page 64.*

Game 26: Sunday 24 September (1.30pm) at the Saffrons, Eastbourne
Eastbourne Town Women 7 Eastbourne Borough Women 1 (SCWGFL Premier)
Weather: sunny and warm
WOM: Geri Burt. Leads the line well and notches two goals

Even before I ask the couple who are standing nearby what the score is (I missed the start because the kick-off time has been moved forward by half an hour), it's pretty clear from the few minutes I have seen that Town are the better side today. Unfortunately I tell them as much before learning that the couple are here to watch their friends play for Borough. Town score as I am standing with them, but I resist the temptation to say, "I told you so".

The home side score another one before half-time and the local derby already seems like a walkover. Geri Burt is looking good upfront, with a goal in the bag already, while the dangerous Dani Parfitt is still looking for her first — much to the surprise of Kevin, whom I have started chatting to behind the goal by the Meads Road.

Kevin is a proper football fan. He tells me he once watched 101 matches in a season (yes, he has a wife) and he is fully up to speed with the Town women's side. Although they now play in the Sussex County Women's and Girls' Football League and didn't enter the FA Cup this year, they were certainly punching a fair bit above their current level a few seasons ago.

In 2011–12, while known as Eastbourne Town Ladies, they missed out on promotion to the National League by just four points. Three seasons later there was glory in the FA Cup when they reached the Third Round, beating Burgess Hill Town, Parkwood Rangers, Gosport Borough, Chichester Ladies, and QPR Girls on the way. They only lost to Derby County Women after taking them to extra time.

Town are now 5–0 up, with goals from Diane Vilciu (2), Geri Burt (2), and Hayley Beattie. I desperately avoid looking at the couple who have come to watch their friends play for Borough. Then Parfitt gets her goal, sliding in after a good solo run, and Poppy Payne blasts home a cracker before Borough get a scrambled consolation goal.

Things are looking good for the Town club overall. The women are clear at the top of their league, the men went top of theirs yesterday, and the U23 and U18 sides have both had excellent starts.
* *For Eastbourne Town Women's next match, see Game 40 on page 84.*
* *For Eastbourne Borough Women's next match, see Game 58 on page 117.*

Game 27: Monday 25 September (7.30pm) at the Saffrons, Eastbourne
Eastbourne Town U23 2 Eastbourne United U23 3 (Southern Combination U23 East).
Weather: a pleasant evening
MOM: Shay Hollobone. The Town keeper 'parries' a couple of shots that lead to goals, but his saves in the first half give his side a fighting chance

Does anyone know what the raised arm signal means when a player is getting ready to take a corner? It's been going on for years and I still can't work out if it means anything more than "I'm about to kick it lads." It's certainly not a secret signal, unless I'm missing a cocked arm or crafty flick of a finger, because everyone does it. Tonight I see the lesser used double-arm version. I'm still none the wiser, but the United number two certainly whips in a mean corner whatever signal he uses.

United are bombarding the goal and Shay Hollobone is doing well to keep them out with a string of diving saves and blocks. It somehow inspires Town and, after a bit of return pressure, one of the club's rising stars, Leo Groombridge, puts them unexpectedly ahead. But it doesn't last long because Koby Farrell makes it 1–1 on the stroke of half-time and just after the break United take the lead through Josh Gould. During the interval I foolishly tell the darts team, who are practising in the clubhouse, that I'll turn out for them if they are desperate. They'd have to be, because I haven't thrown a dart in ten years.

United really shouldn't be desperate for anything after such first-half dominance, but after a slick move, Town's Blake Larby equalises with a measured shot. It's starting to look like it could be one of those games for the visitors. But justice is done in the end, however, and United win 3–2 thanks to a Jordan Pittam winner. The game finishes just before 9.30pm. Added time for everything and anything anyone?

Most of the darts team are still working their way through the doubles in their round-the-clock practice when I get back in the clubhouse. Maybe I will get a game after all.
* *For Eastbourne Town U23's next match, see Game 38 on page 82.*
* *For Eastbourne United U23's next match, see Game 81 on page 157.*

Game 28: Tuesday 26 September (7.30pm) at the Crouch, Seaford
Seaford Town 3 Eastbourne United 2 (Peter Bentley Challenge Cup 2nd Round)
Weather: another lovely evening at the end of the summer
MOM: Callum Connor (Seaford)

I do like an away game, especially visiting a ground for the first time. It makes me feel as if I am an explorer. I've always been in awe of explorers, especially those old ones who set out to be the 'first' to do something. What I've never understood, though, is why some of them explored cold places. After all, there were plenty of nice, warm areas to explore, so why head off to the ice and the snow? The formidable adventurer Ernest Shackleton, who lived in Milnthorpe Road in Meads, Eastbourne, was one of the cold lovers. But the Antarctic? Three times? Surely Newcastle is chilly enough if you like that sort of thing.

Tonight, I'm channelling my inner warm-weather Shackleton and going on an expedition of my own. To Seaford. The trip on the bus to this seaside town passes through beautiful countryside, threading its way through the picturesque village of East Dean and the Seven Sisters Country Park. The grazing land of the farms is a deep green and sheep dot the grasslands with their fluffy whiteness. It's all rather lovely. Then a young girl gets on and sits near me. She starts to share her favourite TV shows and YouTube clips. She doesn't tell me in so many words that she wants to share them, but her speaker is so loud I soon know what she likes. I would keep looking at the sheep to distract myself but they've all run for the hills at the noise, so I try to read some more of Evelyn Waugh's *Black Mischief*, a book that caused some controversy in its day — although that, rather weirdly, was because it lacked normal standards of decency rather than because of its blatant racial slurs and clichés about people from Africa. The dialogue of Waugh's satirical novel, even with its 1932 style, however, is decidedly better than what is coming from the speaker near me. Then I get to a passage in the book where an old guy is moaning about the youth of today, so I put the book down and start to count sheep.

When I wake up I'm in Seaford, so I head off to the Crouch ground. 'Crouch' is a word that comes from Old English meaning 'cross', and according to the club's records there was once a wooden cross near the site — hence the name of the ground.[12] The atmosphere at the ground, which is found down a narrow track, is more like that of a summer fair than a football match. The official attendance tonight is only 74 but there are a lot of youngsters, with their mums and dads, still hanging around after their earlier training sessions, so it's probably a lot more than that. The smell of frying burgers fills the air, and young children are running around excitedly. Seaford Town seem spurred on by it all and look more up for a battle than United, who are strangely sluggish. There are a couple of changes from the usual team, but the bulk of the visiting side are first-team regulars.

In the distant past, Seaford folk had a bit of reputation for using fake harbour lights on the cliffs so that ships would run aground and they could loot them.[13] But worry not, however, most of the 22,000 people who live here today an altogether nicer bunch (for goodness' sake, Dame Penelope Keith went to school here, don't you know) and the only things the locals are enjoying tonight are those fabulous burgers and the football.

Seaford FC (they only added the Town bit later) were formed in 1888, although football was played in the town before that by a team called Seaford Rovers. The game arrived at the Crouch courtesy of a chap called John Plaister, the landowner who made the land available for football for no other reason than "because he happened to like the game and felt it deserved a home", according to the club's records.[14]

During World War I, the ground was dug up and food was

grown on it. I can only assume that the Germans must have heard great things about the vegetables, because during World War II they bombed the Crouch on two separate occasions.

There are certainly no craters on the surface these days but the sloping pitch seems to be causing United some problems, and despite the home side being a division lower than the visitors, they look the better side tonight. The Peter Bentley Challenge Cup — named after a former chairman of the Sussex FA — is the Southern Combination's League Cup, so it's a good chance for Seaford to test themselves against higher ranked opposition.

There are a few fans scattered along the touchlines, but most of the people watching are clustered in the covered area just outside the bar (did I mention the burgers?). The great little bar is adorned with prints of old programmes and they create a fabulous montage for lovers of printed football memorabilia.

Although United grab a couple of late goals they are beaten by a determined home side through finishes from Joshua Wright, Matthew Ford, and the impressive Callum Connor. The result is probably best summed up by a man who limps past me and exclaims with a smile: "Well, I wasn't expecting that!" The Seaford summer fair rolls on.

• *For Eastbourne United's next match, see Game 35 on page 76.*

Game 29: Saturday 30 September (2pm) at the Oval, Eastbourne
Eastbourne United Reserves 6 Westfield 2 (Mid Sussex Premier)
Weather: warm, with some clouds
MOM: Daniel Tewkesbury

My plan for round two of the Eastbourne Football Cheeseburger Challenge is thwarted because there are no burgers on sale today. In fact, the club are using the burger hut to take entrance money. I get a Kit Kat for my lunch instead.

The burger hut is a prominent feature at the Oval, not least because it's right there as you enter the ground, (usually) tempting you with the lovely smell of fried onions. There's a nice patch of grass in front of it and somewhere to sit nearer the pitch, which is handy if you don't like to eat on the go. Burgers with a view. To one side of the hut, just behind the goal, there is a small stand with 62 seats (one side of the stand has rusted away and is cordoned off) while to its right as you view the pitch there is a covered area for standing about 11 yards wide and four terraces deep. Further along, on the other side of the halfway line is the main stand, which has 113 seats in the black and white colours of United. All the stands at United are modular so they could, in theory, be dismantled and shifted elsewhere (except the rusty one, obviously).

These modular stands are popular among lower league clubs, as they can be added to meet the ground requirements of leagues when needed. Funds permitting, of course. A rather nice 40-foot long, 63-seater stand converted from a shipping container for FC Hartlepool, who play in the Northern League Division 2, cost £30,000 in 2023. Or you could pick up a second-hand one from a club who no longer have use for it. A 100-seater stand (some repainting needed) from Aylestone Park FC was on sale for just £7,800 in 2024.[15] You would need to know a man with a big van, though. The converted containers are a great option for smaller clubs looking to add more seating or provide some covered standing, and chances are, if you've watched a non-league game, you will have sat or stood in one of them.

It is still early days in the Mid Sussex Premier — the league's highest level and tier 11 in the pyramid — but United have had a good start and remain unbeaten in their first six matches. The official name of this division is (you might need to take a deep breath here): the Gray Hooper Holt LLP Mid Sussex Football League Premier Division. The sponsors are a well-established firm of Sussex solicitors and have been in practice since 1905.[16] Clearly a firm which does things long-term, they have sponsored the Mid Sussex League since the late 1990s — possibly the longest running sponsorship of its type in English football.[17]

The Mid Sussex League was formed way back in 1900 with seven founding members — Burgess Hill, Crawley, Haywards Heath, Three Bridges, Ardingly, Cuckfield, and Hurstpierpoint, with the latter three still playing in the league today. A Division 2 was added in 1903 and by the 1950s there were five divisions. Today, the league operates 12 open-age divisions, as well as divisions for veterans, and runs 12 cup competitions.[18]

Most people who have played football have turned out for the 'seconds' at some stage in their career. It's a strange experience. Some of the players desperately want to move up to the 'firsts', some are never going to be good enough, while others have done their time and just want to enjoy their football on a Saturday afternoon. But that strange mix binds reserve teams together rather well. Maybe it's that joint feeling of knowing that none of you are really wanted (by the firsts), because some of the most close-knit teams I have ever played for have been reserve sides. There's a determination to prove something, marked by a nonchalant outward display from the players of not caring (they do really).

Westfield is a small village near Hastings, and with only a couple of thousand people living in the village, I admire the fact that they can even sustain a football team. Unfortunately, from what I see of the early exchanges in this game, I'm not sure my admiration will do them much good against this United side.

Westfield football club, however, have no shortage of experience behind the scenes, as the majority shareholder is QPR defender, Steve Cook, who hails from the area. Cook played five seasons in the Premier League with Bournemouth and also had a short loan spell at Eastbourne Borough in 2010.

Eastbourne United have just formed this reserve side and they are pretty good. They are near the top of the league and I'd be surprised if they don't win it. They pass the ball around with confidence and have a string of players who are comfortable on the ball, not least the impressive Paul Rogers, who strolls around like a man who's clearly played a better level of football than this.

United are 2-0 up at half-time, but they really kick on in the second half with goals coming thick and fast. Daniel Tewkesbury adds number three, Rogers gets the next, then Charlie Yeates and Ashley Crabb push their side's total up to six. Despite a couple of late goals for the visitors through Corey Wheeler and Josh

Pickering, it's a convincing win for the reserve side at the Oval
• *For Eastbourne United Reserves' next match, see Game 43 on page 89.*

Game 30: Saturday 30 September (3pm) at the Saffrons, Eastbourne
Eastbourne Town 2 Pagham 0 (Southern Combination Premier)
Weather: still warm and cloudy
MOM: Ollie Davies

This is the first time I've ever seen two games of football on the same day (although I should point out that according to some of the groundhopping 'rules' I've seen, the second encounter wouldn't 'count' as I am not watching the whole of it).

Groundhopping, a hobby which involves fans travelling around the country and visiting (or 'collecting') different football grounds, has become a big thing in recent years. Many years ago, a trend arose among football fans endeavouring to watch a match at each of the 92 Football League grounds (there is actually a 92 club — with rules naturally — which was formed in 1978).[19] But after a while, the 92 become a fairly common achievement. Too many people had done it. It was becoming the norm. So fans started to compete to do it in the fastest time (Ed Wood from Rochdale holds the Guinness World Record at 189 days).[20] Then they started including visits to the National League clubs, pushing the target up to (currently) 116 clubs. Then the National League South and North grounds were added to the target (164). And so it goes on.

Over time fans went in search of a different kind of experience. Gone were the visits to big, glitzy stadiums. The smart thing to do these days, at least among groundhoppers, is to visit smaller non-league grounds — the more obscure the better. To boldly go where no groundhopper has gone before. And because it's a nerdy sort of thing to do, there's a popular app, Futbology,[21] where you can log your visits and compile your stats. Many groundhoppers even post screenshots of their achievements on social media. Yes, I know.

Anyway, I'm not really a groundhopper, except for hopping around Eastbourne plus a few away games thrown in, so I completely ignore the rules and jump on the 3A bus after the final whistle of the Eastbourne United Reserves match (2pm kick-off) and get to the Eastbourne Town game just after the half-time. Don't tell anyone.

The Corner Flag cafe is already shut when I arrive, so my cunning plan to switch the burger challenge to Town, after the disappointment of United not serving hot food, goes up in a lack of smoke. I then get told off by an official for having a peek into the boardroom/committee room (the door is near the cafe), so I decide to move along behind the goal before anything goes really wrong. The netting behind the goal at this end of the ground, set up to save spectators from wayward shots, is a bit distracting to start with, but brains are wonderful things and after a while mine is telling my eyes that the netting is not even there.

My timing is perfect, as it happens, because although the game has been a tight 0–0 affair until now, the action is just hotting up. In the 81st minute Town get the opening goal through Harvey Greig, much to the disgust of the Pagham keeper, who berates everyone within earshot. The lady beside me claps wildly. Then, a few minutes later, Ollie Davies finds a gap and slides the ball home with pinpoint precision. The visiting keeper mouths wildly again but his words don't seem to be coming out. Or is that just because of the noise coming from the Town fans behind the goal? It's eight league wins on the trot for Eastbourne Town and they are sitting at the top of the table.

• *For Eastbourne Town's next match, see Game 33 on page 73.*

Game 31: Sunday 1 October (2pm) at the Oval, Eastbourne
Eastbourne United Women 0 Montpelier Villa Women 2 (Women's FA Cup 2nd Qualifying Round)
Weather: lovely and sunny
WOM: Emma Sweetman. Never stops working

There is programme for this game. It's the first one dedicated to the women's side. For people who love programmes — and oh, how I love programmes — this feels quite special. Like this match really. The FA Cup. The oldest tournament in the world. Born before the rest of the world could even conceive of such an idea. And here I am watching the women's version of the tournament at the Oval along with just over a hundred other people.

The United players look as if they are feeling the pressure because they seem to freeze early on, handing the initiative to Montpelier Villa. Tara Barrett and Saskia Taylor-Doyle are causing endless problems upfront and United can't cope with their threats. Inevitably they get one apiece as the Brighton side go two up early on.

United need to wake up. They are being watched by a lot of mums, dads, and young children (who are coached by one of the United players, I'm told). This is the time to inspire them. Even if teddy, orange drinks, and bags of healthy nuts are distracting the youngsters from the actual action. Come on, there is £3,000 in prize money at stake for the winner of today's match.[22]

The Women's FA Cup, currently sponsored by the software company Adobe (used to put this book together incidentally), started out as the Mitre Challenge Trophy in 1970–71. There were 71 entrants in that inaugural cup (the first men's FA Cup in 1871–72 had 15 entrants, although only 12 actually played) which was won by Southampton, who beat Stewarton Thistle from Scotland in the final (the cup was initially open to teams throughout Great Britain).[23] It was quite a wait for footballing women because the FA had effectively banned them from playing from 1921 until 1970 (clubs affiliated to the FA were not permitted to host women's games).[24]

These days, the final is played at Wembley, with last season's tie between Chelsea and Manchester United attracting 77,390 spectators. A total of 456 clubs were accepted into the 2023–24 tournament and the winning team will bag £430,000.[25] It's quite a turnaround.

United do wake up, and driven on by their tireless captain Emma Sweetman, they stifle Villa's striking threat and start to show what they can do. But huffing and puffing is no good when you have handed the visitors an early two-goal advantage. They never really look like scoring and are left to wonder what might have been, against a side they beat 3-2 in the league earlier in the season.

• *For Eastbourne United Women's next match, see Game 34 on page 75.*

Game 32: Tuesday 3 October (7.45pm) at Priory Lane, Eastbourne
Eastbourne Borough 6 Billingshurst 0 (Sussex Senior Challenge Cup 2nd Round)
Weather: it's getting chilly
MOM: Fletcher Holman. Five goals. Who else?

Billingshurst is a village of just over 8,000 people, so I suspect Borough will fancy their chances of progressing in the county cup. The village side play in Southern Combination Division 1, a few levels lower down the pyramid. They would need to get promoted four times to see Borough on their league fixture list.

As far as football is concerned, Billingshurst can lay claim to James Tilley (he was born in the village and his dad, Kevin, is the chairman), who made one appearance for Brighton before a loan spell with Cork City in Ireland and a career with Grimsby Town, Crawley Town, and Wimbledon.[26] Outside of football, other people who have called the village home are the blonde bombshell Diana Dors, England's answer to Marilyn Monroe,[27] DJ David Hamilton, and comedian Harry Enfield. "Only me!"[28]

I used to play against Billingshurst in boys' football. All I remember is some close matches on a sloping, very muddy pitch. From the images I can see on the club's website and social media links, it looks as if they have made significant progress since then. Off the pitch, they even appointed a director of football in June: Terry Eames, the former Wimbledon professional (1977–80) and later manager of the Dons (2002–04). On the pitch, however, things have clearly not been so good because a new manager was appointed only a few weeks ago and the club are hovering near the bottom of Division 1.[29] They've lost their last four matches. Billingshurst's average attendance at home in the league is just 70, so if Borough are hoping for a bumper payday from this tie, the whole lot of them will need to turn up. And buy a few burgers each.

The Borough full-timers have put a proper side out, with a backbone of first-teamers that includes Billy Vigar, on-loan from Arsenal, and Blackpool loanee Zak Emmerson, fresh from his debut against Worthing. Surely a walkover is looming?

But maybe Billingshurst haven't read about the pedigree of the players they are up against, because they are probably the better side in the first 20 minutes with Ronnie Reeves having a couple of good chances, one of which whistles just past the woodwork. Skipper Matt Rendell also gets into a good position but he can't connect. I fear the village side's moment has passed and so it proves. Fletcher Holman slams home a goal for Borough — and it could well be the first of many more.

Decarrey Sheriff is showing electric pace for Borough and Matt McAlpine is doing his best to emulate that type of run at the other end, but both are being stifled by the respective defences. It's tighter than expected at half-time despite another Holman goal.

But Borough are bigger, stronger, more skilful, and much fitter than Billingshurst. Despite a couple of good saves from visiting keeper Ollie Courtney, Holman fills his boots to grab five and Sheriff adds a sixth with a superb strike. The loan player from Blackpool still hasn't scored.

• *For Eastbourne Borough's next match, see Game 41 on page 85.*

Game 33: Saturday 7 October (3pm) at the Edgar & Wood Stadium, Shoreham-by-Sea
Shoreham 3 Eastbourne Town 1 (Southern Combination Premier)
Weather: lovely autumn afternoon with plenty of sun
MOM: Muhammad Wilson. Ironically signed from Eastbourne Town recently, he causes lots of problems with his skill and trickery out wide

Eastbourne Town are sitting second in the league with 25 points after stringing together a nice run of eight consecutive league wins. Shoreham have yet to win a league game after 11 matches (although they did triumph in a cup match after penalties) and have just two points. But the obvious is not always the obvious in football.

The railway first arrived in Eastbourne way back in 1849, but the lines are such that I need to loop up to Lewes and back down to Brighton before changing for Shoreham-by-Sea. At least the train comes in on the lovely old wooden platform at Brighton, which is a delightful old-school pleasure, and thanks to the waiting time between trains there is time for a pint in the wonderfully eclectic Prince Albert, landing zone for many an excited, squealing tourist to Brighton (of which there are plenty today).

Shoreham town centre and station are not actually 'by-sea' as the name might suggest, but on the north bank of the River Adur, which is handy for me because the football ground is also on this side. Shoreham Beach is on a promontory that loops around to its tip in the east, where Shoreham Fort keeps watch over the English Channel, holding ancient foreign invaders at bay. A short bridge (the A259) — actually two bridges with a small patch of land in the middle of the crossing — links the two parts of the town and is just to the west of the station, which is useful if you want to visit the fort, Chuck's Smokehouse, or Beachcombers Barbers. There's not much else in this part of Shoreham, though, unless you like nice walks I am told. Such delights will have to wait for another day.

Shoreham, the not-quite-by-sea bit, is a mix of modern office blocks, standard small business units, some used-to-be-modernish houses, and colourful graffiti-covered fences hiding wasteland.

The ground (optimistically called a stadium on a sign I see on a board advertising the cafe) is accessed through a park with a couple of open pitches, a playground, and a small car park. It's neat and tidy and has a proper turnstile (just the one), a lean-to covered standing area behind one goal, three rows of the usual plastic flip-back seats on the halfway line (covered), and another lean-to — metal this time — behind the other goal. Plus, the previously mentioned café and a cosy clubhouse. The original floodlights at the ground were donated by Wimbledon from their old Plough Lane stadium in 1981, although new LED ones have since been installed.[30]

Shoreham were formed in 1892 and although they had some success at the turn of the 20th century — winning the county cup and the Royal Ulster Rifles Cup twice each — they have mostly bobbed about various leagues since then, their high point coming with a season in Division One South of the Isthmian League in 2017–18 after winning the Southern Combination Premier the previous year.[31] Anyone who has looked at the excellent programme will have seen the league table. And within 90 seconds it's what they would have expected: Town go ahead, the goal coming from Evan

Archibald. But like all good tales, you need to read between the lines.

A few weeks ago, the struggling Shoreham parted company with their manager after the disastrous start and appointed Paul Ettridge, who was at the club as head coach last year.[32] He's spent the early autumn getting his management team together and overhauling the playing staff with a string of new signings, including the tricky Muhammad Wilson, signed from today's visitors, Eastbourne Town. Captain Tony Timms has also recently returned to first-team action.[33] The Shoreham side of today are nothing like the one that Town dispatched with ease back in August in the Royal Ulster Rifles Cup.

From the friendly banter outside the clubhouse, it seems as if there is a solid group of regulars who follow Shoreham, and they are thrilled when Alex Patching cancels out Archibald's early goal with a header from a whipped cross after just seven minutes. There is a good buzz about the place at half-time. The Musselmen of Shoreham will take on Brighton & Hove Albion in the Sussex Senior Cup in just three days — a game that will undoubtedly attract more than the 192 here today.[34]

As as if warming up the crowd for Tuesday night, Shoreham go ahead — a cracking strike from Jack Hartley, one of the new signings. As time ticks by, the nervous laughter among the home fans grows louder as they start to believe that long-awaited first league win of the season might just happen. And then, against a backdrop of relief, cheers, and spilt beer, it's a penalty to the home side. Patching puts it away in injury time.

Oh, I do like to be beside the seaside. Sort of by the seaside, anyway.

• *For Eastbourne Town's next match, see Game 47 on page 95.*

Game 34: Sunday 8 October (2pm) at the Oval, Eastbourne
Eastbourne United Women 3 Steyning Town Community Women 1 (L&SERWFL Division 1 South)
Weather: and the sun keeps shining in October
WOM: Emma Sweetman. The skipper continues her outstanding form

Things are a lot different at Eastbourne United this week. Just seven days ago the Women's FA Cup match raised the bar, with the club a buzz of activity. This week, there is no one manning the entrance booth, so the money is being collected by an injured player using a cash box from WHSmith (so no card payments); the burger hut is closed (so no bacon butties); there is no programme; and the hordes of youngsters with mums, dads and their emergency bag of wet wipes have found something else to do.

But things are different on the pitch too, because United have no nerves, and despite a few changes — in what looks like a bid to give some of the other squad members a run out against a team lower down the league — they look sharper and smarter from the off. The skilful blonde striker Grace Hill is immediately into the action when a bouncing ball comes across and she nods home nicely for an early goal. A determined challenge on the Steyning keeper sees Rebecca Relf's header bobble over the line not long afterwards to double the lead.

Steyning score just after half-time and I get the lowdown on their team from a man who is here watching his daughter, a stalwart defender for the club. He tells me that a whole bunch of last year's team have left to join other clubs and Steyning are struggling this time around. Worse is still to come apparently, as a few more of the players will be heading back to university soon. Any thoughts this threadbare squad may have of salvaging anything from this game, however, are ended when they concede a penalty (duly converted by Leanne Hawkins).

• *For Eastbourne United Women's next match, see Game 61 on page 121.*

Game 35: Tuesday 10 October (7.45pm) at the Oval, Eastbourne
Eastbourne United 1 Little Common 0 (Southern Combination Premier)
Weather: a beautifully mild evening for floodlit football
MOM: Charlie Ball. Playing a bit deeper than I have seen him previously, he passes and probes for openings throughout the game. Until his sin bin, at least

I do enjoy a floodlit game. Especially when it's not cold. But my mind tonight is firmly on round two of the Eastbourne Football Cheeseburger Challenge. It's good. A meaty burger, with the cheese melted to perfection, plus nice onions, and a brilliant range of sauces. This is going to take some beating.

The much expected bumper crowd has not materialised (there are 140 here), even though Little Common is just up the road. Maybe it's bingo night in the Little Common clubhouse.

The game itself is remarkably even, but as with most even football matches, not much actually happens because the players cancel each other out. I chat to the irrepressible Joe Knight, long-term sports photographer for local newspapers, who now clicks away for pleasure. I do hope he gets a free cup of tea at half-time. Local football ticks along thanks to people like this: Knight with his great photos and many others doing all those jobs that help clubs run smoothly.

Little Common have an extra big gun in their armoury thanks to the long (as in *ridiculously* long) throws of Ollie Black, but the chaos they cause has led to nothing so far.

In the second half I move behind the goal and listen to a few local fans shout abuse at the referee and some of the visiting players, seemingly picked at random. Maybe the game is worse than I think. I chat to a man from Polegate who tells me that he moves around the area to watch whichever local game takes his fancy from the fixture lists and that he thought this one would be nice and even. He's got that right.

But on the hour mark, as I'm trying to get a sort-of-arty shot for the @FishChipsFooty X account, Gary Ingram gets a cross in and Callum Wilson powers home with his forehead from point blank. I post the blurry picture and hope that people view it as arty.

It's a great win for a historic club. Eastbourne United — or Eastbourne United Association FC, to use the club's full name — were born on 5 September 1894 as the 1st Sussex Royal Engineers Volunteers (Eastbourne) FC. There had been a training camp for the Sussex companies of the regiment and they'd enjoyed some success in a local tournament, so on the back of that the new football club was formed. Next year will be the club's 130th anniversary.

The club's name has changed a few times in that time. You'll have to bear with me, but here goes...

In 1913 the club became the 1st Home Counties Royal Engineers (Eastbourne), by which time they at least had a home ground (Gildredge Park in Old Town) after a few years of being nomads. This first name change reflected the merger between the Volunteers and the Territorial Army. However, in 1920–21 the Volunteers were disbanded, so it was on to name number three: Eastbourne Royal Engineers Old Comrades. Three years later the 'Royal Engineers' bit was dropped, and after another three years the 'Old' suffix went as well. The club, now simply Eastbourne Comrades, were on to their fifth name in just 33 years — a change which coincided with the club adopting the black and white colours of today.

By now the club had moved to the Lynchmere Ground, which could possibly lay claim to being the first venue for an 'outside broadcast' of a sports event. The opening match there, against the Royal Signals in the 1920–21 East Sussex Cup final, was relayed back to the Signals' camp. Now granted, the camp was only 21 miles away in Maresfield, but still. Sadly, most of the facilities at Lynchmere had been gutted by the end of World War II. So, after a short spell struggling on at their old ground, the Comrades moved to the Oval in 1947, where they remain.

So ended the 'groundhopping' saga. But for those of you still with me, hang in there because there are still a few very important name changes to come yet, not least in 1951–52, when the club finally became Eastbourne United. At last.

A planned merger with Eastbourne Town a couple of decades later fell through, which is lucky in one respect, because heaven knows what the name would have been. However, a merger did occur when United and Shinewater Association came together in 2001–02. This facilitated the most recent of the name changes, as the club officially became Eastbourne United Association FC. Luckily, most fans just call them United still. And who can blame them.[35]

• *For Eastbourne United's next match, see Game 36 on page 79.*

Game 36: Saturday 14 October (3pm) at the Oval, Eastbourne
Eastbourne United 1 Newhaven 2 (Southern Combination Premier)
Weather: sunny but chilly. Winter is approaching
MOM: Alfie Rogers. The Newhaven no. 10 constantly battles in the centre of midfield, drives home the first to set the tone, and soon afterwards calmly tucks away a penalty

The trains are not running (again), but nobody seems to know if it's yet another strike, maintenance work, or just something random. I don't think anyone cares any more as they cluster around the bus stop for the Brighton route. Train strikes, delays, problems on the track, and the like, are part and parcel of British life, along with rain. We just take it all in our stride.

Luckily, I have discovered since moving to Eastbourne, that there is a Wetherspoon pub — the London & County — right opposite the station. It is an ideal place to kill time when you are delayed. Even better, there is another Wethers just a few hundred yards away — the Cornfield Garage — which is right outside the bus stop for the route to Priory Lane. Bring on your strikes and delays; I can wait in the warm with a pint.

But quite apart from the convenience of these pubs, I find that they also serve up a good helping of local history. The walls of both pubs are full of facts about characters with links to Eastbourne, such as actor Sir Alec Guinness (who went to school here), composer William Sterndale Bennett (who wrote *The May Queen* while staying here), and various royals who made the town 'fashionable'; not least King George III, who stayed in Sea Houses (that'll be Marine Parade today) in 1780 with four of his children.[36] He probably needed a holiday to build up his strength for a last, ahem, push, because 13 of his 15 children had already been born by then.[37]

When the 12X arrives, everyone swarms forward, determined to get a seat, or even just get on the bus to get where they are going. A lady with her disabled child in a wheelchair stands back, ignored and unable to board the bus.

Today's plan is a trip to watch Peacehaven & Telscombe v Eastbourne Town. A nice trip along the coast in some sunshine and a decent game of football at the end of it. But the bus is nearly full already and there is already a crowd waiting for the next one, so I change my plan and decide to watch Newhaven's visit to Eastbourne United just down the road instead. When I head off, I notice that the woman and the disabled child in the wheelchair are still no closer to the front of the queue.

After an electric start to the season, United are having a bit of dip as far as results go. Their list of scores in the programme was once a sea of green (signifying wins) but a lot of red (losses) has been creeping in recently.

After nine minutes another red blob in the programme looms, when Newhaven's Alfie Rogers slides home a beauty from what must be the visitors' first real attack. Less than 20 minutes later the same player slots home a penalty for 2–0. To contort a common saying completely, Eastbourne must be at the races, because they are certainly not here today. Having two players in the sin bin in the first half doesn't help.

But United are a different team in the second half, with Charlie Ball and Gary Ingram constantly probing, and Callum Barlow putting himself in the line of fire upfront as usual. The impending threat to the visitors' lead ratchets up the intensity of the game and the usual tricks and comments from the players descends to the level of a mini-farce that has both me and the man next to me, as the *Beano* comic would say, "chortling".

It's all rather petty, as players start falling over at the slightest touch (argh!), screaming at the officials (another sin bin), and bashing into opposition players with snarled grimaces ("I'm tougher than you"). On one occasion the linesman tells the full-back where the throw is from. He steals a few yards and is told: "That's enough!" He steals a few yards again and a foul throw is given.

"You're supposed to tell him where the throw is from, lino," screams one of the substitutes who is warming up nearby.

"He did," I tell him.

"No he didn't."

"Yes he did."

Join us at the Devonshire Park Theatre this Christmas for some thigh-slapping fun in our upcoming pantomime performance.

United pull one back through substitute Mason Creese and their pressure for an equaliser is relentless. But Newhaven hang on for a win in a cracking game of football thanks to some staunch defending, highlighted by a superb point blank save from their keeper Jake Buss from what looks like a nailed-on Gary Ingram headed equaliser.
• *For Eastbourne United's next match, see Game 50 on page 100.*

Game 37: Sunday 15 October (10am) at Priory Lane, Eastbourne
Eastbourne Borough Women DS 2 Woodingdean Wanderers Women 2 (win 7-6 on penalties)
(Sussex Women's Challenge Trophy QF)
Weather: very warm in the sun, but decidedly chilly in the shade of the main stand
WOM: Mia Connor. Solid and composed at the back for Borough

I do like a friendly bus driver. Who doesn't? The grumpy ones seem to view customers as a nuisance. I feel like apologising sometimes. "Oh, sorry; I made you stop." But the friendly ones know their job is actually to help people — and the way they do that is by driving a bus. Quaint idea really.

There are plenty of drivers with those quaint ideas, thankfully, but my Bus Driver of the Year award goes to the driver of the 1A this morning. My plan is for a double header of women's matches at Borough today — the development side followed by the firsts — are thrown into disarray early on when I realise the Loop bus doesn't seem to be operating, despite the promises from the electronic board in Cornfield Road. Five minutes, four, three, two, one, due… then the bus disappears from digital existence.

But my super driver not only confirms that the Loop is "not on the road", but, once on his 1A bus, also tells me which stop to "alight" (bus driver speak) and how to walk to Priory Lane from there. Quality. Thank you, sir.

The first game, in a morning baked in sunshine, makes all the effort worthwhile. The Sussex Women's Challenge Trophy is the county cup for teams lower down the ladder and they can't come up against bigger clubs such as Brighton or Hastings United, who compete for the Sussex Women's Challenge Cup. With only 15 entrants, the trophy competition provides an excellent opportunity for someone to get their hands on some prestigious silverware this season.

Borough are 2–0 up at half-time thanks to a brace from Abigail Tucker and seemingly in control. Even midway through the second half there seems nothing to worry the home side, with Mia Connor mopping up most of the trouble at the back when her strikers are not threatening upfront. But chances are missed. Slowly the Borough attacks dry up while gaps start to open up in their defence. The keeper makes a series of good saves to ensure that the gaps don't turn to panic.

But the Woodingdean pressure eventually pays off and, with time ticking by, the Brighton side get a goal back through substitute Elise Gallacher, who slides home after a break on the right. A lob in the dying moments from the same player takes the cup tie to penalties which, for some strange reason are taken at the opposite end to where all the spectators are standing. Early clinical finishing from both sides has to crack eventually and, after a couple of penalty misses, Borough DS, who led 2–0 in this match for so long, are out. Oh well, at least the England cricket match will be on in the clubhouse while I wait for the second game.

Except the second game never happens. A message posted on X informs me that it is off.

• *For Eastbourne Borough Women DS's next match, see game 72 on page 142.*

Game 38: Monday 16 October (7.30pm) at the Saffrons, Eastbourne
Eastbourne Town U23 1 Horsham YMCA U23 0 (Sussex U23 Challenge Cup 2nd Round)
Weather: lovely mild evening
MOM: Mark Fox. The Horsham keeper is outstanding, with a series of point-blank saves to keep his side in the game

I'm chatting to a guy from London whose son is playing for Horsham. Well, he's not actually playing, because he's been substituted, but he does represent Horsham despite living in the capital. His dad, who's originally from Bulgaria, is happy to drive his son to matches. This, at the least, is a four-hour round trip for him on top of a full day's work. Respect for that.

Unfortunately for him, his son's side don't look capable of getting anything from this game tonight. Although it's only 1–0, they are hanging on, the bombardment of their goal only kept at bay thanks to a superb performance by their keeper Mark Fox, who produces a series of saves and plenty of verbal, er, encouragement, to ensure that his defence do their bit as well.

But it's not enough, and the first-half goal from that man Leo Groombridge, calmly slotted home as usual, is enough to ensure that Town move on to the next round.

• *For Eastbourne Town U23's next match, see Game 39 on page 83.*

Game 39: Thursday 19 October (7.30pm) at the Saffrons, Eastbourne
Eastbourne Town U23 2 (win 4–2 on penalties) Welcroft Park Rangers 2 (Eastbourne FA Challenge Cup QF)
Weather: another mild evening but with light rain
MOM: Jason Tibble. The defender stands out, controls the backline and delivers some piercing long passes

The Eastbourne and District FA Challenge Cup is an invitation cup that has been in existence since 1893–94. It is one of a series of cups still hosted by the historic body, which at one time also ran leagues. It's a truly local affair, open to teams in an area broadly bounded by Newhaven to the west, Bexhill to the east, and Uckfield to the north.

After the game, Welcroft's manager tells me they are honoured to have been invited to compete in the cup because they are a relatively new club and still climbing the pyramid (they play in Division 2 (South) of the Mid Sussex). But they are clearly a good new club because, after winning Division 4 (South) last season, they were catapulted up two divisions by the league administrators. Tonight, owing to their position in the pyramid, they can put out their first team, while Town's higher status means it must be largely their U23 side which takes the field (they can play four overage players, as can any U18 sides entered).

The visitors go 1–0 up early on, raising the hopes of their fans, who are mostly clustered under the Sid Myall & Taffy Jones stand behind the goal. For a long spell they look the better side, their physicality knocking back the more technically gifted Town youngsters. But defender Jason Tibble is ensuring Town hold firm at the back, and the game ends 2–2 after a late Sonny Walsh equaliser. The better technique of the Town players shows in the spot-kicks and they win 4–2.

The players from the Hailsham club chat amiably in the bar afterwards and are clearly lads who enjoy their football. They are pleased with their effort. At the break before the penalties their manager had told them: "Well done, you've all put a shift in today and can be proud of that performance." And rightly so. These are players who play for enjoyment — though no less determined to win, and they are disappointed to have let the game slip.

Founded in 2018, Welcroft Park Rangers started life in East Sussex Division 5. A third-place finish in a tiny division of just seven teams was enough for the league to move them up a division when their newly formed reserve side joined Division 5. But after a couple of Covid-19 lockdown-hit seasons (they were moved up another division during this time), life for Rangers really took off.[38]

There were two finals in 2021–22 — the League Challenge Cup (Divisions 2 and 3) and the Eastbourne FA Vice President's Cup — and after moving across to the Mid Sussex League, the first team stormed to the Division 4 (South) title in 2022–23, losing just one game all season, while the reserves took the East Sussex Division 4 crown. The club also lifted the Eastbourne FA Vice President's Cup that year.[39]

Despite being pushed up two divisions after their stellar season in 2022–23, Welcroft are thriving at the higher level. They are unbeaten in six matches (they lost two cup games on penalties) and have smashed in 22 goals in those games, with Jake Barker, Jason Bundy, and Bill Coles all filling their boots.

• *For Eastbourne Town U23's next match, see Game 49 on page 98.*

Game 40: Sunday 22 October (2pm) at the Saffrons, Eastbourne
Eastbourne Town Women 10 Whitehawk Women 0 (SCWGFL Premier)
Weather: a beautiful sunny afternoon in the wake of Storm Babet
WOM: Geri Burt. Sniffs out the goal like Gerd Muller

Storm Babet has been battering Britain for a few days. Giving storms names has been a thing since 2015 and the naming cycle runs from September to the end of August, so we are still near the start of the alphabet. Apparently, Agnes has been and gone (in September), but I must have been asleep when she turned up because I can't remember her. Storm Ciarán is up next, but the one I'm really looking forward to is Storm Minnie. Whoever thought that was a good name for a storm? Now, Olga, a couple of storms along, that is scary. But Minnie? It hardly strikes fear into anyone's heart does it? Still, a storm only gets a moniker, according to the Met Office website, "when it has the potential to cause disruption or damage" not by how nasty its name may sound. BBC weatherman Michael Fish, a son of Eastbourne — who famously told the nation that there was nothing to worry about just hours before the worst storm to hit South East England in three centuries unleashed itself in 1987 — knows a thing or two about downplaying storms, so I'm taking no chances.

But it's Eastbourne Town who are doing the damage here today — and the disruption is to the back of the opposition net. The goal tally builds with no mercy, despite Town having to wait over 20 minutes for their first (and that after nearly conceding). Momentum builds and by the end the goals are flying in, as the young Whitehawk side get more and more dispirited. It's a clinical performance, seven of the strikes coming from the bench, with goal-hungry Geri Burt notching four in 15 minutes. But ten conceded seems a bit unfair on a goalkeeper who, ironically, has had a good game.

As for the scorers, I can do better than to quote the X feed from the Town Women's account itself: "Four goals from Geri, two from D, and one each for Molly, Poppy, Loz, and Chappers".
• *For Eastbourne Town Women's next match, see Game 58 on page 117.*

Game 41: Tuesday 24 October (7.45pm) at Priory Lane, Eastbourne
Eastbourne Borough 1 Dartford 1 (National League South)
Weather: dry and pleasant. Is this really the end of October?
MOM: Fletcher Holman. The young man strikes with a stunning solo effort
Borough are in control early on. As has been the case so often this

season, it's Leone Gravata that is providing the spark, and the wide man goes close after two minutes when he jinks his way into space down the left.

I bump into my friend Steve, who has been dragged along to the match by his sports-loving sons, Louie and Charlie. It's Steve's first time at Priory Lane and he's impressed by the standard. Unfortunately for him he won't get to see much more of Borough's danger man, as a crunching challenge floors Gravata, who can do little more than hobble to the dugout once he's recovered. The crowd in the Peter Fountain Stand erupts — you could hear the crack against Gravata's bone on the terraces — when the defender receives just a yellow. I've got a soft spot for Dartford because I used to watch them regularly when I lived there for a few months, but my sympathy is evaporating rapidly. An awful challenge.

I'm hoping that Will Taylor — all acoustic guitar and cheeky smile — who was playing in the Sports Bar pre-match, will be back on stage at half-time to calm down the prevailing mood. His brand of that talky type of vocals that seems to have taken over from actual singing was very soothing before the game, so it's just what we all need now.

But something a lot better comes along. Three minutes into the second half, Fletcher Holman — in the starting line-up after his goal from the bench at Weymouth three days ago — receives the ball inside his own half, and after sliding past a defender on the halfway line as if he doesn't exist, heads diagonally for the goal. Four Dartford players converge on him, but he weaves his way skilfully through them and slides the ball home from the edge of the box. Absolute magic: Will Taylor should write a song about it.

Holman's five against Billingshurst in the Sussex Senior Cup earlier in the month has catapulted him into first-team contention (he's started only one league game all season before tonight) and the way he's playing it doesn't look as if he's keen on going back to playing village teams in the county cup again.

Unfortunately for Borough a sublime display of dribbling skills leads to a cracking individual goal from Dartford's Brandon Brazey and the home side have to settle for a draw, much to everyone's disappointment.

But afterwards in the bar there is great excitement, as Steve's son Charlie spots Theo Baker, social media star of the football world, and gets a selfie with him. Baker is a part of the *Pitch Side* podcast, who are match sponsor of tonight's game. The cheeky trio of Theo, Reev, and Tom have produced over 1,400 videos on YouTube and have 281,000 subscribers.[40] And if you are turning your nose up from antipathy towards digital media, note that the country's newspaper of record, *The Times*, has only 120,000 print subscribers.[41]

Theo Baker is a local lad (born in Eastbourne and raised in Seaford)[42] who has played for Seaford, Newhaven, and Crystal Palace development team,[43] but he is better known for his sporting videos, tweets, and images. Oh, and winning the Boots Baby of the Year competition, aged two, of course.[44]

Cheeky, jokey, affable, and with a fair bit of football talent of his own, Baker has attracted a huge following for his brand of down-to-earth humour. He has a whopping 1.43 million subscribers on his YouTube channel @TheoBaker, over 161,000 followers on X, and a massive half-a-million-plus followers on Instagram. In comparison, Eastbourne Borough have 2,500, 11,700, and 100,000 respectively.[45]

• *For Eastbourne Borough's next match, see Game 45 on page 92.*

Game 42: Saturday 28 October (2pm) at Eastbourne Sports Park.
Eastbourne Rangers 3 Cuckfield Town 0 (Mid Sussex Division 1)
Weather: windy with intermittent rain
MOM: Tony Derese. Controls the middle nicely in difficult conditions

"Proper grassroots football, where the opposition sub has a quick fag before coming on, the attendance goes up ten per cent when a dog walker stops to watch, and the players battle hard before going for a pint," my notes read. And that pretty much sums up my first visit to Eastbourne Sports Park really.

The players do battle hard. But they have to at this venue

today because the fierce wind (Storm Ciarán is on its way), combined with a smallish 3G pitch and a surface where the ball zips around wildly as if it's on speed, means that meaningful football will have to wait for another day. But at least the match is on. Eastbourne United's game at Lingfield is off, their reserves' home game is off, Town's home game is off, and even Borough required a pre-match pitch inspection, despite having a 3G pitch.

The terrible conditions notwithstanding, Rangers are still attempting to play football. Tony Derese is impressing in midfield with his control and passing, while Chris Billin is putting in some telling runs up the left. The Eastbourne side, who are pushing for another promotion after winning the Division 2 (South) title last year, go ahead when, despite a bobbling ball, Oscar Linzey retains his composure in front of goal to score the first. He adds another in the second half. Cuckfield start to press, but just when it feels as if they'll pull one back, a shot from Billin deflects off one of their defenders and loops into the net, ably assisted by the wind. 3–0.

Just over a year ago, today's team formed the backbone of Rangers' reserves. But at the end of the 2022 season, the first team — who had been playing in the Mid Sussex Premier — folded. The determined second team simply scratched out the word 'reserves' and committed themselves to getting the club back into intermediate-level football.

Eastbourne Rangers were formed in 2009 by club secretary Nick Stephenson when, after years of involvement with other clubs, he set out to start a team from scratch. It was obviously a decent scratch side, because over the course of the next seven years they rose from Division 7 of the East Sussex League to the Premier, picking up four titles on their relentless upwards march.

A reserve side was started in 2014, and their rise was so meteoric that they were promoted from Division 6 to Division 2 in just two seasons! (League administrators sometimes take the decision to push a team up more than one division if they feel they are particularly strong.) In 2015–16 the side completed the league and cup double.

In 2017 the firsts moved from the East Sussex to the Mid Sussex League and were placed in Division 1. That season they reached the final of the Sussex Intermediate Challenge Cup and gained an immediate promotion to the Mid Sussex Premier. And there they stayed until they folded and the current team ably took up the mantle.[46]

• *For Eastbourne Rangers' next match, see Game 44 on page 90.*

30 and 31 October, 2023
It's been a sad two days for football in Eastbourne. On the 30th, Eastbourne United announced the passing of their president Brian Jones while a day later Eastbourne Borough announced that Tony Smith, the former owner of the club had also died. Many, like myself, will not have known these men personally, but will have experienced what they built: warm and welcoming clubs that bring pleasure to many people not only every Saturday, but throughout the week as well. RIP.

Game 43: Tuesday 7 November (7.45pm) at the Oval, Eastbourne
Eastbourne United Reserves 1 Polegate Town 0 (Eastbourne FA Challenge Cup QF)
Weather: dry and a bit chilly
MOM: Paul Rogers. A stand out performance

Eastbourne United Reserves are good: six wins and two draws in eight league games sees them top of the Mid Sussex Premier and in a good position to push for the title. They must be favourites for this competition as well. They can probably beat the intermediate clubs invited to take part in this cup, while their experience and strength should be able to counter the Eastbourne Town U23 should they meet them.

Tonight, United are looking good immediately. They move the ball quickly, shifting the opposition from one side of the pitch to the other to create gaps. They pressure them into making passes they don't want to, gently 'persuade' the referee to reconsider his decisions, and control the play. It's the drip-drip effect of it all. The whole game is on their terms.

But make no mistake, Polegate are no mugs. They have recorded four wins in seven matches in the Mid Sussex Championship and sit in fourth place, pushing for promotion to join United Reserves in the Premier. And they are battling here, even if they are up against a team in top form.

The area around the floodlit pylon near the halfway line is, as usual, a bit of a magnet for fans. Are they moths to the flame or is the small box at the bottom just too convenient for resting beers? Either way, it always seems to attract an interesting bunch to chat to. A couple of them admit they have no idea who is playing, or what competition this is, but just decided to come along to watch a midweek game. At just £3 to get in, those not of the same mind have missed out on a very good, and well-priced, match.

• *For Eastbourne United Reserves' season summary see page 216.*

Game 44: Saturday 11 November (2pm) at Eastbourne Sports Park
Eastbourne Rangers 3 Crawley AFC 1 (Mid Sussex Division 1)
Weather: bit of spitting rain but it mostly holds off
MOM: Tyriece Whiteoak. An impressive and strong young player who is battling for every ball today

I'm not really feeling it today. The weather's not too bad but it's hardly lifting my gloom, and with winter taking hold there's not much to look forward to on that front. And Eastbourne Sports Park, a site with a mishmash of derelict building and overgrown vegetation, is hardly the place to lift anyone's spirits.

But I've been taken by the story of Eastbourne Rangers (see Game 42) and I want to watch them again. The club's first team may have folded, but the reserves (now the first, and only, team for Rangers) have simply rolled up their sleeves and vowed to get the club back into intermediate football. What's not to admire?

The sun is low in the sky and piercingly sharp, its light pulsing across the bright green of the plastic pitch. It's difficult enough to see anything watching from pitchside, so goodness knows what it's like for the players when the ball is coming out of the sun. Rangers take an early lead. I chat to a spectator who plays football for Eastbourne Hospital. They play friendlies, apparently. A useful team to be up against if you break your leg during the game, I suppose. There's also a young family cheering on their son/brother who is playing today. The gloom is lifting. Football is wonderful again.

Now, if you are ever at Eastbourne Sports Park and fancy a beer at half-time, you have only one option: Eastbourne Rugby Club. There are two ways to get there from the 3G pitch: the easy way or the quick way. The easy way involves a walk around some of the forlorn buildings on this site until you get to the pitch used by the rugby club's second and third teams. Then it's back round to the main pitch and, hey presto, you reach the bar. But by the time you have done all of that, you'll need to head immediately back to the football if you don't want to miss the start of the second half. The quick way is to climb over a wire fence, bash through some bushes, and clamber over a ditch. Not too difficult really. Except when the ditch is full of water. Leap, you say? It's pretty wide and I don't want to get wet, I reply. So, I build a bridge with bits of wood and hope my Scouting skills have not deserted me. They haven't and I enjoy a bottle of beer in the clubhouse without having to rush it.

Eastbourne Rugby Club is a lovely, friendly club. Next week, I am told by the staff behind the bar, Eastbourne are playing local rivals East Grinstead and they have 60 visiting fans booked in for lunch. Coaches are expected. I'm invited to return. I decide to accept the invitation because I'm planning to come to watch Eastbourne Athletic at the Sports Park next week anyway. Things are all falling into place.

Back on the 3G pitch things are coming together for Rangers as well. They win 3-0, with goals from Josh Kyte, Artur Mendes, and Tyriece Whiteoak to seal an important victory in their bid for promotion. Rangers go top of the league and are now very much in control when it comes to their aim of a return to intermediate football. I feel guilty for not being up for it earlier. The players certainly are.

• *For Eastbourne Rangers' next match, see Game 66 on page 131.*

Game 45: Tuesday 14 November (7.45pm) at Priory Lane, Eastbourne
Eastbourne Borough 0 Tonbridge Angels 3 (National League South)
Weather: cold and dry
MOM: Jordan Greenidge. The striker's a handful and seals the win with the third goal

Borough is an impressive football club for the sixth tier and they are clearly on the up and up. Businessman Simon Leslie became a majority shareholder in June[47] and soon announced that they were turning professional, with their sights set on the Football League.[48] There was even a sprinkle of Hollywood celebrity dust with the news that actor Oliver Trevena — *The Paradox Effect*, *The Bricklayer*, *The Plane* — had invested in the club.[49] But it wasn't always this way.

Eastbourne Borough were formed in 1964 as Langney FC, and an article in *The Argus* describes how it was in the early days. "They played on council pitches in front of one man and his dog in the Eastbourne and Hastings League, put up their own nets and washed the kit themselves."[50] In the article, one of those players, Len Smith, who would later become chairman, admits that their ambition at the time extended no further than getting a full team on the pitch each week.[51]

But no matter how many they had playing, that team must have been pretty decent because Langney Sports — as the club had been known since the 1968–69 season — moved steadily through the local leagues and were admitted to the Sussex County League in 1983, the same year they moved to Priory Lane. The club had previously played at various recreation fields before a spell at Princess Park next to Eastbourne United's ground, the Oval.[52]

It was from these earthy foundations that Borough (the club's name from 2001)[53] reached the National League (where they played from 2008 to 2011) — just one step from the Football League.[54]

But to reach those heady heights again requires points and 'The Sports', as they are still known on account of their former name, aren't picking up too many of them right now. However, for a team near the relegation zone, I don't think they have been playing badly at all. They are certainly not getting tonked every week.

Even without the electrifying Leone Gravata tonight, the goalscoring form of Fletcher Holman since his five in the county cup provides cause for optimism. But like ambition, optimism must eventually bear fruit. Despite being the better team in the first half, Borough fall behind to a goal on the stroke of half-time, and in the second half the Angels start to control the match and add two more. It's not exactly a tonking, but 3-0 is Borough's biggest defeat of the season.

• *For Eastbourne Borough's next match, see Game 48 on page 96.*

Game 46: Saturday 18 November (2pm) at Eastbourne Sports Park
Eastbourne Athletic 3 Polegate Town Reserves 5 (Mid Sussex Division 3 South)
Weather: windy, with rain in the air
MOM: Richard North. Looks composed throughout for Polegate

Is that Ederson in goal? Some early, confident passing from the Polegate keeper seems to indicate that his side are not fazed by the respective positions of the teams in the league table. Eastbourne Athletic are second with 14 points and a very healthy goal difference while Polegate Town Reserves are some eight points adrift, albeit with a couple of games in hand. But the visitors certainly look determined in very windy conditions (Storm Debi has just passed, but it feels like she is making a return visit).

Athletic, however, quickly show why they are pushing for promotion in consecutive seasons by taking an early lead. I'm back at the 3G pitch at Eastbourne Sports Park, home not only to Eastbourne Rangers, whom I watched in the Mid Sussex Division 1 last week, but also Athletic, a side who are somewhat lower down the ladder in Division 3 (South), in a league system that goes down to Division 6. This would be definitely be described as grassroots football — if there was any grass on the pitch.

According to the FA, there are more than 660,000 male adults who play organised football for 27,770 affiliated teams[55] — and most of them play grassroots football. I love it. I cut my footballing skills (or should that be ankles?) playing for a village side in Surrey. The pitch sloped horribly and the middle became a quagmire when it rained. As I was playing in the centre of midfield, I could barely move more than a couple of steps in the mud, and I swear that there was one game when I never left the centre circle. At least that sort of thing won't be happening today, thanks to the 3G surface.

Athletic's early lead is pegged back and a combination of the unpredictable wind and Polegate's fierce determination turns the game into a topsy-turvy affair, with the visitors grabbing first-half goals through Finlay Kelly, Perry Ford, and George Sambrook. Richard North, the tall Polegate defender, is one of the few players who appears to have any time on this pitch and his calmness on the ball is opening up spaces.

Eastbourne Athletic were formed in 2007 and have a rather nifty badge in yellow and black featuring a hornet (designed by Liz Hadfield, wife of player Dan Hadfield, one of the club's early kit sponsors). The founder, Lee Boniface, is a Watford fan if you are in any doubt where the inspiration came from. Boniface was part of another Eastbourne team, White Knight, but wanted to start "a new club with the main ethos that football at that level should be for anyone regardless of ability, the key ingredient being positivity towards each other and respect towards officials and opponents". And so, helped by a few players from his former club, he brought his new club into being.

Most of the usual suffixes (Town, United, Borough) had already been claimed in the Eastbourne footballing world, but Athletic was a good traditional choice for a football club name — and although 'Hornets' was also considered, Boniface had to settle for its use as the nickname.

The club joined the East Sussex League, and although they moved up from Division 7 to Division 2, most of that was due to league restructuring, so the Hornets have only one runners-up trophy (2008–09 Division 6) to show for their steady ascent. In 2017–18, after playing the same teams for so many years, Athletic made the decision to move to the Mid Sussex League and were admitted to Division 6. More restructuring helped them rise again, and last year they finished runners-up and were promoted to Division 3 (South).

I take my half-time victuals at Eastbourne Rugby Club, which is warm and still packed with lots of lunchers wearing East Grinstead club ties, even though today's game has already started. I don't think many of them have any intention of getting their shoes muddy by actually going outside to watch the match, because they are still tucking into cheeseboards and ordering fresh bottles of red. A few hundred spectators are braving it, however, all no doubt hoping to spot the next Joe Marler, the Harlequins and England prop who started his career at Eastbourne as a youngster.[56] There are lots of posh wellies on show. Eastbourne are winning — or at least they are when I venture through the mud on my way back for the second half of the football.[57]

Back at the match I watch Elliott McWilton and Samuel Eaton add more goals for Polegate as they head towards an unexpected victory. The high-flying Athletic have had their promotion hopes dented, and despite goals through Jim Pyle, Oliver Albertella, and Jake Lambert, they crash to a 5-3 defeat in a highly entertaining game.

• *For Eastbourne Athletic's next match, see Game 56 on page 113.*

Game 47: Saturday 18 November (3pm) at the Saffrons, Eastbourne
Eastbourne Town 0 Hassocks 3 (Southern Combination Premier)
Weather: windy
MOM: Liam Benson. The man who breaks the deadlock

The wind is blowing but at least it's not raining. 'Postponed' has been pasted across local fixtures for the past few weeks thanks to the endless rain, and it's been seven weeks since Eastbourne Town have had a home game. I'm determined not to let the rain rob me of more football so I dash down the hill at the end of the Athletic game at Eastbourne Sports Park to catch the second half at the Saffrons. A cyclist has stopped mid-ride to see what's going on. "I didn't realise football was played here," he's probably thinking.

Hassocks are fifth in the league and Town sixth, both on 28 points, so it's no wonder the game is locked at 0-0. The poor weather means most of the crowd has clustered together to take shelter in the Sid Myall & Taffy Jones stand behind the goal. It's creating a good atmosphere, and a man with an antique rattle is urging the players on. *Clack, clack, clack.* "Come on Town!"

The stalemate is broken just after the hour when Liam Benson strikes for Hassocks, but there is still optimism behind the goal as Town push to pull it back. A shot from Ollie Davies goes close. James Stone and Evan Archibald both threaten too. Then, finally, with just a couple of minutes left, Town have it in the net and the rattle goes crazy. But it's offside. The wind has dropped at last — but only out of Town's sails. The effort for the equaliser, coupled with the disappointment of the goal that never was, is too much and Hassocks add two more goals in injury time. It's not often that a team narrowly lose 3-0.

• *For Eastbourne Town's next match, see Game 51 on page 102.*

Game 48: Tuesday 21 November (7.45pm) at the Crabble Athletic Ground, Dover
Dover Athletic 1 Eastbourne Borough 1 (National League South)
Weather: windy and drizzly
MOM: Fletcher Holman. The bursting run, followed by his patience for the pass that set up the goal, and later his overhead kick, is pure class

It's impossible not to start humming it when you see those chalky cliffs. So, here goes... "There'll be Bluebirds Over, The White Cliffs of Dover".

Sorry, Vera Lynn's famous wartime classic will be buzzing round your head for the rest of the day.

I've always liked Dover and places similar to it. A town passed through by many but visited by few, I always think. It's Europe's busiest passenger port, with 13 million people passing through every year,[58] and yet there were only 34,000 'staying visits' by holidaymakers in 2022, according to Visit Britain.[59] I'll be adding to that tally though, because there is no way to watch the match and get back to Eastbourne on the train tonight.

Dover are second bottom in the league with just one win to their name — and that was back in August, away to Slough Town

— and they have a goal difference of -16, so I'm feeling optimistic for Borough tonight. They could do with the three points because they are hovering uncomfortably near the relegation zone.

The new Dover Marina only opened a few months ago[60] as part of the revitalisation of the waterfront area. It's shiny new and impressive, but it's the old — the 1870 Clock Tower and the lifeboat station next to it — which stands out the most on the Esplanade, where a kiosk advertising South African fusion food is closed. It's no surprise really, because apart from a man walking his dog, the scene is deserted. Maybe everyone is up at Dover Castle today. Or more likely on one of the ferries I can see chugging out across the Channel.

Luckily, it's a bit busier in the town and I run into a couple of Borough fans in the Admiral Harvey, a friendly, down-to-earth pub. The two fans come from London and, although they have no connection with Eastbourne other than that they like it, they have adopted Borough as their team and watch them as often as they can. It seems as good a reason to support a team as any.

We share a cab up to the ground, which is wonderfully named 'the Crabble', a word which comes from the Old English *crabba hol*, meaning 'hole in which crabs are found'.[61] There's a steep hill up to the pitch itself from the entrance and the club have laid on golf carts to ferry people up. Only two seats are available, so I volunteer to walk. I trudge upwards slowly as the crabs of ancient times might have done.

Inside the clubhouse, the travelling Borough fans are clustered around a couple of high-top tables and my two new friends know them all. You quickly start to recognise faces if you follow the same club in non-league football, especially at away games. These are fans brought together by shared experiences of last-minute victories and painful losses after a journey to watch their team.

The Crabble has been a sporting venue since the late 19th century when it was used for cycling, athletics, and cricket. Marylebone Cricket Club played here in 1899 and Kent hosted more than a hundred first-class games between 1907 and 1976. That was on the 'lower pitch', which Dover FC used before moving to the 'upper pitch' in 1951.[62] The current club were formed in 1983 and took over the use of the ground after Dover FC folded.

The wind and rain are not the easiest of conditions for the players but there are a few chances being created at both ends. Iffy Allen and Dontai Stewart are a threat for the home side, and despite the early loss of Leone Gravata, Fletcher Holman and Zak Emmerson are ensuring that Dover have plenty to think about too. And it's Holman and Emmerson who link up to give Borough the lead. Holman bursts through on the right with speed as Emmerson races to get into position. But Holman, showing a great footballing brain, is able to slow down his run and time his delivery to the on-loan Blackpool striker to perfection for the tap-in.

At half-time I hear a couple of Borough fans say: "I'd settle for a draw," which seems a bit odd considering the scoreline and Dover's position in the league. Let's hope the players are bit more ambitious.

But Dover equalise through Dontai Stewart and despite a few chances to snatch the victory, including a lovely overhead kick from Holman that just goes over and a shot that is parried by the keeper, the Borough fans do indeed have to settle for the draw.

• *For Eastbourne Borough's next match, see Game 53 on page 108.*

Game 49: Thursday 23 November (7.30pm) at the Saffrons, Eastbourne
Eastbourne Town U23 0 Peacehaven & Telscombe U23 2 (Southern Combination U23 East)
Weather: dry and pretty mild
MOM: Michael Lloyd. His two goals decide an otherwise closely fought match

I've been impressed by Town U23 this season. They run hard, work for each other, and have fast strikers like Sonny Walsh and Leo Groombridge (although he's out tonight) who know where the goal is.

But Peacehaven & Telscombe have not lost so far and they seem to have that little bit extra when it matters. It's a barely noticeable difference, just the odd touch here and there, but Michael Lloyd is able to get the ball in the net twice to decide what is otherwise a remarkably close game.

Thursday night used to be the deadest of dead nights when it came to football. Not any more. Apart from the entertainment of the U23 action, Thursday is now the chosen day for the Europa League and the Europa Conference League, while the occasional Champions League match gets shifted there as well, to avoid two clubs from the same city playing on the same night. Increasingly, the Premier League and the FA Cup have started using Thursdays too, usually for TV broadcast reasons. But it wasn't always so.

When Sheffield FC took on Hallam FC in 1860, a match believed by many sources to be the first ever inter-club match,[63] it was actually played on a Wednesday, as that was when the chosen day — Boxing Day — fell. The first recognised international (Scotland v England in 1872)[64] was played on a Saturday (a 2pm kick-off, incidentally), as was a match between the two countries two years earlier (not recognised because the 'Scotland' team were made up of players based in London with Scottish roots).[65] The first league matches came along in 1888 when the Football League was formed, and gloriously for you traditionalists, the opening day (8 September)[66] was a Saturday (although before you get too excited, the 3pm kick-off was only a guideline, so the games actually started at different times).[67] There was one match on a Monday that season and one on a Wednesday (Boxing Day), but all the other games were on a Saturday, which became firmly established as football's chosen day. And, apart from the occasional match (usually on a public holiday), that is how it remained for decades.

Then, in the 1950s, after years of experiments with artificial light, football suddenly found itself able to play at night thanks to better quality floodlights and a more reliable electricity supply, due to the introduction of the national 'supergrid'.[68] European competition saw midweek matches become frequent events.

Sunday football followed (the first professional match played on a Sunday was between Cambridge United and Oldham on 6 January 1974), an initiative that came about because of electricity supply problems during an oil crisis sparked by war in the Middle East.[69] A new fixture pattern emerged: Saturdays and Sundays were for weekend football, while Tuesdays and Wednesdays (usually cup matches) provided the midweek fix. With a few exceptions during that time, Mondays, Fridays, — let alone Thursdays — didn't get much of a look in. Presumably people amused themselves in other ways.

Then along came the Premier League in 1992[70] — the year that the European Cup became the Champions League. The associated TV deals grew more lucrative, and so the next phase of televised football began. Football matches became commonplace on the first night of the working week, thanks to Sky's *Monday Night Football*,[71] and in 2014 the *Guardian* reported plans for "regular Friday night live matches on TV" in the Premier League.[72] With the Champions League expanding, the UEFA Cup also getting bigger under its new brand (the Europa League), and the launch of the Europa Conference League, even Thursday was eventually sucked into the fixture schedule.

On the evidence of tonight, Peacehaven & Telscombe U23 are probably very glad that it was.

• *For Eastbourne Town U23's next match, see Game 82 on page 160.*

Game 50: Saturday 25 November (3pm) at the Oval, Eastbourne
Eastbourne United 2 Loxwood 0 (Southern Combination Premier)
Weather: dry, but without much cloud cover, and the temperature hovers around zero
MOM: Alfie Headland. Commanding at the back, as always

The Oval is a suitable place to bring up my half-century of games this season because it's where I've seen some of the best football so far. United started the campaign on fire, remaining unbeaten in their first 12 matches and losing just one in their first 15 (to Berkhamsted of the Southern League in the FA Cup 2nd Qualifying Round). But a lackadaisical away defeat to Seaford Town in the Peter Bentley Cup signalled a bit of a slump. Drubbings at Midhurst & Easebourne and Crowborough followed, in a run of nine games that included just three wins. Although things have picked up in the league recently, United were knocked out of the RUR Cup in the week by Hayward's Heath.

The West Sussex village of Loxwood is in the north of the county, up near the border with Surrey. The population is a mere 1,597 according to the 2021 Census,[73] but they are certainly a savvy PR bunch. Owing to 'political turmoil' in the country, reports the *Daily Mirror*, the village declared independence in 2019 and appointed a new ruler — Queen Adelina. Bless 'em. As far as I can tell, the new 'country' is still awaiting recognition from another state and have yet to secure a seat at the United Nations, although the move would certainly have gained a lot of publicity for the village's 'Loxwood Joust'. The realm also claimed to have raised an army and launched its own currency — the Loxwood Groat.[74] But if any of these 'foreigners' think they are getting into United with their groats, I think they will probably be disappointed. I reckon Tracey on the entrance gate will be wanting eight proper British pounds today.

Loxwood football club have been in existence since 1920 and the Southern Combination Premier is the highest level they have played at. They have been at this level for a decade and have had two sixth-place finishes in that time, so they are certainly not here to make up the numbers.[75]

But small is not always beautiful in football. Along with proximity to other clubs and the population of the surrounding catchment area, the size of the place where a club are based is a key determinant of how high they can climb. The smallest town with a Premier League club, in terms of population, is Burnley,[76] with just over 78,000 people.[77] It does, however, have a number of places such as Manchester, Liverpool, Leeds, and Bolton all within an hour or so as a catchment area for fans. And, once at this level, players can be drawn from all over the world, of course. But when it comes to villages, few can match Forest Green Rovers in recent years. For the past seven seasons, the League Two club have sustained themselves in the top tiers — including a season in League One — from their base in Nailsworth, which has a population of fewer than 6,000 people.[78] Bigger than Loxwood for sure, but a village, nonetheless.

There's no game at Eastbourne Town today, and I spot a few familiar faces from the Saffrons standing in the small covered area near the entrance who have come to watch their rivals. One of the Town fans, who plays in the Sussex Disability League, is berating his younger cousin because he has stopped playing football. Ross and Liam are good company.

To amuse ourselves during a lull in play, we think up ridiculous possible scenarios that could occur in a match and what would happen as a result. Would a game be abandoned if a flock of seagulls invade the pitch, for instance? We are soon presented with a real-time (and much more common) scenario, however, when the referee starts talking to one of the managers and it begins to look as if he may be sent off. If he were 'sent to the stands', as they say in professional football, he wouldn't actually be much further from the pitch than he is while sitting in the dugout. Is he allowed just to stand on the other side of the barrier a few inches away from the pitch? Or must he stand by the burger hut? Or sit in his car? The debate soon spreads around the stand (football fans do like a good discussion) but there is obviously no agreement (football fans don't like agreeing on anything).

Later I check on the RefChat forum, but there's no definitive answer on there, although one poster does point out that Law 12 in the Laws of the Game indicates that when a player is sent off, he or she should leave 'the vicinity[79] of the field of play and the technical area'. However, the Law doesn't mention managers or define what 'the vicinity' actually is.[80] Unfortunately there is no thread on flocks of seagulls.

United are as entertaining as ever for my 50th game of the season, taking the lead through the goal machine Callum Barlow, and wrapping it up with a Hayden Beaconsfield strike at the end, with the goals coming either side of a penalty save by James Broadbent.
• *For Eastbourne United's next match, see Game 54 on page 110.*

Game 51: Tuesday 28 November (7.30pm) at the Saffrons, Eastbourne
Eastbourne Town 0 Crawley Down Gatwick 1 (Southern Combination Premier)
Weather: it's a fairly fresh November evening
MOM: Jack Ryder. His runs upfront are a constant threat for the visitors

I'm standing on the open terracing by the bowls club. The linesman running this side is very good. Now, those are eight words you're not likely to see written too often.

There are three types of official at this level. There are the old guys (I've not seen a woman officiate in the Southern Combination yet) who can't stop pulling on the black. These are the officials who love football so much that they won't retire, viewing it as a wonderful reason to get out of the house every so often. They've officiated in umpteen matches, may have been at a higher level at some stage, seen everything that can be seen, and received all the abuse possible. If a bench descends into screaming and shouting following one of their decisions, they just smile as if placating children having a tantrum. They are pretty decent officials.

The second type look as if they are just doing it for the money and give the impression that they'd rather be anywhere but on a football pitch. They go through the motions in every game and want to get to the end of it with as little hassle as possible. That's why they get angry when a player questions them. It makes no sense to them that someone should actually care. It's only a game after all. They will never progress up the pyramid and, frankly, never have the ambition to either. They are pretty useless.

The third type are the officials who are on the way up. They want to go to a higher level and have the talent to do it. They make decisions firmly, but aren't afraid to admit it if they don't see something or make a mistake. But best of all, they talk to the players. They don't want to be their friend; they are just man-managing the game. They are pretty good. But don't get used to them because they'll be moving on to higher things.

Tonight's linesman is the third kind. I hear him ask a player who is taking a corner if he is right- or left-footed, before positioning himself accordingly for the kick. He informs a player where a throw must be taken in such a way that the player actually listens.

Sneaking a few yards at a throw-in is a compulsion for most players, even though it rarely makes any material difference to the game. But it's important for them to try their luck because it tests the boundaries of the officials, enabling them to see how far they can be pushed and what they can get away with later. Officials mostly deal with this in two ways: scream and point like a schoolteacher or ignore it and hope it'll stop. Those who adopt the former approach get accused of being petty and lose respect immediately, while players simply take advantage of those who pursue the passive line. But both have lost control by going to extremes too early. Tonight's linesman, by contrast, is the archetypal 'firm but fair' official, displaying this on one occasion by cocking his head and smiling, as if to say: "Come on, we both know how this works. Now take that throw back a couple of yards." It works too. And the player smiles back, knowing he's been caught.

But enough about officials because it's round three of the Eastbourne Football Cheeseburger Challenge. I head off to the Corner Flag cafe. The service is excellent and the burger is pretty good. It's tasty, with proper mustard, but the onions are more boiled than fried, so it doesn't quite top the pile and it's Eastbourne United's superb cheeseburger which takes the title.[81]

The game has been fairly even so far, but Crawley gradually start to edge it. Town are working hard but they are clearly missing the experience of Evan Archibald. I'm chatting to him behind the goal and it doesn't sound as if his injury will keep him out for long, which is good news for Town fans because their side look a bit flat tonight. Archibald is a decent goalscorer, but it's his often unnoticed hard work off the ball that really makes a difference. It's a very young-looking bench, with Matthew Myall, Calum Pollitt, and Leo Groombridge joining Anesu Sisimayi in the dugout, so I'm not expecting a string of changes from manager Jude McDonald.

Marc Pelling is full of energy and pushing forward from the back for Crawley, while Jack Ryder's laconic dribbling style upfront is causing trouble for Town. But marshalled by skipper Frankie Chappell, Town are, as usual, defending well. Suddenly they have to because there is a flurry of chances. A deflected shot from Crawley looks like it is looping in but is just cleared off the line. Then Chappell puts in an amazing last gasp block that thwarts what looks like a clear chance. Then a save. Then another block. Something has to give — and it does. In the 65th minute Pelling scores with a good strike. Without Archibald it doesn't feel as if Town will get this back and they lose a game they surely would have expected to win.

• *For Eastbourne Town's next match, see Game 52 on page 107.*

3
When the Watchin' Gets Tough

Game 52: Saturday 16 December (3pm) at the Saffrons, Eastbourne
Eastbourne Town 1 Steyning Town Community 0 (Southern Combination Premier)
Weather: cloudy with some wind, and rain in the air
MOM: Chris Winterton. You need your keeper to be on top form in tight games like this. And he is

After a week off from *Fish, Chips & Football* to watch my own side, Aldershot Town, trounce Swindon 7-4 in the FA Cup, I'm back at the Saffrons to watch a match between two teams pushing for a play-off position. Only the champions are automatically promoted from the Southern Combination Premier to the Isthmian League, while the next four teams must battle it out in the play-offs (assuming those clubs meet the various Isthmian League ground requirements). These are one-off ties. The second- and third-place teams get a home tie against fifth and fourth respectively and the winners of those games play a 'final' to see who will join the champions in Isthmian next season.

Every football fan has heard of the Isthmian League — even those who only follow the Premier League — probably because it's not a word you can forget easily (although spelling it is another matter). Even the casual supporter is likely to sit up and take notice when 'a team from the Isthmian League' has a run in the FA Cup. Derived from both Latin and Greek, an 'isthmus'[1] is a narrow strip of land, bordered on both sides by water, connecting two larger landmasses, and its adjectival variant pulses with nostalgia and romance. In Ancient Greece there was an Isthmian Games named after the famous Isthmus of Corinth with athletics events like there are in the Olympics (although it was always scheduled in such a way that the two never clashed). So if history had taken a different turn, it's quite possible we would be watching the Isthmian Games on TV every four years rather than the reincarnation of its rival.[2]

But the league with the romantic name — inspired by that long-ago feast of sporting prowess with its amateur ideals — must wait for these two teams a while longer. For now, it's the Southern Combination and a chase for a play-off place.

It's all quiet on the western stand, with Steyning having a few off-target shots and Town unable to set up any chances at all. Their first shot comes only on the half-hour thanks to a Tom Vickers curler. It's a precursor of what is to come, however, because it's Vickers who dispatches a penalty for Town eight minutes later. After that, some fine goalkeeping from Chris Winterton in the home goal ensures nothing more is needed for Town to close the gap at the top. And start dreaming of Ancient Greece.

• *For Eastbourne Town's next match, see Game 54 on page 110.*

Game 53: Saturday 23 December (3pm) at Priory Lane, Eastbourne
Eastbourne Borough 0 Yeovil Town 1 (National League South)
Weather: mild and overcast
MOM: Frank Nouble. Like a true striker, he doesn't hesitate to slot the ball home despite the circumstances that led to his chance

Yeovil are strong, fast, and very clever. That's why they are top of the league and looking good for promotion. Tonight they are very clever (or sneaky, depending on your viewpoint) as they grind out a victory in front of 1,736 fans.

The solitary goal comes in the 35th minute — and it's controversial. A Yeovil player goes down holding his head, and because the referee is obliged to stop the game for a possible head injury under FA guidance,[3] he blows up. The game restarts with a drop ball 'to' Borough, the referee dropping the ball at the feet of Freddie Carter while the Yeovil players stand back. This is one of football's unwritten rules: the ball goes back to the team who were in possession at the time of the stoppage and the opposition allow them to have it. But Carter lingers, and Yeovil's Rhys Murphy whips the ball away before racing down the right wing and setting up Frank Nouble for the goal. Ho, ho, ho! Merry Christmas.

According to the Laws of the Game, it's a goal. So the referee, although looking a bit perturbed, points to the centre circle. However, as advocates of those weird unwritten rules, some fans think that a lightning bolt should instantly strike the transgressors. Giving the ball to the opposition at the restart remains a firm fan favourite, and failure to adhere is guaranteed to provoke a loud chorus of boos. Slicing the opposition striker down? Well, that's just 'taking one for the team'. Wasting time when you are ahead? That's just 'managing the game'. But not giving the ball back? Let those lightning bolts commence. The trouble with unwritten rules, of course, is that they are not really rules at all. How long must you give the opposition before you are allowed to challenge them? Presumably Murphy believes it's a second or two. Carter obviously thinks it's longer. In any case, Carter hardly mitigates his indecision by choosing to flap his arms in protest rather than chase after Murphy.

Afterwards, both the Borough website[4] and its Yeovil counterpart[5] politely call the goal "bizarre". Yeovil's independent *Goverscast* at least stretches the description to "controversial".[6] Needless to say, Borough manager Mark Beard, left raging on the touchline, might be using slightly different words.

Like a lot of people who went to school when there was still free milk in the mornings, I'll always associate Yeovil with the infamous sloping pitch they once had[7] and their celebrated FA Cup runs, when they were flying the flag for non-league football seemingly year after year. That pitch was one of those novelty stories the BBC used to wheel out on *Football Focus* every couple of years, along with the story of the Isles of Scilly Football League, made up of only two teams. Unlike Yeovil, though, neither Garrison Gunners nor Woolpack Wanderers, who play on those western islands, wear green.

In fact, Yeovil are one of the few teams in the top seven divisions of English football to use green on their first-choice kit (for those racking their brains right now, the few I can think of are at the back

of the book).[8] And it's quirky trivia like green kits and sloping pitches that stick in our football minds. For the 2023–24 side, you can now add an interesting brand of cleverness to the list of Yeovil distinctives.
• *For Eastbourne Borough's next match, see Game 71 on page 140.*

Game 54: Tuesday 26 December (11am) at the Oval, Eastbourne
Eastbourne United 2 Eastbourne Town 2 (Southern Combination Premier)
Weather: a mild and clear Boxing Day morning
Men of the Match: (come on, it's Christmas): Brett Patton (United) and Nathan Jenkins (Town)

With stomachs full and heads still spinning, there's a steady stream of people drifting towards the Oval. Few buses are running, but the reward for a therapeutic walk along the seafront is the Boxing Day local derby. And a pint.

Not that it's all plain sailing, because there are queues outside the Oval. Yes, queues. And stewards. It's the first time I've seen either at the ground, despite some very appealing games here in the past few months. But then nothing beats a local derby and an excuse to escape your (insert the name of your least favourite relative). United have set up two entrances to the ground (in itself a novelty); one taking cash, the other accepting cards. A voice comes over the PA system (is that new as well?) to announce that the game will be delayed by five minutes to ensure that everyone gets in before kick-off. The mood in both queues is friendly and relaxed — until a card-carrying supporter realises that he is in the line for cash payments, sparking a dash to a friend for a tenner. People are enjoying the fresh air and are catching up with friends after what must have been, oh, a good 36 hours or so. A young boy, who hasn't been to a local game before, tells me that he's supporting "Eastbourne". Not unlike a lot of the new faces here, no doubt. Let's just hope that one day that young boy starts to watch one of his local sides regularly — regardless of whether it's the whites or the yellows he decides to adopt.

I'm supposed to be meeting two people this morning. Neil doesn't make it because he's still asleep, but Steve is here — a 50 per cent turnout seems decent enough, given that it's Boxing Day morning.

It's an even first half, and certainly not lacking in purpose or energy, but it is missing the blood and thunder usually associated with derby games. The 734[9] spectators seem more than happy though, and after a half-time break in a crowded bar, they are rewarded with plenty of typical derby-type action.

As the temperature rises to a heady 45 degrees, so does the heat on the pitch. Tackles are getting fiercer and there are even a couple of scuffles. This is more like it. If the first half was one of jabbing and probing, then the second half is one of trading blows. Ollie Davies opens the scoring for Town on the hour, but it takes only two minutes for Charlie Ball to equalise. There's time for Town's Jack Murphy to be sent to the sin bin before a Callum Barlow goal turns the game around and gives United the lead with ten minutes remaining. Again, the lead only lasts two minutes as a penalty is put away by Tom Vickers for Town to make it 2-2. But it's not quite over yet. There's a goal-line clearance from United's Alfie Headland in injury time, then Vickers gets shown his second yellow and is sent off. Barely has he reached the tunnel before it's all over, leaving the crowd to work out which queue they'll join for the exit.

- *For Eastbourne United's next match, see Game 79 on page 152.*
- *For Eastbourne Town's next match, see Game 59 on page 118.*

Game 55: Sunday 14 January (11am) at the Saffrons, Eastbourne
Eastbourne Town U18 7 Newhaven U18 1 (Southern Combination U18 East)
Weather: bright piercing winter sun with barely a cloud in the sky
MOM: Flynn Sweeting. Full of energy and two goals after coming off the bench

The Premier League's version of a winter break — in which each team gets a full week off — is in progress. In reality, it's more of a two-week staggering (half the teams get the first week off and the others are free the next). Players can at least head to Abu Dhabi to do their shuttle runs in the warm. To add to the confusion, however, the games that *are* scheduled, are spread throughout the week, so there seems to be a match on every day. Presumably this is to ensure that fans don't suffer from EPL withdrawal.

I've had my own (enforced) break from football after a recurrence of an African lurgy I picked up some years ago, but sadly there was no Abu Dhabi for me. It's nice to see some live football again. Hello 2024! Most of the spectators are standing on the long east terrace at the Saffrons by the Roger Addems stand (named after the Town legend, a former manager and president) which is bathed in lovely morning sun.

Newhaven's hopes of holding back the league leaders are quickly put to bed when Sonny Walsh tucks away an early penalty. An injury in the build-up to the incident signals the arrival of Flynn Sweeting off the bench, fresh from his selection for the first-team squad yesterday, when Town beat league leaders Crowborough. It's not going to get any easier for the visitors. Their keeper is under bombardment and it's the substitute who gets Town's second, somewhat fortuitously, when the ball hits him following a corner. He's fired up and full of energy. It's infectious, and from then on the game becomes a procession, and there are two goals apiece for Sweeting, Walsh, and Noah Titterton-Manos.

There is always a bit of spice in these local U18 games because players on opposing sides have often been to school or college together, and many of them have probably played in the same team at some time during their early careers. And even though this game is one-sided, these do not look like players who want a winter break — Abu Dhabi or no Abu Dhabi.

If they *do* need an extra incentive to run around with vigour and enthusiasm, however, this month's signing of Fletcher Holman — a former Eastbourne Town U18 and U23 player — to a Premier League side from Eastbourne Borough shows that there is 'gold in them thar hills'. In Holman's case it was Wolves, hence the gratuitous California gold rush reference. I've been waiting years for an opportunity to use this fabulous phrase, so you'll have to forgive me.

In fact, Holman is not the first to have gone on to bigger things after spending his early years at Eastbourne Town. Between 1892 and 1903, left-half George Topham represented Eastbourne (he also played for both Corinthian and Casuals, clubs who later merged to form the famous Corinthian Casuals) during which time he was selected to play for England in a British Championship game against Wales at the Racecourse Ground in Wrexham.[10]

A year later, Eastbourne goalkeeper William Meates moved to Small Heath (later Birmingham City), while Jack Carruthers turned pro for Brighton & Hove Albion after a spell for the club in 1929–30. In the 1960s and '70s Tony Buck played for Oxford United, Newport County, and Rochdale after a youth career here, while Brian Clarke played for Gillingham from 1988–92 following a similar start on the sunshine coast.[11]

In more recent years, Nigerian Yemi Odubade scored over 70 goals for Town in his two-season spell, and later made 135 appearances for Oxford United from 2006–09 before moving on to Stevenage and many other clubs besides. And in 2009, local lad James Norwood joined Exeter City from Eastbourne Town. The striker has gone on to make nearly 400 appearances for clubs such as Tranmere Rovers, Ipswich Town, Barnsley, and Oldham Athletic, as well as representing England Schools and England C.[12]

And if the young lads of today ever go off football, William Grevett provides a very early reminder that there are other sports out there as well. He made over 100 appearances for the club, managed them between 1931–39, and also made a cameo appearance for Sussex County Cricket Club along the way.[13]

• *For Eastbourne Town U18's next match, see Game 90 on page 174.*

Game 56: Saturday 20 January (2pm) at Eastbourne Sports Park
Eastbourne Athletic 3 Nutley 2 (Mid Sussex Division 3 South)
Weather: very chilly
MOM: John Clarke. The big man is solid and commanding at the back and snags two crucial goals
and
Game 57: Saturday 20 January (2pm) at Eastbourne Sports Park
Jesters Town 4 Battle Town Reserves 1 (East Sussex Division 1)
MOM: Musa Camara. A constant threat upfront and two goals

Today, Eastbourne is considered to be a large town[14] — the 69th largest built-up area in the country by population, in fact[15] —

and all its individual parts are joined up by development. From the town centre to Meads, to Langney and Sovereign Harbour, to Willingdon and Hampden Park, it's all one big conurbation. But, of course, it wasn't always like this. Way back in the mid-1900s, the area was just four hamlets divided by pastureland: Meads (whose residents still think it is a hamlet), Bourne (the Saxon settlement around Motcombe Gardens where entertainer Tommy Cooper had a holiday home long after the Saxons arrived), Southbourne (around what some people today call Little Chelsea), and Sea Houses.[16] Now, the last one is so easy to work out that I won't bother putting anything in brackets to explain it.

It seems strange today that so many people chose to live inland when the sea was so close, but the clever ones (rich too, no doubt) would have plumped for Sea Houses. One of those shrewd individuals was Charles Darwin, who I think we can all agree, was a pretty clever chap. When he stayed here in the 1850s, the lovely coffee and ice cream shop, Gelato Famosa, had yet to appear on the seafront. But that was a good thing, probably. Darwin could scarcely afford to spend his day mulling over his choice of ice-cream flavour as he was busy writing the earth-shattering *On the Origin of Species*, published in 1859.[17] No doubt he wrote the best bits here.

At that time there would be little of interest in the area just to the north of what is now Eastbourne District General Hospital. Luckily for me, this site is now the home of a thriving and busy sporting facility — Eastbourne Sports Park, which is where Eastbourne Athletic are playing today.

But when I arrive, there are *two* games about to kick off. Athletic have an important game for their push for promotion in the Mid Sussex League on the 3G pitch, while on the adjacent grass pitch Jesters Town are about to play Battle Town Reserves in the East Sussex League. It might just lead to the type of cross-border co-operation that would have globalists singing "We Are the World" and advocating the free movement of players between games and clubs without restrictions.

I've seen a few matches on the 3G pitch this season, but there has never been any action on the grass pitch next to it — which is officially Pitch 1, according to the board that shows teams which dressing room they have been allocated. There have been a lot of storms in the past few months (we are up to Storm Isha, if you haven't been following), so Jesters — named after a sports bar in Eastbourne — have presumably had a lot of games on their grass pitch called off, while Athletic bounce along happily in wind and rain thanks to their plastic surface. As if to emphasise the point, the league fixtures reveal that Athletic have, remarkably, just two more league games to go after this one — while Jesters are only halfway through their fixtures.

In the world of groundhopping, watching more than one game a day is like the holy grail. Hoppers watch one game, then race across the country to fit in another that's kicking off later. There are even hoppers who manage three games in a single day. An organisation called GroundhopUK[18] arrange trips (along with accommodation and transport between grounds) so fans can watch six or seven matches over a weekend while meeting up with fellow groundhoppers. As well as watching the games, these hoppers gather to buy programmes and pin badges — important prizes in the groundhopping community, along with photos of the ground that can be posted on X or Instagram. And this sort of thing is not as niche as you might think. As a rule of thumb, these trips "add a couple of hundred extra to every game" according to GroundhopUK's Chris Berezai. I like the sound of it. Groundhopping is a hobby that involves travel, fresh air, and meeting new people around the country. I might sign up for a weekend myself.

In fact, seduced by these smooth-talking groundhoppers, I've already succumbed to temptation and tried out the two-game thing myself this season, as those of you who have read this far will know. It's fun, but it is a bit exhausting. But today I may have stumbled across a solution to all this running about: simply watch two games at the same time. I am actually thinking of launching Groundstay, a new organisation enabling you to stay in one place while different teams come to you. Way more practical, don't you think?

Watching two games at once is pretty difficult, however, and my neck is certainly getting a good workout. I soon realise that the trick to following both matches simultaneously is to watch long chunks of each match to get a feel for the ebb and flow of what's happening, only turning around to the other one when there is a pause in play. Everything I learn will be included in the welcome pack for new members of Groundstay.

The sports bar side, who are top of Division 1 out east are strolling it in their game. The grass in one corner of the pitch is so long that the ball nearly disappears completely at times — but when it does emerge, it's usually Jesters that have control. They are quicker and sharper than their visitors and striker Musa Camara is the main threat, especially when Jesters are attacking the end where the grass is not ankle-high.

Meanwhile, Athletic are making heavy weather of it against bottom side Nutley, who look better than their league position suggests. Nutley have just five points this season, so it's a big surprise when Jack King scores for them in the first minute against their promotion-chasing hosts. But Athletic are a determined bunch and they bounce back. One player in particular is standing out on the 3G. I ask the sub/linesman the name of the player at the back. It's 'big' John apparently.

John Clarke is indeed a big man, but don't be fooled; he has plenty of skill and is solid and composed at the back. He is also a great header of the ball and he celebrates with some vigour when his first-half equaliser flies off his head at pace and into the goal. Another for the home side follows from Andy Ratcliffe. It's crucial that Athletic win today, but the bottom side aren't playing ball and are putting up a fight. Cue another priceless celebration from Clarke as he grabs his second. Athletic hang on for a crucial win despite another Nutley goal and some late nervy moments.

Over on Pitch 1 it's a lot less dramatic. Jesters are coasting after going 4-1 up a few moments ago, with their goals coming from the impressive Musa Camara (2), Reece Davey, and Jake Barker.

Good stuff. It's certainly been worth a trip from Sea Houses, Mr Darwin.
* *For Eastbourne Athletic's next match, see Game 73 on page 143.*
* *For Jesters Town next match, see Game 69 on page 135.*

Game 58: Sunday 21 January (1.30pm) at Priory Lane, Eastbourne
Eastbourne Borough Women 5 Eastbourne Town Women 1 (SCWGFL Premier)
Weather: cold with clear skies and no wind
WOM: Charlotte Gurr. A top player who knows how to finish

Things are certainly different at Borough since these two teams met in September and Town were the runaway victors 7-1. There have been a number of changes at Priory Lane. The women's manager has been sacked and replaced by Billy Wood — and there are more than a few new players wearing Borough red thanks to his recruitment skills. They are very good players too, not least the talented pair of Kellie Larkin and Charlotte Gurr. Larkin is a former England U19 international, who was previously with Chelsea, Brighton, and Lewes.[19] She joined Borough in October. Gurr, another player with an impressive footballing CV, has Brighton, Arsenal, and Charlton Athletic among her previous clubs,[20] and signed at the same time.

Town are struggling to cope with the onslaught from players of this calibre and even the usually commanding defender Sarah Da Silva can't stem the tide, as the home side grab five goals. Gurr scores two and Larkin one, to add to a double from Abigail Tucker. The September scoreline is almost reversed.

The 3G pitch suits Borough's fast passing style, and love or hate this type of surface, there is no doubt that it makes this a non-stop working football club. There is a decent crowd of 169 — an impressive turnout for a match in this league — and there are plenty of youngsters all kitted up and waiting their turn to play on the shiny surface once this game finishes.

Borough's 2023–24 campaign has definitely been a 'season of two halves': since their pointless first five matches when they leaked goals for their opponents' fun, they have strung six wins

together with a free-scoring goal tally of 36. Gurr has ten of them, failing to score only once in the run. Today's win takes Borough above Town, the early league leaders and last season's Division One champions.
• *For Eastbourne Borough Women's next match, see Game 85 on page 164.*
• *For Eastbourne Town Women's next match, see Game 70 on page 138.*

Game 59: Saturday 27 January (3pm) at the Saffrons, Eastbourne
Eastbourne Town 2 Peacehaven & Telscombe 1 (Southern Combination Premier)
Weather: chilly, but the shivering only kicks in towards in the end of the match
MOM: Tom Vickers. The man is everywhere, throwing himself into tackles and driving the team on in search of the winner till the end

My friend Tim has been visiting his family in Eastbourne for over 50 years, but this is the first time he has been to a game of football in the town. We've known each other since we were proverbially knee high to grasshoppers and for some reason, we still theatrically put our hands just above the ground when we tell people this fact, just in case they are unsure about the height of a grasshopper's knee.

"What a friendly bunch of people," he soon declares after chatting to a few fans at the game, quickly followed by: "Oh, you can drink a beer while watching the game. That's civilised." As fans who go to local football more than once every 50 years already know, of course. Just as they know that today it's too cold to be holding a plastic cup of cold beer outside. But novelty wins the day with my friend.

Three London exiles greet me and Tim decides that they remind him of Bob Hoskins, as we all swap tales of life beside the Thames. The London lads are part of a decent crowd that has turned out for today's match, in part no doubt because there's no game at the Saffrons for the first team till March after this one (remarkably the next six games are away). There are also plenty of black and white scarves; Peacehaven is only 15 miles away, after all. But it seems that one of the visitors has chosen a bad place to leave his car.

A man in the bowls club, which is separated from the football ground by only a small wooden fence, is optimistically scanning the crowd, searching for the driver before the club shuts. "I'm looking for the guy who left his car in our car park," he tells me. He goes on to describe him. But there are more than 200 people here. While we are chatting, Peacehaven & Telscombe take the lead with a scrappy but nonetheless effective finish from Aaron Capon. They all count. I take the opportunity to get the lowdown on joining the bowls club (*Fish, Chips & Bowls* anyone?) before going in search of the PA system announcer.

Mackenzie Whitehouse, the Town PA man, is without doubt my favourite announcer. His relaxed style, his honesty when he lacks information, and the occasional bit of unashamed bias towards his team, never fails to raise a smile in an ever-more regimented world of clones. I eventually find him (he is on the terraces) and he reads out the registration number of the car that is parked in the bowls club, after wedging himself between the gap between the boardroom and the Corner Flag cafe. "It's the only place where I don't get feedback," he tells me. What's not to admire about this young man?

The car driver never arrives and the man at the bowls club decides to give up waiting. So, to the owner of the navy blue VW, I'm sorry, but I did try. The club will be open again on Monday.

Meanwhile, back on the pitch, things are looking up for the home side. They have won a penalty, duly dispatched by Tom Vickers just before half-time, and their neighbours are down to ten men for the rest of the match, with goalkeeper Nathan Stroomberg shown red. His replacement, pulling on the Day-Glo number 13 shirt, doesn't look like he usually does this goalkeeper stuff.

Harry Docherty, has in fact, been playing in midfield alongside former Town player Max Hollobone. At least until the referee's card is flashed. I was always the go-to replacement keeper in my playing days and quickly learnt that it was a no-win situation. If you make a mistake, your teammates forget that you are just a stand-in, but if you make a few saves, you are stuck with the job the next time the real keeper is injured. Docherty has practically secured the stand-in keeper role at Peacehaven because he does pretty well throughout and makes a cracking diving save towards the end of the match to back up a determined defensive display. Town, however, are not really testing him as they should be.

There are seven minutes of injury time, the voice tells us all over the PA system, rounding it off in indomitable style with a rousing, "Come on Town!" Inspired, perhaps, by their cheerleader, the home side push on. After a frantic session of pinball in Peacehaven's box, the ball is eventually cleared. But it is soon whipped down the right and the low, hard cross is rammed home by Brazilian Lucas Rodrigues, newly signed on loan from Horsham. Peacehaven's X account, which puts the goal at precisely ten seconds from the end, calls it "cruel". It is. Particularly on stand-in keeper Docherty.

• *For Eastbourne Town's next match, see Game 63 on page 125.*

Game 60: Sunday 28 January (11am) at the Oval, Eastbourne
Eastbourne United U18 4 Bexhill United U18 0 (Southern Combination East U18)
Weather: sunny with mostly clear skies
MOM: Sami Gadah. His hat-trick leads the way

Sunday mornings are football mornings for many young men. It is, of course, the traditional time of the week for pub league 'action' (if it can be called that). This is when players drag themselves out of bed at the last minute, shake off their headaches, remember that they have to pick the new bloke up, then race to a muddy pitch to discover they have only nine players.

But there should be no hangovers here this morning (at least, not from the youngsters running about on the pitch). Eastbourne United U18 are taking on their neighbours from Bexhill United in the Southern Combination League. There are some decent players in the U18 East Division, with a few of those on display today occasionally appearing on the team sheet for the firsts.

While neither of these sides has set this small league (just eight teams) on fire, neither is struggling either. Middly-diddly. It should be a close game. Except it's not. Eastbourne take an early lead and much as Bexhill battle to bounce back, they soon realise it's not going to be their morning. While both sides appear comfortable knocking it about at the back, the killer balls are thin on the ground. But when they do come, it's inevitably from the white shirts of United and, led by a Sami Gadah hat-trick, the home side are clinical with their finishing.

There is more to this win than the Gadah show, however. The home side's defence is solid, the impressive Arthur Grout — who has way more time on the ball than anyone else — is running the show in the middle, and the goals steadily mount.

"I thought this was going to be a close game," I tell a couple who are here watching their son play for Bexhill.

"So did we," they reply, shaking off their headaches.

Middly-diddly indeed.

• *For Eastbourne United U18's season summary see page 217.*

Game 61: Sunday 28 January (3pm) at the Oval, Eastbourne
Eastbourne United Women 2 Welling United Women 2 (L&SERWFL Division 1 South)
Weather: dry and mild, but pretty cold once the sun goes in
WOM: Kim Dixson. Class throughout

Following the U18 game, there is a break for a couple of hours before Eastbourne United Women take on Welling United. This will be my first double header at the same ground this season. But what to do in the break between games?

The club at the Oval doesn't often show football because it doesn't have Sky, but as it's the FA Cup today, there is a game on terrestrial TV. Liverpool are banging in goals against Norwich while the regulars get ready for bingo, but I soon get bored of that, so I decide to take a stroll around the lake in Princess Park. The water is like a magnet for families this afternoon, with lots of children busily feeding swans, trying to control little boats (mostly unsuccessfully), and badgering their parents to buy them some sweets.

Luckily, by this point, I'm not far from the Fishermens, a social club of which I am a member. When I walk in, I initially think the club must be holding a tattoo convention. Or is it a big, shiny shirt show? But no — it's neither of the above. Tattoos and shiny shirts are in plentiful supply this afternoon because the Fishermens is hosting the three-day Eastbourne Darts Open. The place is packed. The main hall, usually shaking with salsa dancers on a Sunday, is now filled with rows of tournament darts boards; the room that usually shows football on the big screen is hosting the merchandisers; the snooker hall is a practice room for the darts players; and the bar is doing a roaring trade in cheese sandwiches and beer. It's the perfect place to kill some time before the women kick off at the Oval.

According to the FA: "The first recorded women's match took place on 7 May 1881." It was played in Edinburgh between 'Scotland' and 'England'. Note the quotation marks. In fact, some historians doubt whether the players representing the sides were actually Scottish and English at all. They may, in fact, have been from the theatrical community "acting out these team roles". Nonetheless, the 'Scotland' team won the match 2-0. There is an image in the National Football Museum entitled *The Girls of the Period — Playing Ball*, which appears to be from that era, in which the women are all wearing long dresses, smart hats, and sturdy looking boots with heels.[21]

I'm pleased to see that there is no such nonsense for the women when they run out for the start of this afternoon's match. Eastbourne are in white shirts and black shorts, while Welling are in all-red. Not a hat in sight. Kick-off is at three o'clock, an hour later than most of the women's games at the Oval. Let's hope those floodlights are warming up, because once that sun goes in it's going to get gloomy.

It takes me until midway through the second half to discover the name of Welling's classy, diminutive midfielder. Kim Dixson wears her shorts really low and her socks really high, so you can barely see her legs when she runs. I start to think this is because they are bionic. Her energy is endless, and those hidden legs have a fair turn of pace in them. She's a class player, and as well as the hard running, her passes — many of them made while feinting to go the opposite way Ronaldinho-style — are sharp and precise.

Dixson spent a large part of her career at Charlton Athletic, and according to the linesman I chat to she also has an England cap, no less, which probably explains why she's so good, even at the back end of her career.

Despite facing a former international, however, Eastbourne are confident on the ball and open up a two-nil lead, thanks to first-half goals from Grace Hill and Laura Stew. But just past the hour mark, driven on by Dixson, Welling push forward and Hannah Baker pulls one back with a looping header. The home side's composed play from earlier starts to become more fragmented as the time ticks by, and their defending is increasingly frantic. With only a couple minutes left, Baker determinedly chases a ball down the right and crosses for Kate Doherty to equalise. It's probably no more than Welling, and in particular Dixson, deserve.

• *For Eastbourne United Women's next match, see Game 76 on page 148.*

Game 62: Friday 2 February (8.15pm) at Priory Lane, Eastbourne
Eastbourne Borough Recreational Squad 7 Seaford Town Women 3 (Women's Flex Ultra League)
Weather: cold, but not too bad for the time of year
WOM: Katie Wise with a hat-trick

Flexible, *adj*: 'capable of being changed or adjusted to meet particular or varied needs' (*The Free Dictionary*).[22] When it comes to football, the recently developed concept of flexible leagues is such a good idea that it's a wonder it wasn't introduced earlier. Teams receive a fixture list, but it is up to them to arrange the exact date and time of each game within a three-week window. Can't do that particular afternoon? Can't do that morning? How about a Friday night then?

The Eastbourne Borough Women's Recreational Squad book a regular slot on Fridays for training sessions and they use that same slot to play if they have a match arranged. But because these flexible leagues tend to be small, and therefore sparse on fixtures, players aren't tied to turning out every week if they have other commitments. When it comes to matches, it's organised but not too organised; regular but not *too* regular. Adaptable and variable.

'Flexible football' made its first appearance as an official concept in the *FA Handbook 2017–18*[23] and is described as providing "players with an additional way to participate in 11-a-side football". Although there are some specific basic rules outlined by the FA (players must be over 16 and competitions should not last more than 20 weeks, for instance),[24] the exact format of the league is left to the organisers and the precise fixture scheduling to the teams themselves. In November 2018 the Surrey FA announced that it had launched the first ever women's flexible league[25] and there are now similar leagues across the country. This is the inaugural season of the eight-team Sussex league, and because it is mostly geographically compact — as well as Borough and Seaford, there are teams from Bexhill, Pevensey, Newhaven, and Heathfield — travelling is fairly light too.

The Eastbourne team came together in 2018 "as a small group of players who just wanted to learn the basics of football and have a kickabout", according to Karen Parsons, the captain and secretary. They were "players who had never kicked a ball before or had played when they were young and wanted to return to football". A lot of them had children playing at Borough, but like a lot of mums with responsibilities, they themselves had been lost as participants in the world's most popular sport. But they still wanted a hobby. And so through word of mouth, the recreational club was born. Meanwhile, as the appetite grew for recreational football in the area, the Sussex FA started a Festival of Football, held monthly,[26] followed by a league.

There are a lot of black leggings and gloves out there tonight, but if it stays as lively as the first few minutes they'll be shed soon. It's one-one after just seven minutes, with Seaford's early goal cancelled out almost immediately by Eastbourne. A few minutes later Seaford's no. 17, who is making some lovely runs, delivers a delicate chip that dips just over the despairing keeper. Seaford add more pressure and although Borough are defending well, the visitors start to take control of the game.

The Borough right back, Billie-Jo Anderson, is getting plenty of encouragement from her family and friends who have come to support her and are standing together in the Peter Fountain Stand.

"Come on, mum!" shouts her son. "Get stuck in!" She obliges with a lovely, well-timed tackle and gets a big cheer. It has to be well-timed because, when it comes to 'getting stuck in' there are no sliding tackles allowed in this league, so as to limit the number of injuries.

The visitors add another goal before half-time and their keeper is looking impressive with a number of excellent blocks and stops, including a penalty save.

As a further feature of flexibility, the duration of matches can be adjusted by the teams, and Eastbourne Borough play only 40 minutes each half due to the number of over-35s in their team — a shortfall which at least means we are heading to the bar a bit earlier than usual for the half-time break.

There is a party in the large Sports Bar, with beams of coloured light bouncing off the clusters of balloons decorating the room and 1980s hits blaring out. The partygoers sing along to a string of old favourites with gusto. "Holiday!" they all scream, channelling their inner Madonna. "Celebrate!"

The small but enthusiastic crowd from the football gather in the Founder's Bar at the back of building instead. I chat to the group who are here to watch Borough's right back and we dissect the first half as if we are pundits on Sky. Madonna has been replaced by Wham! "Wake me up before you go-go" comes the cry. I peek into the main bar, half expecting to see some people wearing leg warmers.

But I've come here search of flexible football and that's exactly what I get. In a complete turnaround in the second half, Eastbourne bounce back to win the game 7-3, their goals in the game coming from Katie Wise (3), Joelle Woodhouse (2), Hayley Chapman, and Caroline Pate.[27]

• *For Eastbourne Borough Women's Recreational Squad's season summary see page 211.*

Game 63: Saturday 3 February (2pm) at the Withdean Stadium, Brighton
Varndeanians 0 Eastbourne Town 4 (Southern Combination Premier)
Weather: dry, with no wind
MOM: Tom Vickers. Some great shots and cracking crossfield passes, as well as his usual hi-tempo work rate

In 2008, Brighton & Hove Albion played Manchester City at the Withdean Stadium in a League Cup 2nd Round tie. They beat a side that included Kasper Schmeichel and Vincent Kompany after penalties in front of 8,729 people.[28] The next year, Leeds United were among the visitors in League One. The crowd for that match was 7,615.[29]

The stadium is now home to both Varndeanians and Brighton Electricity of the Southern Combination Premier and Division Two respectively — and the official attendance today is 105 (boosted slightly by a few latecomers who didn't know that the kick-off time had been brought forward an hour to two o'clock). The turnout for the last Brighton Electricity game was 25. Just a few miles to the east of us this afternoon, 31,345 fans are at Brighton's Amex stadium — the club's home since 2011 — to watch the Premier League game against Crystal Palace.[30]

At the entrance to the Withdean today optimism reigns: no fewer than three people are ready to collect money from spectators when I arrive 20 minutes before kick-off. They joke that they might introduce face-recognition software soon in case they can't cope with the numbers. The earlier kick-off is a cost-cutting exercise, apparently, obviating the need for floodlights. A couple of other clubs do this as well, and I honestly can't see why it's not standard practice in this league.

The players are warming up on the pitch. The ground is like a giant bowl, and from high up there's an impressive view. But my immediate sense is that this large facility, initially built for tennis in the 1930s,[31] could do with a bit of tender loving. In the 1950s, the Withdean was converted for athletics (it was the home track of Olympic athlete Steve Ovett),[32] which explains why it has only one stand — the long north stand — along the home straight. Additional temporary stands were built when

Brighton played here, parts of which are now dotted around various local non-league clubs who took advantage of their neighbour's subsequent move to snaffle the stands and upgrade their own modest grounds.[33]

These days, the other three sides at the Withdean are a mishmash of decaying concrete terracing, grass banking, fencing, and a car park. Dotted around the site are prefab buildings, metal and canvas storage containers, and some machinery. The seats in the north stand don't look like they've been wiped down since Brighton left.

There's a carvery-type pub next to the stadium, but I soon find out that you can't access it from inside the ground, so I'm rapidly heading back out and past the three gatemen to kill some time before kick-off. The Sportsman is a large, sprawling pub and restaurant that includes a sports bar, a pizza place, and the carvery, and at just £8.49 for the latter it's not difficult to understand why the place is busy. A wonderful black and white photograph from *Brighton and Hove in Pictures*[34] entitled 'Police sportsevent [sic], date unknown' shows that people were, in days gone by, able to move freely from the mock-Tudor building to tables shaded by umbrellas outside, indicating that this may have been more of a clubhouse-cum-pub at one stage.

These days, however, the paved garden area outside the Sportsman is separated from the Withdean by a tall, green, security mesh fence. The people in the pub garden can peer through the fence and have virtually the same view of the action as those watching the game at the back of the stand *inside* the ground. There are quite a few who have chosen this option.

Town, wearing light blue today, take an early lead with a James Hull goal from a corner. And before I've had time to stir my tea from V's Tea Bar, former Polegate Town player Nathan Hover adds a second. Tom Vickers is running the show and it's looking as if Varndeanians, who were formed in 1929 and take their name from the fact that they originally only accepted players if they had been to Brighton's Varndean School, could concede a hatful. The travelling Eastbourne fans, now swollen in numbers by the "we didn't realise it started at two o'clock" latecomers, are belting out their version of a popular football chant:

Oh Eastbourne (oh Eastbourne),
Is wonderful
Oh Eastbourne,
Is wonderful.
It's full of old people and seagulls,
Oh Eastbourne is wonderful.

Hull adds a third in the second half, and by the time the home side's Alfie Proto-Gates is shown a red on the hour, it seems as if nearly every Town player has had a shot at goal. With Town chasing a play-off place and Varndeanians near the bottom — and coming into this fixture off the back of five straight defeats — this was never going to be an even match. But this is *really* uneven. Lucas Rodrigues gets number four late on with a tap-in, but even the 4-0 scoreline flatters the home side.
• *For Eastbourne Town's next match, see Game 68 on page 133.*

Game 64: Sunday 4 February (2pm) at the Saffrons, Eastbourne
Eastbourne Town Women DS 0 Mile Oak Ladies 7 (SCWGFL Division 1)
Weather: windy, with a cold bite in every gust
WOM: Ingrid Gismarvik. A stand-out player for Mile Oak. She has loads of time on the ball and lights up the game with lovely passes and some great Cruyff turns

Town Development Squad (the Town women second team) have only one point this season, but I have a lucky feeling about today. I was in a team that lost every single match one season, so I'm rooting for them.

My optimism helps for all of 13 minutes. After a few offside calls, the Mile Oak winger times her run better and charges through on goal in plenty of space. Her shot is well saved by Town keeper, Summer Mooney, but the ball then falls into the path of Vanessa Gauerke, who taps in. Towards the end of the first half, Mooney somehow fumbles a long shot from Jade Samways that she seems to have under control and it trickles in for number two. It's unfortunate because she has had an excellent game and shown some good handling skills until now. I'm not feeling so lucky any more.

Town are struggling as Mile Oak start to move the ball about — and one player stands out. Student Ingrid Gismarvik is playing for fun in midfield; twisting, turning, passing, and shooting, seemingly at will. She's perfected the Cruyff turn and is using it to good effect to open up space. The turn, where a player drops their shoulder and feints to pass in the direction they are facing before dragging the ball back past their standing leg, was made famous when the Dutch Master, Johan Cruyff, performed it and left Sweden's right back Jan Olsson floundering in a 1974 World Cup match.[35] Gismarvik is clearly too good for Division 1. Expect to see her in a higher league next year (sorry Mile Oak).

In the second half, although there are barely 20 people watching, Kevin — who loves non-league football — somehow manages to find out from one of them that Lucas Rodrigues, one of yesterday's scorers for Town men, is coming to the end of his loan spell from Horsham. Oh, how Town Development could do with a striker like him right now.

But no matter how good they are, forwards need the ball in forward positions. This afternoon, Town's strikers are now alone and adrift on the halfway line as their midfield drops ever deeper to try and stem the flow from Mile Oak. The ball has become a hot potato for the yellows and each clearance is coming back with interest. Despite more great stops from Mooney, Mile Oak add four more, with Gauerke completing a hat-trick and substitutes Ali Clements (2) and Taylor Chamberlain joining in the fun towards the end.

That Town DS win will come one day. But it will need more than my optimism to secure it.

• *For Eastbourne Town Women DS's next match, see Game 67 on page 132.*

Game 65: Wednesday 7 February (2pm) at Priory Lane, Eastbourne
Eastbourne Borough Academy U19 0 Welling United Academy U19 6
(National League U19 Alliance Division B)
Weather: dry and fresh
MOM: Omar Kamara. Nice work on the left and a couple of goals

The National League U19 Alliance is an 11-division competition, featuring mostly non-league sides plus a few better-known names (notably the West Ham Foundation). At the top of the tree is the National League South (including the likes of Dartford, Eastleigh, and Southend United), and the National League North (featuring York City, Chesterfield, and Blyth Spartans, among other similar clubs). There are nine other divisions, A–I, which are regionalised. Borough are in a league comprising clubs from Sussex, Kent, and South London.

Many of the players on show today are already playing senior football with clubs such as Eastbourne Town, while others turn out for Borough's U18 side. They will be hoping this provides them with a launch pad to Borough's senior team and a professional career. One of the most interesting things about watching academy football is spotting a talent and being able to follow the player's career as he or she (hopefully) moves upwards. It's the nature of the sport that some will not make it, but for those that do, it's always fascinating to see how far they can progress. But however they do, they will do well to have such interesting and varied careers as Daniel Carr and Darren Lok, two other players who appeared for Borough early in their football lives.

Carr joined the Langney club after being released by Reading Academy, and although he only played a few games here, it was the start of an intriguing journey for a man who clearly has itchy football boots. After a few years with Dulwich Hamlet, a short interlude at Huddersfield Town, and loan spells with six other clubs such as Fleetwood Town and Mansfield Town, Carr embarked on a world footballing cruise. First came Karlstad BK in Sweden, then Dublin-based Shamrock Rovers, followed by clubs in Cyprus, Finland, and India. A few international appearances for Trinidad and

Tobago further boosted his CV, before Carr returned to Ireland and finally made it back home.

Hailsham-born Lok, meanwhile, made 140 appearances for Borough at the start of his career, but after a couple of games on loan at Horsham he moved to the country of his father — Malaysia. Despite a bit of a hold-up while waiting for his Malaysian passport, he was soon playing for Johor Darul Ta'zim in the Malaysia Premier League and being picked for the national team (he's made 34 appearances so far). In 2022 he joined Super League side Sabah and, earlier this year, was part of the national team squad for the AFC Asian Cup in Qatar.[36]

Try beating that.

• *For Eastbourne Borough Academy U19's season summary see page 209.*

Game 66: Saturday 10 February (2pm) at Eastbourne Sports Park
Eastbourne Rangers 4 Nutfield 2 (Mid Sussex Division 1)
Weather: drizzly but no wind
MOM: Josh Kyte. The substitute is constantly buzzing when he appears and never lets the opposition settle

Eastbourne Sports Park seems particularly forlorn today. The place has a lot going on, but this sprawling site feels disconnected at the best of times, let alone on a day of miserable drizzle on top of a week of endless rain. In bureaucratese, the park would be described as "a multi-purpose complex providing leisure and sporting facilities for the wellbeing of the whole community" — the type of PR sentence which simply washes through the brain without registering any real meaning.

Although the sports park itself is neat enough, the area around it feels ramshackle and neglected. The entrance is via Cross Keys Road, which heads towards Hampden Park's level crossing — one of the busiest in the country.[37] There is an athletics track, a gym, a reception/cafe, a large hangar-style sports hall for indoor sports such as tennis and badminton (and a roller disco on Saturday afternoons), plus football pitches — grass and 3G.[38]

The park can also be accessed from King's Drive, just up from the Rodmill, the busy Greene King pub. Entering this way, you'll pass a couple of football pitches (although I've never seen anyone use them); various buildings belonging to East Sussex College; a large, disused structure with its windows boarded up; a few areas for parking; plus plenty of wild brambles and patches of overgrown grass. It's not very Eastbourne at all.

To the south is Eastbourne District General Hospital, to the north the excellent Eastbourne Rugby Club, and beyond this Hampden Park. Everything I have described sits snugly between the railway line and the A2021, both of which lead to Polegate.

This is the setting for today's all-important top-of-the-table clash between Rangers and Nutfield in Mid Sussex Division 1. The visitors are in third, seven points behind leaders Rangers with a game in hand, so a win here would really open up the promotion race. And the players know it. The match is fast and furious, but despite the pace, it lacks neither skill nor entertainment. The sides are cancelling each other out as half-time approaches, and the urgency on the field only heightens the tension. Then the bubble bursts. The constantly buzzing figure of Josh Kyte wriggles into space in the box and is brought down. Penalty. 2-1.

By the time Kyte latches onto an error from the Nutfield keeper and rolls the ball home to make it 4-1 in the second half, it looks all over. But the visitors still believe they can get something from the game and they push forward with even more insistence. Rangers know what is at stake and are taking no chances: strong tackles, huge clearances, precious moments wasted. They see it out to go four points clear at the top and well clear of Nutfield in third. The venue may be disconnected, but that's certainly not true of today's performance.

• *For Eastbourne Rangers' next match, see Game 78 on page 151.*

Game 67: Sunday 11 February (2pm) at the Saffrons, Eastbourne
Eastbourne Town Women DS 0 Worthing Town Women 7 (SCWGFL Division 1)
Weather: the rain holds off except for a heavy burst in the second half
WOM: Worthing's Jamie Lee-Ledger. Smashes in two early goals and is a constant menace with her runs

It's been raining most of the weekend so I abandon any ideas I might have had of seeing a game today and turn my thoughts to lunch.

But there he is as I wander past the Saffrons on the way to Tesco: the referee. He's squelching about on the field with the sort of look you get on your face when you really don't want to make a decision but you know you have to eventually. There's a stony-faced man with him (who I later learn is his assessor for the day). When I raise my hands upwards and shrug questioningly the referee gives me the thumbs-up. The game is on. I've got just enough time to visit the shop, get my shopping home and make it back for the kick-off. Sunday lunch will have to wait.

Eastbourne Town Women's Development Squad have already conceded 59 goals this season, seven of them in their last game at home to Mile Oak. Facing a team who have banged in 71 goals in 15 games just a week later is not the fixture they would have chosen.

It only takes a few minutes for the game to settle into what becomes a familiar pattern during the 90 minutes. A Worthing player wins the ball in midfield, finds a bit of space and slips a pass through a gap in the home side's flat back four. One of the visitors' nippy strikers strides onto it as the defenders give chase. Then one of three things happens: 1. The striker misses her shot at goal. 2. The keeper saves it. 3. The striker scores. And so the game continues. Pass, run, chase. Jamie-Lee Ledger, who has a ferocious shot, grabs the first two, Dulcie Elder snaffles a hat-trick, and Katie-Jane Henderson adds two more. Drip, drip, drip. But it's not the rain.

• *For Eastbourne Town Women DS's season summary see page 214.*

Game 68: Saturday 17 February (3pm) at the Trafalgar Ground, Newhaven
Newhaven 0 Eastbourne Town 4 (Southern Combination Premier)
Weather: mild and dry with no wind
MOM: take your pick from any of the Eastbourne Town players. This is a complete team performance

My friend Ben is a football obsessive. He once told me he'll watch every game he possibly can because they'll always be one moment — a pass, a shot, a run — that makes it all worthwhile. This game's moment comes halfway through the first period. The ball is bouncing awkwardly at pace on the right and it looks to be heading out of play. But Town are on top, and right back Leon Greig clearly wants to keep their foot on the pedal. With his back to the ball, he flicks his leg out and, using the side/back of his foot, keeps the ball alive and puts it into the path of an onrushing midfielder. The midfielder runs forward and lays it into the path of Ollie Davies whose shot goes just wide.

"That was like watching Barcelona," the man sitting next to me says. My friend Ben would just say: "I told you so."

That bit of skill from Greig is certainly a gem, but this game is overflowing with creativity. Newhaven are top of the league, and it's not hard to see why. They play at pace and their passes are crisp and precise. But they've met a team that are purring. Every time a home player gets the ball, an opponent is snapping at his heels. Every time a Town player gets it there are runners off the ball in every direction. It's a near-perfect team display. Everything is going right.

Davies gets the first goal after selling a defender a dummy pass and clipping home from the left, and Nathan Jenkins adds a sublime second from a similar angle. In the second half, Greig — he of the beautiful flick — makes it three after a bursting run and James Hull completes the misery for Newhaven. The previously busy main stand is now deserted. Town's X account sums it up perfectly: "The Dieppe ferry is now leaving the port. They've had enough!"[39]

To anyone who doesn't know the area, the name 'Newhaven' might conjure up images of a quiet little fishing village with gnarled, long-bearded men fixing their fishing nets. The reality, of course, is something much different. The town of nearly 13,000[40] is a significant container port and regular ferries run to France from here.

Split in two by the River Ouse, Newhaven is further fragmented by the wide service roads and other facilities required for the large port area, leaving it with no real focal point. Heading into the town from the east there is a giant out-of-town retail park, which is ideal if you need a new bed or a bucket of chicken, but not the most aesthetically pleasing of developments. What's left of the traditional type of shops can be found along the narrow, steep High Street, which runs down to the water on the west side of the river. Although it's a fairly short road, it has a nice, local feeling to it and is a pleasant enough place in a rough-and-ready, port-town type of way. The Rose Cafe certainly serves a good fry-up.

Fort Road, Newhaven's football ground, is situated south of this at the top of the Castle Hill Local Nature Reserve, where you'll also find Newhaven Fort and West Beach. The ground looks out across the marina and the port area, with plenty of boats — including the previously mentioned Dieppe ferry — within sight of spectators sitting in the impressive, although unfinished, two-tier main stand. Construction on this stand started in the 1990s[41] but on the top level the door and window openings are boarded up. The north stand behind the goal near the entrance is only four rows deep, but it runs almost the full width of the pitch, while the end is completed by one of the quirkiest stands you're ever likely to come across. A small wooden-framed structure, with Perspex windows and a metal roof, it has just two rows of terracing (plus two large dice when I visited).

Behind the other goal, just outside the ground, is a skatepark, with plenty of banking to attract those who want to watch the game without forking out the £7 entrance fee. They must have enjoyed a wonderful view of that flick.

• *For Eastbourne Town's next match, see Game 75 on page 146.*

Game 69: Saturday 2 March (1.45pm) at Hailsham Community College
Jesters Town 6 Battle Town Reserves 0 (Robertsbridge Charity Junior Cup QF)
Weather: clearing rain then sunny, but still a bit cold
MOM: Jake Maynard. The wide man looks dangerous from the start and grabs a late goal

Schools and colleges are always a bit gloomy on the weekends. Although they are no longer as deserted as they used to be, because a lot of them now provide community-use facilities, there's still a bit of a forlorn feeling about them. Their very reason for being —

teaching young people — is on hold, so the usual buzz of activity is missing, and the functional architecture, built to accommodate hundreds or thousands of people, towers imposingly over those few dozen souls who use it on the weekend. I've never been a fan of playing or watching football at multi-use facilities. Everything is there, everything works, but the 'club' feeling that is such an integral part of visiting a 'real' ground is missing. Where's the bar, for one thing?

Hailsham Community College is no different. It does, however, have two superb 3G pitches, and after a ridiculous amount of rain this winter and a string of postponed games, Jesters Town from Eastbourne have given up waiting for the pitch at Eastbourne Sports Park (another multi-use facility) to dry out, and have moved to Hailsham. I don't blame them. Who cares about the functional architecture when you can actually get a game in without the groundsman worrying that you'll cut up a field that is enclosed by squiggly white lines?

I've already seen Jesters take on Battle Town's Reserves in the league this season and it was a bit of a stroll in the sports park. This time, in a quarter-final, it's a stroll on a beautiful artificial surface, with the ball zipping around nicely to suit Jesters' style of play. Jake Maynard, in particular, is enjoying a lot of the ball out on the wing, with the defender marking him getting caught out of position time after time.

After just seven minutes, Maynard makes a nice run down the right and cuts in, but his cross is not met cleanly. The defender (supposedly) marking him doesn't heed the warning and the winger's threats continue as the rest of the team keep pinging the ball to him. Still, Jesters only go in 1-0 at half-time, thanks to a late penalty — beautifully dispatched by Travis Parks — despite their obvious dominance. The goal comes just in time to ease the nerves of the league leaders, clearly frustrated that they are not overpowering the lowly placed Battle who, I am told later, "have a more or less new team from last year".

The visitors may have a lot of new players in the team but

Battle itself has no shortage of history. Home to fewer than 7,000 people,[42] it is located near the site of the famous play-off of 1066 between the Anglo-Saxon King Harold and the French-backed claimant to the throne, Duke William of Normandy. The duke's arrival in England with his fleet at Pevensey Bay is depicted on the Bayeux Tapestry,[43] a sort of *Le Figaro* of its time.

So, what the teachers taught us at school was nonsense then. It wasn't the Battle of Hastings at all. It was the Battle of Battle. Although, as Battle as a town barely existed then, it should probably be called the Battle of Some Forlorn Hilltop (or of nearby Senlac Hill).[44] Not very catchy, I'll grant you. But wait, I have an altogether better suggestion, thanks to a 19th century historian who spent a fair bit of time on the subject. Edward Freeman, a liberal politician during the age of William Gladstone, wrote six volumes on the Norman Conquest. He believed that the invaders might well have nicknamed the area around that forlorn hilltop as 'Blood Lake'. So, the Battle of Blood Lake it is. Now, that's a proper name for a battle.[45]

Battle the town only grew up after the bloody clash itself, when the new King William (yes, he won, and according to the Bayeux Tapestry Harold appears to have got hit in the eye with an arrow, so the teachers were right about that bit) gave instructions for the construction of an abbey to commemorate the battle and atone for the slaughter.[46] And so it was, *Monsieur* and *Madame* reader: the start of the Norman Conquest and the occupation of England.

But back to the present. Not only does Hailsham College not have a bar, it doesn't even have a place to get a half-time cup of tea. The young man at the reception is politely apologetic and directs me instead to the rather excellent Grenadier pub, just a couple of minutes down Battle Road (no, I didn't make that bit up). The Grenadier, which still has the names of the old-style bars — 'Saloon Bar', 'Public Bar', and 'Private Bar' — etched into stone outside,[47] boasts just two these days, and although I'm not sure which one is which, I choose the posher side as I'm having a pot of tea. It's one of those brilliant pubs in which you could while away many hours if you didn't have to get back for the second half of the football.

And at the football, the floodgates open. Parks adds another goal almost immediately after the restart and player-manager Louis Osborne gets two more quick ones, so that by the 53rd minute it's 4-0. The frustration has well and truly evaporated and Jesters are playing keep-ball with a swagger and a smile. They add another two goals later on — Osborne completes his hat-trick with a header from a corner and there's a well-deserved goal for Maynard — to head to the Robertsbridge Charity Junior Cup semi-final.

During the goal fest I chat to the Battle defender who was given the runaround in the first half. He seems relieved to have been substituted.

• *For Jesters Town's next match, see Game 96 on page 186.*

Game 70: Sunday 3 March (3.30pm) at Culver Road, Lancing
Eastbourne Town Women 1 Saltdean United Women DS 9 (Sussex Women's Challenge Trophy final)
Weather: sunny
WOM: Billie Phillpot. A clinical hat-trick in a clinical Saltdean display

When it comes to cups, people often say that "getting to the final is all that matters". Which is fine when you win. I'm not so sure Town Women will be feeling that way as they line up at Culver Road, home of the Sussex FA, for the Sussex Women's Challenge Trophy final. They are up against a very good Saltdean side, who have romped to the Sussex County Women's & Girls' Premier title and banged in 52 goals in 13 games. Town have already been beaten 3-0 by Saltdean in the league this season — and that was when they were in good form themselves. Sure enough, it doesn't take long before they are 2-0 down this afternoon as Cate Hann and Billie Phillpot score for the Tigers.

Town won Division 1 last year, and they started this season in blistering form in the Premier, with five wins and a draw, including a 10-0 victory and three other matches when they scored seven. At the end of October, they were sitting pretty at the top of the division. But then things changed. Players were unavailable, the manager and assistant manager resigned, and the defeats rolled in. Since that loss to Saltdean in November, the Town Women, who once looked so dominant, have registered only one win (although they have also had a couple of 'walkovers').

Culver Road, very near to Lancing town centre, is an impressive little ground with a capacity of 1,800. The main stand-cum-office block is covered and stretches about three-quarters of the way along the west side of the ground, with the 250 seats[48] spread out either side of the players' tunnel. The rest of the building houses offices, meeting rooms, and changing rooms.[49] There is also a decent-size clubhouse with a little food hatch to the side (which serves a good sausage and chips by the way). There is some grass banking on the opposite, open side, which provides slightly elevated views of the pitch if the setting sun is not in your eyes.

The ground is home to Lancing FC, currently playing in the Isthmian League South East Division, who moved here in 1952. The Sussex FA purchased Culver Road in 1981[50] before making the place their headquarters, but Lancing stayed on as tenants. Although founded in 1882, the Sussex FA had waited nearly 100 years to own this dedicated HQ. In 2007, a £1.35 million redevelopment of the ground started, and in 2015 new LED floodlights and the 3G pitch were installed.[51]

Thanks to the durability of the 3G pitch, games are being played throughout the day. Some of the players for the next match have already arrived and there's an eight o'clock game scheduled after that, so the artificial surface is certainly earning its keep.

And out there on that surface, things are going pretty much as expected, although there's a brief glimmer of hope for Eastbourne supporters just before the break when striker Geri Burt scores an absolute screamer of a goal after a through ball from Dani Parfitt.

But in the second half, the goals for the young Tigers of Saltdean (the side has an average age of 18 today)[52] start going in at regular intervals and despite a fine display, the Town goalkeeper Ell Fenner can do little as the Saltdean youngsters rack up nine. Phillpot rounds off her hat-trick, before Farrah Dorey, substitute Dani Jacobs (2), captain Emily Towner, and Mollie Copper complete the rout.

But, of course, that's not the end of the action. No sooner have the Saltdean side collected their trophy and had a little jig of celebration, than the players for the next game on the Culver Road conveyor belt take to the pitch and start limbering up. Next please!
* *For Eastbourne Town Women's next match, see Game 72 on page 142.*

Game 71: Saturday 16 March (3pm) at Priory Lane, Eastbourne
Eastbourne Borough 2 Taunton Town 0 (National League South)
Weather: the early warmth from the sun fades and a nasty chill fills the air by the end of the game
MOM: Yahya Bamba. Battles and battles, and then tucks away the decisive second goal beautifully

The drums are beating, but the voices accompanying them have not broken yet. The young Borough fans are keeping up the appearance of optimism with their efforts behind the goal on the small bit of terracing behind the goal. A new manager, Adam Murray, has been at the helm since early January following the dismissal of Mark Beard.[53]

He joins a distinguished list of ex-bosses: Mark McGhee, who played under Sir Alex Ferguson at Aberdeen and won four Scotland caps, as well as turning out for Hamburger SV in Germany and Newcastle United; former Manchester City and Portsmouth player Lee Bradbury; Tommy Widdrington, who made 75 appearances for Southampton and approaching 400 at the top level in total; not to mention Beard himself, who represented Sheffield United and Southend United among various other clubs. But Murray has plenty of pedigree himself in the professional game, having made more than 500 appearances for ten different clubs — including Derby County in the Premier League — in a career spanning 17 years.[54] And he's going to need every ounce of that experience in the run-in because things are not looking bright.

The youngsters may be beating their drums merrily, but the older fans all know that their club's situation near the bottom of the National League South is perilous. It's the last chance saloon. Every game is now. The only noises coming from the seasoned supporters are the sound of fingernails being bitten and the odd grumble of encouragement, soon followed by howls of anguish and despair.

Eastbourne Borough are third from bottom, with 34 points, and they have a tough fight for survival ahead of them. Truro City are only four points ahead of Borough but with five games in hand, while Welling United and today's visitors Taunton Town (with four games in hand) are on 40 points. Torquay, the 'giants' of this league and stalwarts of the Football League for decades, are on 41. No wonder the sound of crunching nails gets louder as the game progresses.

In the Premier League, the points target for safety is often said to be between 38 and 40, but there are fewer teams and matches in that shiny, rich world. The average number of points needed for survival in the National South over the past decade is 41, sometimes with fewer than this year's 24 teams competing.

2022–23: 49 points were needed for survival
2021–22: 37 points
2020–21: no relegation due to an unfinished league because of Covid-19 lockdowns
2019–20: no relegation due to Covid-19 and league reorganisation
2018–19: 40 points
2017–18: 43 points
2016–17: 37 points
2015–16: 48 points
2014–15: 31 points
2013–14: 41 points

It would be handy for Borough to be back in 2014–15, but judging by the table in today's programme, this season's safety target looks more like 50 points. And even that is being optimistic. Can Borough win five or six games out of the handful they have left? The drums beat away and the unbroken voices scream out their chants, confident that they can do it. Maybe they don't buy a programme? That would show them that the Sports have only nine wins from their previous 37 matches. If the big bookmakers offered odds on relegation from this league, the odds on Borough going down would be very short.

The team, however, don't seem fazed by what is ahead of them. They don't even seem to have noticed that they've lost their best player, Leone Gravata (recently sold to York City), and they go one up with a goal from David Sesay, who cuts in before curling home just before the break. The older fans' nail-biting stops momentarily and the squeaky voices screech even higher on the terraces. The bar at half-time is a buzz of relief and anticipation. Can they do it after all?

Although Gravata's transfer is a big loss to Borough, it is well deserved for a player who has shone all season in a struggling side at Priory Lane. He's not the first Borough player to move to bigger things in 2024, of course, with Fletcher Holman having headed to Wolves in January. Since then Holman has scored for the U21 side and been drafted into the first-team squad as an unused substitute in both the FA Cup and the Premier League.

Meanwhile, back in Eastbourne, it's tension alert for everyone in the second half. Chances come for Borough. And they go. Taunton have plenty of games in hand and their players seem to know it; there is not the same level of urgency in their play when compared to that of Sports. Finally it comes. And it's a beauty. Yahya Bamba scores Borough's second in injury time after latching onto a clearance from David Clarke and running from his own half before sliding home. The high-pitched voices ring out again, louder than ever.
• *For Eastbourne Borough's next match, see Game 77 on page 149.*

Game 72: Thursday 21 March (7.30pm) at the Saffrons, Eastbourne
Eastbourne Town Women 6 Eastbourne Borough Women DS 1 (Eastbourne FA Chairman's Cup QF)
Weather: cold but no wind
WOM: Gemma Vince. Adds a goal to a solid performance

It's the big one: the Eastbourne derby. Well, sort of. Town have drawn Borough's development side (that's their reserves, to the rest of us) in the Eastbourne FA Chairman's Cup.

The winners of this game could go on to meet Borough's first team in the next round. I overhear someone saying that Billy Wood, the man who has led that first team's resurgence after their poor start, is here to watch the game. If he is, then it doesn't take too long for him to realise which team his first XI will meet, assuming that they can overcome Bexhill United in their quarter-final match. Town take control early on and the contest is pretty much over before it's even got going.

The ever-reliable Diane Vilciu and Gemma Vine grab a goal each but it's the usual goalscoring suspects who do the real damage, with Geri Burt and Dani Parfitt bagging two apiece as Town take the opportunity to fill their boots after their drubbing in the county cup final only a couple of weeks ago. Burt and Parfitt are prolific scorers and both average a goal a game — impressive at any level. Having one player in a team who scores that regularly is a rarity. For a side that finished third from bottom in the league to have two of them is remarkable.

In the second half I wander around the pitch and spot one of Borough's young players, Wen Jiang, in goal after pulling on the gloves for the second half. Last time I watched Borough's DS side she shone as a very decent left-sided player. The sort of player the opposition don't like: a real battler, constantly snapping at their heels and breaking play up. She's not the tallest, though, so it's a surprise to see her between the posts. She has a few friends watching from behind her goal, joking about her new role but supporting her at the same time. As it turns out, the 'reluctant goalkeeper' is actually pretty good and helps stem the bleeding. Town are only able to add one more to their total, but still run out easy 6-1 winners as they head to the semi-final.

• *For Eastbourne Town Women's season summary see page 214.*
• *For Eastbourne Borough Women DS's next match, see Game 82 on page 161.*

Game 73: Saturday 23 March (2pm) at Eastbourne Sports Park
Eastbourne Athletic 1 AS Crawley 5 (Stratford Challenge Cup SF)
Weather: it starts as a beautiful, warm spring day, but it turns into a bitterly cold and rainy afternoon
MOM: Jermaine Neathey. Too much of a handful for the home side

Hope is often followed by disappointment in life. And this afternoon it only takes 20 minutes for that to happen for Eastbourne Athletic. The Crawley side are sharper, fitter, and stronger — and they are three up after half an hour to extinguish the Stratford Cup dreams of Athletic. The competition is open to teams playing in Divisions 3 and 4 (South and North sections) of the Mid Sussex League.

For today's clash, Athletic are representing Division 3 (South) while Crawley are flying the flag for Division 3 (North). Both are near the top of their respective divisions, so I was expecting a close game. Judging by the angry, reddening faces of the Athletic outfield players, and the understandable frustration of their keeper when the third goal hits the back of the net, so were the Eastbourne side.

Despite appearing in a number of semi-finals during their 17 seasons of existence, Athletic have yet to reach the final of any competition — and it's looking unlikely that today will be the day to crack that nut. But it will come eventually, because this is a club of longevity. So far 15 players have reached the 100-appearance milestone, seven of whom have played 200 or more games for the club. James Hanoman, the all-time record holder with a whopping 321 appearances, is on the bench today. Sadly, Will Brooke, the club's all-time top goalscorer (131 goals) doesn't look like he will add to his total this afternoon.

I'm chatting to a referee who's had his game called off, and so I'm getting a running commentary on today's reffing performance, which provides some distraction from the disappointment in the air. Tackles start to fly in and at one stage the opposition manager is on the pitch remonstrating with the match referee. I'm not sure if Crawley scoring a couple more would calm things down, or whether it would simply raise the already high frustration levels of the (not-so-far-from) seaside team. At the end it's 5-1, but by then I've only half an eye on Athletic's pain, as I've wandered over to the adjoining pitch to watch the match in the East Sussex League.

• *For Eastbourne Athletic's season summary see page 207.*

Game 74: Saturday 23 March (2pm) at Eastbourne Sports Park
Parkfield 7 Catsfield 1 (East Sussex Division 3)
Weather: see previous game
MOM: Lee Chittick. Comes off the bench and grabs a hat-trick

"This is the arse-end of East Sussex football," I'm told by a spectator standing next to me. Which, to be fair, is not strictly true, as there is an East Sussex League Division 4.

I quite like "arse-end" football, as the spectator calls it, not least because I played a fair amount of it myself. It's also because the players are underestimated. Hidden behind the usual snobbery about "fat bellies and statuesque defending" are some pretty decent players with the occasional nice touch. Okay, they won't be called up by the England manager any time soon, and certainly not if they are as slow as I was, but there are sometimes little glimpses of skill and technique — the brilliant penalty taken by Parkfield's no 29 for instance — that raise a nod of appreciation among the handful of spectators and make it all worthwhile.

Park football — and make no mistake, the grass pitch at Eastbourne Sports Park is an archetypal park field — can also be entertaining. Sometimes for the wrong reasons, admittedly — a misplaced pass that ends up by the corner flag or a hefty clearance that's still coming down at half-time — but there are usually plenty of goals in these games and there is always passion.

Parkfield are facing second-placed Catsfield (a village just south of Battle, if you are wondering), their nearest rivals for the Division 3 title, albeit some way adrift when it comes to points. It's not surprising that at 3-0 down the visitors realise they are running out of lives and start to argue among themselves. At the end of the game, a 7-1 win for Parkfield — who are now 15 points clear with only a handful of games remaining — their feline lives are all but done. Barring some remarkable results, Brian Chambers, the manager of the impressive Parkfield side, will be moving the club another step away from the 'arse-end' of East Sussex football.

Chambers is an absolute legend of longevity when it comes to park football. Indeed, any level of football. This Eastbourne man founded the club in 1970, when he was just 20 years old, and immediately assumed the role of player-manager. Remarkably, he is still the manager today, aged 74. Yes, 54 years as manager of the same club. It took *me* some time to process that fact. Promotions, relegations, cup wins, cup defeats, leagues changing names, leagues folding, players joining, players leaving: he's seen it all many times over. And certainly more than most.

Take a bow, Mr Chambers. Even at a conservative estimate of Parkfield playing 20 to 25 games a season, that is a run of well over 1,000 games at the helm — and probably closer to 1,250. Chambers himself is not even sure, but he knows that he played over 800 games for the club because he has "a shield commemorating that, tucked away in a cupboard somewhere". He was in his 50s at the time and remembers those latter playing days fondly because he had to go in goal (which he'd never done previously) and saved a penalty in two consecutive matches.

To put Chambers's run as manager into perspective, Sir Alex Ferguson was in charge of Manchester United for 'only' 27 seasons (although that resulted in him managing a nice, round total of 1,500 games, due to the higher number of matches a professional team plays each year).[55] After 27 seasons Chambers was still getting warmed up.

• *For Parkfield's next match, see Game 89 on page 172.*

Game 75: Saturday 23 March (3pm) at the Saffrons, Eastbourne
Eastbourne Town 0 Shoreham 0 (Southern Combination Premier)
Weather: the awful weather has cleared and it's bright sunshine by the time I arrive
MOM: Sam Marsden. Leads a fierce defensive display to halt Town's run of nine wins

Wolves striker Fletcher Holman is at the Saffrons watching his former club. The 19 year old was catapulted into the big time a few months ago after just a handful of games with Eastbourne Borough in the National League South. But prior to that he was playing here in front of a hundred or so fans each week. It'll be Jamie Vardy stuff if he makes it — and with his goalscoring touch there's no reason to think that he hasn't got a good chance. Holman scored on his debut for Wolves Academy with a deft touch from an inswinging cross, and last week he made the squad for the FA Cup 6th Round tie against Coventry.

This is an exciting moment for me because it is the first time I have watched three matches in the same day (well, part-matches, at least). And there's certainly no shortage of excitement at Eastbourne Town right now. The yellow and blues have won an incredible nine on the trot and are wedged firmly in play-off contention. The run has seen them topple the (then) league leaders Newhaven 4-0 in a near-perfect away display, as well as pull off similarly impressive wins over fellow high fliers Haywards Heath and Crowborough Athletic.

But it's another Athletic causing the biggest stir at Town today: Athletic Club have donated a retro shirt to be raffled off as part of 'non-league day' (that's when fans of the big clubs get bored because England are playing a meaningless friendly and they are encouraged to keep themselves amused by watching their local side). Athletic Club! Yes, the La Liga club from Bilbao.

There's a very good reason for this shirt to wind up on England's south coast: the two clubs have played each other in the past. Okay, so it was in 1912, but they all count. Town were Eastbourne FC[56] in those days, but the 'Gentleman Amateurs', as they were also known, must have had a bit of money because they "regularly toured Europe", according to the Athletic website.[57] And on that particular tour they took on the fiercely proud Basque Country club twice, the home side winning on both occasions (3-2 and 5-3).

Eastbourne FC not only regularly toured Europe at that time, but they even won a couple of international tournaments. In 1904 they won the first Tournoi du Nouvel An Paris, a competition which ran until 1935, when they beat Racing Club Paris (5-0) and Racing Club Roubaix (4-2).[58] Then, in 1909, they triumphed in the Challenge International du Nord after beating Le Havre Sports (2-0) in the semi-final and Racing Club Roubaix (5-1) in the final.[59]

This week, Athletic Club also donated shirts to the other English non-league clubs they have played in the course of their history — Civil Service, United Hospitals, Merton, Bromley, Corinthian Casuals, and Dulwich Hamlet — as well as exchanging flags with all of them. The English flags are heading to the Athletic Club Museum after this weekend, something to note, if you are ever visiting the northern Spanish city of Bilbao.

This admirable initiative by Athletic Club is part of the celebrations for Euskal (Basque) non-league day, an idea launched in 2023 — inspired by its English counterpart — to celebrate grassroots football in the Basque Country and to thank smaller clubs for developing Basque players.[60] It's hard not to admire this club.

Driven on by their motto *Con cantera y afición, no hace falta importación* ('With home-grown talent and local support, you don't need imports') [61] Athletic are famous for selecting only Basque players or those with heritage from the region. They may not have won La Liga since 1983–84, but it seems that they still have something sadly missing from top-league football these days: principles. Nice shirt too, by the way.

Town come close to scoring on a number of occasions today, but a fierce defensive display — and a bit of luck — means Shoreham deny the home side a chance to make it ten wins on the trot.
• *For Eastbourne Town's next match, see Game 80 on page 155.*

Game 76: Sunday 24 March (3pm) at the Oval, Eastbourne
Eastbourne United Women 0 Bromley Women 6 (L&SERWFL Division 1 South)
Weather: sunny with no wind
WOM: Bromley's Charlotte Lee

It's a bit early perhaps, but there's an end-of-season feel to this game. Watching the United performance at least. They are mid-table with only a slim chance of going down, with seven wins and eight defeats in the league, and facing a team that smashed them 8-0 last time out. So who can blame them, really? But it's been that sort of season on Sunday afternoons at the Oval. Mid-table stuff. One week United are on fire — and the next week it's hard to believe you are watching the same team.

But there are two things I am getting used to. The first is that captain Emma Sweetman will run and run and battle to her last breath. The second is that Grace Hill gets better with every game she plays. She knocks some lovely passes around early on today and I briefly think there might even be a contest. Then the onslaught begins.

Perhaps the home side are blinded by the Bromley kit. While United players are wearing a classic strip — white shirts, black shorts, and white socks — the South Londoners are dazzling from every angle. To be fair, Bromley usually wear white too, so this is their change kit. But what a change it is.

Their shirts are predominantly baby blue at the top, fading into pink at the waist on one side and also at the chest on the other, creating an angled effect on the bottom half of the shirt. Thin lines run diagonally in one direction and thick lines in the other. The arms are pink with thin black stripes and there are pink neck and arm trims as well.

But wait, there is more. On the front of the shirt is a bright yellow Kappa logo, the club badge, and the sponsor's name. The arms have more kit-maker logos and another badge. Deep breath… The shorts are similarly multicoloured in pink and baby blue with thin black lines and more silhouettes of a man and a woman sitting back to back in case you doubted that this creation was by the famous Italian apparel firm.

Kappa first introduced its distinctive logo in 1969. Apparently it promotes 'equality between the sexes', while representing the company's values of 'quality, humanity, and authenticity'.[62] As if we were in any doubt. The socks for Bromley are a relatively muted pink with black trim, by the way.

Faced with all that, and a quality team with an outside chance of the title, it's no wonder United lose 6-0.

• *For Eastbourne United Women's season summary see page 217.*

Game 77: Friday 29 March (3pm) at Priory Lane, Eastbourne
Eastbourne Borough 1 Maidstone United 5 (National League South)
Weather: dry with no wind
MOM: Lamar Reynolds

The Maidstone winger goes down after a challenge from Sam Beard and — judging from the reaction of the Borough fans — they believe some 'simulation' might have been involved. Needless to say, this actual word is not one of those that is currently bouncing about the open bit of terracing beside the Peter Fountain Stand. The Borough defender is shown a yellow, and as he was shown the same card only two minutes ago, he's sent off.

When it comes to disputing decisions against their team, Borough fans are no more reasonable with officials than any other fans in the world — but this tirade is like nothing I've heard at Priory Lane before. They are not happy, and the linesman is told in no uncertain terms who his father isn't.

A lady leaning against the barrier just in front of us turns around and stares at the source of the abuse that is coming from the crowd behind her. At this point most of the fans decide to shut up and pretend that they are grown-ups for a while. But it turns out that the lady is Beard's mum. Clare is probably as angry as the rest of us who saw what happened, although she's certainly not as verbally colourful as the rest of the terrace. During the following few minutes, the referee gives a few 50-50 decisions Borough's way and there are some ironic cheers. "Balancing things out, he is now. He knows he made a bad decision," is the inevitable cry.

A really early penalty already has the Kent side ahead, so things are looking bleak for Borough now they are a man down. This year, Maidstone is the adopted 'plucky' non-league side of ITV and the BBC. They've enlivened the little bit of live football they still have on their channels by beating Ipswich Town to make it to the FA Cup 5th Round, where they met Coventry City. Funnily enough, I'm not sure I remember much interest from the same TV people following Maidstone's wins over Steyning Town, Winchester City, Torquay United, Chesham United, Barrow, or Stevenage.

Still, all non-league fans will say "good luck to them". It's Maidstone's year and they have sprinkled the famous cup with the non-league 'magic' we all like to pretend still exists, before the rich clubs dominate the rounds that really matter and scoop up all the big prize money. Maidstone's famous run netted them £120,000 prize money for the conquest of Ipswich, plus £231,375 for their wins in previous rounds.[63] The Premier League team that wins the cup (West Ham's triumph in 1980 was the last by a team from outside the top division)[64] will net £3.9 million.[65]

But back to today's National League South match, which has

attracted a bumper bank holiday crowd of 2,229, including a decent number of fans from Maidstone. To the surprise of the Kent contingent who have made the 90-minute trip to the coast, Pierce Bird brings Borough level with a rocket of a shot in the 35th minute. But the brief sense of optimism at Priory Lane is burst when Bird is sent off as well, just after half-time, and Matt Rush restores the lead for the visiting team in yellow. However, it takes a nine-minute hat-trick in the dying minutes from Lamar Reynolds (who scored against Ipswich but started on the bench today) to kill all hope. He lashes in three goals as if he's trying to bust the ball, wrapping up the 5-1 away win with a blockbuster of a penalty. It is certainly not a Good Friday for Borough.

• *For Eastbourne Borough's next match, see Game 87 on page 167.*

Game 78: Saturday 30 March (2pm) at Eastbourne Sports Park
Eastbourne Rangers 4 Crawley United 4 (win 3-0 on penalties) (Edgar German Challenge Cup SF)
Weather: warm and muggy
MOM: Tyriece Whiteoak. A solid all-round performance

It's a weekend of meeting players' mums. Lisa, Tyriece Whiteoak's mum is among the slightly larger than usual crowd, the numbers no doubt boosted by a brief improvement in the weather. She's chosen a good day to watch because her son is having a great game for Rangers. The youngster occasionally turns out for Eastbourne Town U23, but for Rangers he's playing in a more advanced role. He grabs one of the goals in what turns out to be a topsy-turvy goal fest of a match.

The Edgar German Challenge Cup is one of the oldest competitions run by the Mid Sussex League and was first competed for in 1938.[66] It is a cup for teams who play in three different divisions of the league — Division 1, Division 2 (South), and Division 2 (North).[67] It's a relatively small field of 29 entrants (even the slimmed down version of the Grand National, which is coming up in a couple of weeks, has more starters), so it's a good opportunity for the clubs to grab some silverware. Rangers will be fancying their chances against a team from a division lower than them, especially with home advantage in their favour.

But things aren't going as expected and at half-time the 'northern' side are leading 3-2. Rangers bounce back with two goals to take the lead after the break, but they can't hold on and let it slip back to 4-4. Then in the dying minutes Rangers are handed a chance to nail a place in the final when they are awarded a penalty. However, seeing the words 'penalty', 'cup' and 'German' together is not usually a good omen. The penalty is duly missed. And it gets worse.

In the penalty shoot-out, Rangers' kickers fail to hit the back of the net once and it ends in a 3-0 defeat for the Eastbourne side. It's like watching England taking penalties in the 1990s. On steroids.
• *For Eastbourne Rangers' season summary see page 211.*

Game 79: Saturday 30 March (3pm) at the Oval, Eastbourne
Eastbourne United 0 Crowborough Athletic 0 (Southern Combination Premier)
Weather: warm and muggy
MOM: the whole United team

Tiger and Scorcher was one of my favourite comics when I was a youngster. Comics were what passed for entertainment in an era when there were just three TV channels to choose from and our phone number (a landline obviously) had only four digits in it.

The comic's jewel in the crown was a strip called Roy of the Rovers, which first appeared in *Tiger* in September 1954.[68] Roy was a swashbuckling blond striker for Melchester Rovers, a famous team in the fantasy world Roy lived in. All my friends thought Roy was the best character in the comic because he was a top player in a top side. But ever a supporter of the underdog — it was a time when I still believed that football was fair and all teams had a fighting chance — my favourite feature was Hot Shot Hamish, which had started life in *Scorcher* in August 1973 but moved over when the two titles merged.[69] In this comic strip, Hamish Balfour played for Princes Park, a lowly Scottish team. He had a pet sheep called McMutton, and the hardest shot in the world because he'd grown up kicking rocks around his little Hebridean island. Princes Park were mostly rubbish and they only survived various scrapes (and enjoyed the odd bit of success) thanks to the brilliant Hamish, a loyal man who stuck with them despite offers from bigger clubs.[70] A sort of Scottish Matt Le Tissier.

One episode, and one frame in particular, still sticks in my mind. His team are down to eight men, so Hamish has dropped into defence because the Princes Park goal is under bombardment from the opposition. The giant man is illustrated rising high in the air and heading the ball off his own line in a desperate attempt to keep his team from conceding. "Come on the eight men," a speech bubble from the crowd urges. It's pure battling spirit. Backs to the wall, Rorke's Drift, a refusal to lie down — choose whichever cliché you prefer. It's great stuff when you are ten years old.

Somehow, I'm not sure the crowd at the Oval thinks being down to eight men is as much fun as I did when reading that comic a few decades ago. Harvey Mapstone is off, Max Thompson is off, and Alfie Headland is in the sin bin. Then the referee tops it all off by marching over to the United dugout and flashing a red card at the bench. I'm later told by a United player walking around the edge of the pitch that the card was for "Bailo [Camara]", the stand-in manager for Anthony Storey today.

The United players scrap and fight for every ball, defending their goal with everything they have as they battle for a point, holding up a Crowborough side that still have their eyes on the title. The supporters, both incensed and frustrated at the same time, are roused by the red cards, and the encouragement for their side (coupled with a few words of 'advice' for the officials) goes up a few notches. Suddenly it feels as if there are a lot more than 158 along the sidelines today. The sense of determination to hang on, both on and off the field, is palpable.

Fittingly for my memories, the Oval ground is situated in Princes Park, the name of the club for which Hot Shot Hamish gave his all. Today the big man may not have actually headed the ball off the line, but I'm sure I saw some speech bubbles with "come on the eight men" hovering in the air.

• *For Eastbourne United's next match, see Game 80 on page 155.*

4
We've (still) Got a Good Game Going

Game 80: Monday 1 April (11am) at the Saffrons, Eastbourne
Eastbourne Town 3 Eastbourne United 0 (Southern Combination Premier)
Weather: mostly dry except for one burst of rain. Welcome to April
MOM: Ollie Davies. Tops off another fine display with a late goal

Non-league football fans in Eastbourne have been talking about this game for some weeks. It's not often that a contest at this level is as eagerly anticipated as the Town v United derby. Kick-off is on a bank holiday morning, which is always a nice time to watch a game, and today there is the added edge of play-off places to fight for. Town are sitting in fifth place, so they are currently in a play-off spot, and although United are eight points adrift, they have a game in hand and are certainly still in the mix. A win for the visitors today will shake things up.

For me, the sense of anticipation has the added ingredient of believing that I will be able to go through the turnstiles in the lovely 1914 building that faces out to Meads Road for the first time. There will be an entrance open at that end of the ground today, as well as the usual one by the cricket field, I've heard. And there is too. Sadly, it's the gate, not the turnstiles, so the £7 entrance fee is paid at a table just inside the ground. At least I am able to snaffle the last available programme from chairman Dave Shearing, who is on duty at this end.

I love programmes at the best of times, but this is a gem because today it is the 100th staging of this historic fixture, a fact which is proudly displayed on the front of the special commemorative edition. It has a great cover, too, featuring players from both teams in various poses of celebration and moodiness as if they are in a boy band music video. Top design. It's also nice to see that Caffyns, the motor retailer, is sponsor for this game, along with Audi. For anyone who visits the Saffrons, it's hard not to notice the fabulous old cars on display in the Caffyns showroom — a 1913 Wolsey, a 1914 Morris Oxford Bullnose, and a 1933 Rolls Royce among others — as you walk to the ground.

A full list of the previous 99 football clashes between the two sides is included in the programme, courtesy of Ed Copping, who puts the stats together, and it provides an interesting record for history lovers. The first ever fixture was on 1 May 1920 when Eastbourne (Town) beat Eastbourne Royal Engineers Old Comrades (United) 3-1 in the East Sussex Challenge Cup at the Saffrons. A 'forward' called Steve Tugwell scored two that day, apparently. The next year the Royal Engineers overturned the result to claim the same cup. Mr Tugwell failed to get on the scoresheet. But the first fixture between sides actually named Eastbourne Town and Eastbourne United was not until 1971.[1]

This has been a fairly regular encounter over the years — its longest break coming because of World War II (there were no matches between 1940 and 1948) — and apart from a 6-0 win for United in 1956 and an 8-1 win for Town in 2017, the games have generally been fairly even. There have been meetings between the two clubs in famous competitions such as the FA Cup, FA Amateur Cup, and FA Vase, and the overall tally stands at 45 wins to Town, 40 to United, and 14 draws.

But today, all eyes are on winning three points in the Southern Combination Premier. Early on, a Leon Greig cross from the right sails across the goalmouth and nestles into the back of the net. Even Jim and John, regulars on the open terrace near the halfway line, and not usually prone to more than the odd shrug and smile, look impressed. It's a lucky goal and the Town supporters aren't complaining. But it's United who take charge of the game, with Tigana Quebe serving up his usual mixture of trickery and pace out wide, and youngsters Ed Ratcliffe and Max Thompson probing for gaps as the visitors look to fight back. Delwin Duah, the Town defender, nearly scores an own goal, goalkeeper Chris Winterton saves well from a Callum Barlow header, and then United hit the bar. It's hotting up nicely.

It's also nice and warm in the bar, with Neil and Harry, the Saffrons' very own Peter Cook and Dudley Moore, pouring pints rapidly as the queue grows. The crowd of 687 is good for the Saffrons club, as well as for the football club. But if anyone is spending ten minutes in the queue in the hope of getting a coffee or a tea, they are in for a disappointment.

"No, sorry. Hot drinks are out there in the ground," the bar duo keep repeating on autopilot in between pouring beers, wines and Cokes.

The tide turns in the second half and the momentum swings back towards the home side. James Hull drills home from the spot after being brought down himself to make it 2-0. Despite a bit more jousting it looks like the game is already settled, but Ollie Davies wraps things up with a goal at the end just to make sure. Derby number 100 goes to Town, just like the first one in 1920. Steve Tugwell would be proud.

• *For Eastbourne Town's next match, see Game 99 on page 193.*
• *For Eastbourne United's next match, see Game 98 on page 190.*

Game 81: Wednesday 3 April (7.45pm) at the Oval, Eastbourne
Eastbourne United U23 2 Crowborough Athletic U23 2 (Southern Combination U23 East)
Weather: dry
MOM: Anthony Storey. Great to watch such skill and technique

The U23 teams in the Southern Combination are allowed to put out four overage players in their matches. Tonight, manager Bailo Camara has selected a rather good one.

Anthony Storey, the Eastbourne United first-team manager, was on the books at Middlesborough[2] during the era of Gareth Southgate, George Boateng, and Juninho. In 2003 he was transferred to Dunfermline Athletic, who were in the Scottish Premiership at the time, and thereafter played for top non-league clubs including Lewes, Eastbourne Borough, and Basingstoke.[3]

Storey is 40 years old now,[4] but to say he's still pretty good is an understatement. Tonight he is sitting in the centre of midfield spraying pinpoint passes to his younger teammates. He takes all the free kicks and all the corners, and every one of them, without fail, hits the mark. On one occasion he strolls over to the ball for a corner and, despite hardly looking down at it, he swivels and delivers a cross right onto the head of one of his players. Most of us need to scuff up a bit of turf so that the ball 'sits up', and then take a bit of a run-up, even to have a chance of delivering such a cross. It's a pleasure to see such technique up close. And, it seems, there are even bigger things ahead for the Storey family. Anthony's daughter, Gabriella, not yet 14, already plays for Chelsea U15.[*]

Storey has been the manager at United since taking over in the 2021–22 season.[5] He's following in famous footsteps because United have had some top names in charge over the years. Most significant of them all was Ron Greenwood, who went on to manage West Ham United for 13 years and then, from 1977 until 1982, England.[6] Greenwood took over at United in 1956, despite suggestions that he might be heading to Fulham,[7] and moved on in December 1957 to take the assistant manager job at Arsenal.[8]

But even before Greenwood, there was George Smith (1952–55), who played for Brentford and QPR, and turned out for England in a wartime international.[9] Then in the 1960s, there was Gordon Jago,[10] who made 147 appearances for Charlton Athletic and went on to manage the USA, QPR, Millwall, and Tampa Bay Rowdies, where he had players such as England internationals Rodney Marsh and Frank Worthington on the books.[11] Later, United were managed by Micky French, who played for Brentford, Swindon Town, and Aldershot. This footballing son of Eastbourne, also managed Hailsham Town.[12] Other bosses at United

---

[*] Gabriella Storey was selected for the England U16 squad for the Nordic tournament held in Finland in July 2024.

have included Bill Lansdowne, who made 57 appearances for West Ham between 1956 and 1962,[13] and Roger Wedge (manager from 1980 to 1982), who played for Orient.

It's quite a line-up for a non-league club, but as Barry Winter recalls in his book *Inside United*, having such famous names could sometimes cause problems. On one occasion, the club were trying to sort out the paperwork for a player who'd been playing in Germany, only to receive a fax asking for a transfer fee because the German club had been struck by United's impressive managerial roll call.[14]

Winter wrote his book of United memories to mark his 50 years' involvement with the club as a supporter, player, manager, and committee member.[15] He's a good man to stand next to if you need information about Eastbourne United. He tells me that they are resting a few players with niggling injuries tonight because they have the county cup final coming up against East Grinstead.[16]

However, with the likes of Mason Creese, Ollie Hull, the ever-improving Kobe Agbude, and Max Thompson on the bench, plus Storey in midfield, United U23 will be expecting a win tonight against second-bottom Crowborough, who have picked up only one point on the road this season. So, it's a surprise when they go behind in the 22nd minute to a Robert Elliot goal.

At half-time, by which stage Blake Larby has equalised for United, I chat to the dad of the Crowborough goalkeeper, a young man who has recently returned home after a few years of playing college soccer in the USA. Although college soccer attendances don't compare with those of the 'American' sports, some of the top colleges were pulling in average crowds pre-lockdown that would shame a lot of our League Two clubs, so it must be a bit of a change to be playing on a Wednesday night in front of 21 people.

Max Thompson puts United ahead in the 70th minute after coming on as substitute. He's not a bad player to have on the bench. The young player, who is a regular for the senior side (he has scored nine goals for them this season), was on the books at Crystal Palace aged nine, and then joined Chelsea (where he played with Germany's current superstar Jamal Musiala, as well as

Levi Colwell, who is still with the London club), before moving on to Watford. But just as it seems as if United are coasting to the top of the table, a mistake at the back lets in Slavi Chakarov for a surprise equaliser and a draw.

After the game, the Crowborough keeper tells me he's never had to deal with so many pinpoint crosses in his life.

• *For Eastbourne United U23's next match, see Game 86 on page 165.*

Game 82: Thursday 4 April (7.45pm) at the Saffrons, Eastbourne
Eastbourne Town U23 5 Hailsham Town U23 3 (Southern Combination U23 East)
Weather: windy and wet
MOM: Mackenzie Stiles. Delivery is his middle name

Town's U23 side are bobbing about in the middle of the table with seven wins and six defeats in their 13 games so far. As you'd imagine with a team that doesn't do draws, their matches are always entertaining; they average more than two-and-a-half goals a game and concede more than two. It's a case of you score, we score.

There are goals from Sonny Walsh, now a regular in the first-team squad, the hard-working Flynn Sweeting, Harry Murphy, and Lee Connolly. Add to that an own goal, a sin bin (for Sweeting), plus three goals at the other end courtesy of Louis Osborne (2) and Jose Agrela Cornwall, and the spectators who have braved the wet, windy night certainly get their reward.

The terrible weather of this past winter is showing no sign of wanting to give up just yet, and many regulars will be thanking the Sid Myall & Taffy Jones covered stand to the north of the ground for their survival tonight. It was built in 1994, some 25 years after the original wooden grandstand was destroyed by an arsonist in March 1969. The 'temporary' stand that replaced it had its roof blown off in the 1987 hurricane.[17]

The present stand stretches the whole width of the pitch behind the goal at what used to be called the Larkins Field End,[18] which is a fascinating hive of activity. I can think of few areas in a football ground with so much going on in so small a space.

To the west of the stand (or the left if you are looking at it from the pitch) is the Saffrons' clubhouse (opened in 2007) and the cricket field. This is also where you will find the main entrance to the football ground, and a small wooden hut for the people who collect the entrance money (although this is not actually used and the 'gatemen' stand by a table just inside the ground). This end of the stand has 84 (yes, I counted them) blue, flip-down plastic seats in three rows. A sign declares that some of these seats are reserved for the directors, although I have never seen any directors use them. There is then a small stretch of terracing for standing, 19 more flip-down seats in two rows, the entrance to the changing rooms, a park-style bench, the entrance to the toilets, the entrance to the committee rooms and players' lounge, five more benches (with commemorative plaques, including one engraved with 'There is only one Roger Addems'),[19] and a small hatch serving hot drinks. The hatch has a small metal grille in front of it to protect buyers from wayward shots.

Phew! I told you it was busy. But there's more. There are then another 58 of those flip-down seats, and to the side of the stand is another entrance to the boardroom, a storage shed, and the Corner Flag cafe. Just over the perimeter fence is Eastbourne Bowls Club. I might have missed something, but you get the picture.

It is in this wonderful stand that most of tonight's spectators are huddled. Sid Myall, who still holds the record for the most appearances with Town — turning out 602 times between 1962 and 1979[20] — and Taffy Jones, who had two stints as manager,[21] are legends of the club. With the weather as it is today, everyone here is grateful for the stand which carries their names and their memory.

• *For Eastbourne Town U23's next match, see Game 95 on page 184.*

Game 83: Sunday 7 April (1.30pm) at Priory Lane, Eastbourne
Eastbourne Borough Women DS 3 Woodingdean Wanderers Women 3 (SCWGFL Division 1)
Weather: the early glorious weather takes a turn for the not-so-glorious
WOM: Lucy Lomax

Sunday is usually a busy time for children's football, with matches stretched throughout the day. And there is certainly no shortage of it on the former day of rest at Borough, where the football never seems to stop. There is a decent-size car park at the front of the Borough ground and to its right as you look at the stadium, a large area of grass. This is where the children's matches are played. Young bodies race around with more energy than I've mustered in quite a few years, and I watch as a blond boy gets mobbed by his teammates after scoring. It's a cracker from about six feet out. Parents clap enthusiastically from behind the rope which is a couple of yards back from the touchline. 'Respect barriers' were introduced a few years ago in children's football to keep parents back from the pitch. Some of them do get very excited, you know.

It's a welcome move. I was once tripped by a parent (not my own, I should add) in an U12 match as I dribbled down the wing in the days before the barrier was brought in. The other parents laughed. At Borough there are no thoughts of such parental 'gamesmanship', of course, and everyone heads happily off to Spooners, the on-site coffee hut, for a hot drink and a sausage roll.

I leave them to it as the women's match is about to start. Woodingdean are a decent side, but they are up against a determined and fast-moving Eastbourne Borough DS team who have the wind in their sails; they've lost only one of their last six games and in their last outing they demolished their neighbours, Town DS, 6-0. The runaway leaders, Worthing, have already disappeared over the hill, but with games in hand, the runners-up spot looks to be within the grasp of Borough.

And it certainly seems as if grasping it is their aim, because in the early exchanges the keeper from the Brighton side is facing an onslaught. Two blocks with her feet, a double-handed save (from a shot so hard that it is more like another block), the bar, the bar again — it's relentless stuff. Such moments can determine a match. Borough do eventually get the ball past the Wanderers stopper but their three goals are matched, courtesy of two first-half strikes from Amy Creedon and a late one from Ella Baum. Those few minutes' inspiration from the Woodingdean goalkeeper in the first half have gone a long way to earning her side the draw. I hope

she gets a good pat on the back from someone on the other side of the respect barrier.
• *For Eastbourne Borough Women DS's season summary see page 210.*

Game 84: Monday 8 April (7.30pm) at the Saffrons, Eastbourne
Welcroft Park Rangers Reserves 3 Seaford Town U18 3 (win 4-2 on penalties) (Eastbourne FA Junior Cup QF)
Weather: not too cold, but it's a bit blowy at times
MOM: Daniel Fox

Welcroft Park Rangers Reserves are not having the best of seasons. They are currently second bottom of East Sussex Division 3 with only two wins all season, and were knocked out of the Hastings FA Lower Divisions Cup by the Crowhurst third team back in October. They did reach the 2nd Round of the East Sussex Challenge Cup (Divisions 3 and 4) but that was only thanks to a bye in the 1st Round. And, despite leading 3-1 at half-time, they lost that game 7-6 after conceding two late goals to Ticehurst. Yet this is not a team that gets tonked every week. They haven't lost by more than two goals all season, and five of the defeats have been by just the odd goal. They have also secured two draws with second-placed Bexhill Amateur Athletic Reserves and smashed champions elect Parkfield 8-4, albeit with the useful addition of the first-team's goal machine, Bill Coles, who scored a hat-trick.

Their leading goalscorers this season, James Burnett and Steven Cherryman, have a useful nine each, while George Jones has eight, so they are hardly struggling upfront. It's certainly a disappointing campaign for a team that romped to the Division 4 title last season. But also, a frustratingly close one in many ways.

Tonight's game at the Saffrons offers a test of another kind, as they are up against a skilful Seaford U18 side. Teams at the level of Welcroft certainly aren't lacking in determination, but they play football because they love playing; U18 players at the level of Seaford love it too, but they are dreaming of higher things. It makes for an interesting clash. And a very even one, too.

Burnett, Jones, and substitute Charles Fairweather score for the Hailsham side, but the Seaford youngsters match them and the Junior Cup tie heads to penalties. The technique of the youngsters is enough to ensure they go through in the shoot-out. It's another frustrating night for the Welcroft lads.

Game 85: Wednesday 10 April (7.45pm) at Priory Lane, Eastbourne
Eastbourne Borough Women 4 Bexhill United Women 0 (Eastbourne FA Chairman's Cup QF)
Weather: cold and dry
WOM: Charlotte Gurr at the double

I say hello to Wen Jiang, the 'reluctant goalkeeper', as I've dubbed her. She's in the Founders' Bar this time and not in the goal she occasionally keeps. She tells me that she's here to support the first team, some of whom she has played with in the DS side. The Founders' Bar is the cosy smaller bar at the back of the large Borough clubhouse, accessed from the back of the building by the indoor bowls facility. It's the only place open for spectators tonight because there's a big charity quiz in the main bar.

"And for your next question, who will score Borough's first goal tonight?" the quizmaster doesn't ask. But if he had, few (who watch Borough Women regularly) would have got the right answer. It's the ever-reliable skipper Kellie Larkin, the former England U19 player, and instrumental in Borough's transformation under Billy Wood, who breaks the deadlock — not Charlotte Gurr, who has been banging goals in for fun since joining back in October.

Considering the long history of the Eastbourne FA, the Chairman's Cup is a relatively new competition. It has only been held twice — Eastbourne Strollers won it in 2014–15 (when it was a competition for walking teams) and Newhaven Ladies triumphed in 2022–23 (when it was a women's competition). The Chairman's Cup was introduced as a flexible competition, so who competes for it might change again in the future.

Bexhill, who play in the higher London & South East Regional Women's League, should be favourites to go through tonight and have a shot at adding their name to the short list of winners, but judging from their body language, it doesn't seem as if they really believe it. Borough are just too fast and slick for them, stringing together some beautiful moves and producing some of the most polished play I've seen for a while. Gurr, who averages more than a goal a game, gets two, and youngster Megan-Rose Griffiths — not shy of finding the net herself — adds another for a comprehensive victory. Borough's semi-final opponents, neighbours Eastbourne Town, are unlikely to be relishing a meeting with a team in this kind of form.

• *For Eastbourne Borough Women's season summary see page 210.*

Game 86: Thursday 11 April (7.30pm) at the Polegrove, Bexhill-on-Sea
Bexhill United U23 2 Eastbourne United U23 3 (Southern Combination U23 East)
Weather: dry
MOM: Ollie Hull. Returns to his former club and hits a cracking goal for Eastbourne

I'm greeted by an abandoned small bicycle as I head towards Bexhill United's ground. Has a youngster got fed up with his Christmas present already and dumped it to rust away in the overgrown grass? I say 'youngster' because the bike is quite small, but I suppose it could belong to anyone these days, when so many grown people pedal around crouched over undersize bikes like bad-dude characters from *Grant Theft Auto San Andreas*. Come on, that's *sooo* 2004. And this is Sussex.

The abandoned (or likely stolen) minibike is just inside the entrance to the Polegrove Recreation Ground, a popular public space that is shared by the football club, the cricket club, and the bowls club, as well as hosting events such as the Bexhill Horse and Dog Show and the Bexhill 100 Classic & Custom Car Show.[22]

Because the football ground can be accessed through a public park, Bexhill United have permission to shut the park entrances for their senior matches, so they can collect money from spectators. But tonight anyone can just stroll into the ground for free, passing little bikes on their way.

The blocks of flats along the West Parade probably offer residents some impressive sea views from the front, but it's the unremarkable rears of these uniform 1980s-era[23] buildings that tower over the largely open football ground. The pitch is enclosed, as is the requirement at this level, and some vinyl banners advertising the club's sponsors flap loose from their ties on the metal tubing, battered by a season of wind and rain.

But there, standing tall among all of this, is one of the most remarkable old stands you are likely to come across. Bexhill's large, mock-Tudor stand was opened in 1929 and provides rows of fairly steep wooden-bench seating, while tall glass panels on the sides let in light, and some ornate fascia at the front of the pitched, tiled roof completes the effect. Either side of the old stand are two smaller toilet blocks, both built in a similar style, and at the front are the fairly utilitarian dugouts and the players' entrance to the pitch. It's a glorious piece of football history. And a popular hangout for youngsters at night, apparently, courtesy of the public access to the grounds.

First-team centre back Alfie Headland has been drafted in to bolster the Eastbourne defence, but all the talk from the two scarf-wearing Bexhill fans I'm standing next to is about Ollie Hull. He's recently joined Eastbourne from Bexhill after playing 28 games for their senior team and seven for the U23 team, scoring three goals for each. He's obviously a big loss from the way the Bexhill fans are talking. I don't know what to say when their former player gives Eastbourne United the lead with a cracking shot after just six minutes.

At half-time, a lady comes into the impressive clubhouse with her granddaughter. The clubhouse — the Polegrove Sports Bar — has been refurbished in recent years and the lady, who used to work here when her husband was on the club committee, wanders around pointing out where things used to be. "The bar was here before, right at the end," she tells me. Then she starts examining the old photos on the wall, before excitedly pointing out old friends in the pictures, including her husband, to her granddaughter. One photo shows the teams when the famous Arsenal came to play the then Bexhill Town in a charity match. The London club actually took on Bexhill twice in the 1940s, once on 20 September 1948, when the First Division side ran out 8-1 winners in front of 3,000 people.[24] Five days later Arsenal played Wolverhampton Wanderers at Highbury, a game watched by over 56,000 spectators.

It's certainly not as one-sided tonight, and in a highly competitive game Nathan Corke and Joseph Simonian grab a goal each for Bexhill. But T'yano Wilson scores two off the bench to add to Hull's early effort and ensure that Eastbourne United U23 take three points to move into second place, closing the gap on the league leaders Peacehaven & Telscombe.
• *For Eastbourne United U23's next match, see Game 101 on page 196.*

Game 87: Saturday 13 April (3pm) at Priory Lane, Eastbourne
Eastbourne Borough 3 Chippenham Town 0 (National League South)
Weather: dry
MOM: Moussa Diarra. A giant of a performance from a giant of a man

When I was a youngster, a 'project' was something you did at school. You'd immerse yourself in Elizabethan England, the Middle Ages, frogs, the Suez Canal, seemingly anything that took the teacher's fancy. The whole class would study the subject for a while and then we'd have to submit our project, often a few scratchy words and some pictures in a shiny new folder from WHSmith, or for the more enthusiastic in the class, a whole elaborate display they'd lug into school to show off and pretend it hadn't been put together by their parents. They were quite good fun, projects. Except the frog one. I'm not sure many of us were all that keen on hopping down to the local ponds in search of slimy creatures.

Today, you can't turn on the TV or open a sportsfeed on your phone without hearing mention of some club's 'project' by the manager or chairman. The FA are so fond of the word that in 2020 details emerged that they even had a Project Big Picture (a proposal put together by Liverpool and Manchester United to redistribute money to EFL clubs, trim the size of the Premier League, and abolish the EFL Cup and Community Shield). According to a BBC source at West Ham, the plan was no more than a "power grab" by the Big Six.[25]

Even players are using the P-word now. "I am pleased to have signed for Albion and I hope to play a big part in their exciting project," they might declare, as if that makes any sense. I know times change, but I can't remember Bob Paisley or Sir Alex Ferguson referring to Liverpool or Manchester United as anything other than football clubs.

The big 'project' in Eastbourne football circles at the moment is at Borough. It's a slick operation, and while some of the old timers who remember the days of Langney FC might not like it, there is an air of professionalism about the place. Recruitment is obviously good (with players sold to Wolves and York City this season), the match day 'experience' is excellent, the social media is smart, and the players are on full-time contracts. It's only on the pitch that the 'project' has been close to coming off the rails. Borough have been in the relegation zone, or hovering near it, for most of the season. And relegation to the Isthmian League would not do any good for that word in quotation marks.

But just when it looks like the cause is lost, the players find their mojo. They have lost just one in eight, picking up a useful 15 points. The arrival of winger Yahya Bamba as a dual registration signing from Cray Wanderers in March[26] (and his four goals for Borough since then), plus the addition of the excellent Northern Ireland U23 international, Pierce Bird, on loan from AFC Fylde,[27] have certainly helped. But it's at the back where the difference is really stark: Borough have kept five clean sheets in those eight games, compared to just two previously this season.

This turnaround is down, in large part, to Moussa Diarra, the 34-year-old French centre back who joined Borough on loan from Barnet in January.[28] The man is a giant. But not just because of his height — which, granted, is a towering 6' 5". He's a giant because he exudes energy, effort, and presence. Plus, he's chipped in three goals in his 11 starts. Football fans aren't the most forgiving of people, but the thing they hate the most is when it looks as if players are not giving their all. This is something that could never be levelled at Diarra (not that too many people would be brave enough to try).

Today, against a Chippenham side that are playing their fourth game in eight days[29] — and, according to a Town committee man

I chat to, "are resting a few players for Tuesday's county cup final" — Diarra strides tall. Bamba's speed and unpredictability up front might provide the thrills for this revolutionised side, but it's Diarra who ensures there is some good, old-fashioned stability at the back. Moreover, not content with holding court in defence, he seems keen on showing off his other talents. He rises high to nod home a goal from a corner in the 37th minute, adding to Sam Beard's acrobatic early finish, and then languidly celebrates with a pointy sort-of-Usain-Bolt celebration followed by the urban loose-wristed finger snap. Interesting. But quite frankly, he can do whatever he wants today. Then, when Borough are three up in the second half (Bamba, naturally, after a cracking run from Finn Ballard McBride), he takes a little wander up front to display his skills with his feet, even showcasing a silky, albeit fairly slow, feinted step-over. There are ironic cheers from the Borough fans packed behind the goal at the River End.

By this stage it's all carnival and celebrations, with the Borough fans singing "We are staying up! We are staying up!" Most of the 1,627 in attendance are delighted at the prospect. The 'project' lives on.

• *For Eastbourne Borough's season summary see page 208.*

Game 88: Tuesday 16 April (6.15pm) at the Polegate War Memorial Recreation Ground
Polegate Town 3 Sovereign Saints 1 (Mid Sussex Championship)
Weather: sunny, hail, gloomy. And dark by the end of the game
MOM: Thomas Gregory. The youngster stands out for Saints in a disappointing defeat

There's a windmill nestled among the trees that form the backdrop to Polegate Town's War Memorial Ground. The Ovenden Mill was built in 1817 and was still operating by wind right up until 1943, and then by an auxiliary engine and electric motor until 1965.[30] Today, it's a Grade II* listed building.[31] It's a fabulous sight from the Wannock Road side of the ground. But I doubt if the players even notice it anymore. They've got a match to concentrate on. There's no time to be looking at windmills.

Teams in the Mid Sussex League rarely play matches on any

day other than a Saturday. But it's been a wet winter, with a lot of games postponed, so league officials and clubs are battling to wrap up the fixtures towards the end of a long season. And because the football club does not have floodlights, Polegate is hosting tonight's match at the unusual kick-off time of 6.15pm. But the early start has not put off the fans and there is a decent crowd of about 70 here tonight. Saints are struggling near the bottom, so Polegate are certainly favourites. And the favourites go one up.

The Horse & Groom is close to the football ground and it makes a decent enough pit stop during a wander in the half-time break. These days, the place belongs to one of those chains that are more food than pub, but it's been serving beer to this village of just over 9,000[32] for quite a few years, as evidenced by the fact that a 34-year-old man called John Clare from Hailsham is listed as innkeeper in the 1851 census.[33] He probably didn't serve an all-you-can-eat buffet with a side salad and buttered roll in those days though. Situated on the busy junction where the High Street crosses the A2270, and only a short distance from the train station, this Grade II listed building is a popular village landmark nonetheless.

Major thoroughfares have passed this way for hundreds of years. The Roman road that ran from Pevensey to Lewes came through here,[34] and in 1846 the railway arrived when the London and Brighton Railway built the Brighton to Hastings line. For many years, Polegate was an important junction and the town attracted a large number of railway staff.[35] Things change though. The Romans left about 1,600 years ago when they decided they had more important places than Britannia to worry about, while the Beeching and subsequent cuts of the mid-1960s put paid to the town's importance as a junction.[36]

By then, however, Polegate's population was around 8,000[37] and the football club were celebrating their 50th anniversary. They were already firmly established at the War Memorial Ground, having moved here in 1923, and Polegate FC enjoyed a run of success in the 1970s, with a league title and four cup wins. Two decades later the club secured the Eastbourne FA Challenge Cup in 1995–96 (ending a particularly long wait since their first success in 1933–34) and, the following season, picked up the East Sussex Premier league and cup double.[38]

However, this was the prelude to the club's downfall and they folded at the start of the new millennium. They were reformed in 2006 and two years later the club were renamed Polegate Town. They celebrated by reaching the final of the Sussex Challenge Junior Cup that year, and more success was to follow. Two seasons later Town secured promotion back to the East Sussex Premier and lifted the Eastbourne FA Junior Cup, and while the decision was made to move to the Mid Sussex League at the end of 2010–11, the club signed off in style from the eastern front by winning the East Sussex Challenge Cup. The club centenary came in 2015 and the next season Polegate picked up the much-coveted Eastbourne FA Challenge Cup for the third time in their history. More recently still, the reserve side won a cup double — the Parsons Cup and the Testers Cup — in 2018–19, and then lifted the Eastbourne FA Vice-President's Cup in 2021–22. The first team secured promotion to Mid Sussex Championship in 2022–23.[39]

Two quick goals after the break — one apiece, with Jack Griffin scoring for Saints — makes it 2-1 on the pitch. I chat to a guy whose son is playing tonight and we swap tales of when we played ourselves. Like retired boxers past their prime, we wonder if we could still hack it out there. We know we can't, of course, but there's always the dream of a comeback, however fanciful it might be. Once a footballer always a footballer.

Then, suddenly, hailstones pile down in bullets, a farewell gift from a winter that is determined to keep on giving. As the rest of us scramble for cover, the Sovereign Saints chairman, Paul Garnell, stands unmoved against the black fencing that surrounds the pitch. He's been through this and more during the 21 years since he started the club, having previously been involved in the youth section at Eastbourne United. What's a bit of hail when it comes to running a local football club day in, day out?

Saints will have 16 teams (plus Soccer Tots and Mini-Kickers) next season, stretching from U7 to U18 and through to two senior sides, Garnell tells me. The senior sides are not having a good time of things in 2023–24. The reserve team sits second from bottom in the East Sussex Division 2, with just three wins to go alongside their 11 defeats. And there's a real chance of a double relegation for the club, because the first team are also second bottom — in the Mid Sussex Championship — with just four wins and 11 defeats of their own. Actually, make that 12 defeats, as the referee blows up for a 3-1 win to Polegate, the windmill disappears into the gloom of the clouds and Garnell shrugs off the hail from his jacket.

• *For Sovereign Saints' next match, see Game 91 on page 175.*

Game 89: Wednesday 17 April (7.30pm) at the Saffrons, Eastbourne
Parkfield 3 (win 4-3 on penalties) Sovereign Saints Reserves 3 (Eastbourne FA Junior Cup SF)
Weather: spits of rain but otherwise clear with no wind
MOM: Samuel Winston

The opening goal of the game is a gem. Saints' big number nine Jordon Funnel (who also plays for Eastbourne United U23) bustles down the line, shaking off two or three challenges and rounding the left back to put in a perfectly floated gem of a cross from the left. The ball hangs in the air for what seems an eternity, but when it eventually settles, the header from skipper Nicholas Barden is deposited into the bottom corner.

This comes as somewhat of a surprise, despite the fact that Saints' Reserves play in a division higher than Parkfield in the East Sussex League. Winning can become a habit in football and Parkfield have certainly acquired it this season, cantering to the Division 3 title with games to spare. Saints, meanwhile, are near the bottom of Division 2, and when it comes to results, they have the habit that no one wants — losing. They've lost 12 of their 17 games so far this season (one was a walkover) and have conceded six goals or more six times. The wait between their first win in September and their second in March was 189 days. Upward momentum is everything in a season and it's emphatically Parkfield who have it.

Tonight's match at the Saffrons is a rerun of last year's final (which Parkfield won) and it promises to be feisty. And so it is. Sort of. The usual banter, bullshit, and barbed comments that are part and parcel of most matches fly around.

"Why are you wasting time already?" the Parkfield keeper, a stand-in I'm told by a spectator, shouts to his opposite number from afar. "There are still 60 minutes to play." With Sovereign Saints Reserves 1-0 up, their keeper is in no rush to collect the ball after it has been fired past him pointlessly by a frustrated Parkfield striker long after the referee has blown the whistle for offside. I don't think anyone seriously thinks he is wasting time so early on, but hey, it's worth a shout.

As fate would have it, Parkfield knock the ball into the net legally a minute or so later for an equaliser. The follow-up comments that bounce about the Saffrons are fairly predictable, but they are funny, nonetheless.

It's still all-square at half-time, but as the game approaches its conclusion Parkfield have edged ahead 3-2, thanks to goals from James Graham, Julian Pareja, and Samuel Winston, while Luke Maglennon has added to Barden's early goal for Saints. Clearances become more frantic as the time ticks by and more than a few are deposited deep into the bowls club next door, as Parkfield chase another shot at winning the Eastbourne FA Junior Cup. But the more frantic it gets, the more Saints push, and in the dying seconds the hard-working Alfie Morris brings things level. The game's been pretty even throughout, so it's a reasonable end. Except this is a cup match, so the real end only comes after penalties.

I've met an unlikely spectator among the 40 or so people watching the game tonight. Chris is from Melbourne but is thinking of relocating to Eastbourne, which I'd guess is one of the world's lesser-travelled paths. He's fascinated by the pyramid of English football — "there's nothing like this back home" — and is using his trip to catch up on some grassroots games. His knowledge of the various steps in the pyramid is encyclopaedic. "This team are there" and "this team play at that level", he tells me. It's impressive because the exact workings of the pyramid remain a bit of a blur to even the most hardened of non-league fans — or at least to those who haven't bought themselves a wall chart showing where each league slots in.

The penalties are pretty decent by both sides and, despite one that's blazed over by a Parkfield player (which I manage to capture on video and replay later in the bar, much to the pleasure of his teammates) and some gentle behind-the-goal barracking from the Saints fans, the Junior Cup holders, Parkfield, head to the final again with a 4-3 shoot-out win.

• *For Parkfield's next match, see Game 97 on page 188.*
• *For Sovereign Saints Reserves' next match, see Game 92 on page 178.*

Game 90: Friday 19 April (7.30pm) at the Saffrons, Eastbourne
Eastbourne Town U18 2 Seaford Town U18 1 (Eastbourne FA Junior Cup SF)
Weather: a mostly clear evening
MOM: Jack Hammond. Tops off another reliable performance with a goal

Parkfield have already secured their place in the final of the Eastbourne FA Junior Cup, and midway through the game I chat to Adam Smith, their big defender, who has come to see whom his side will meet. "They both look pretty decent!" he tells me, laughing. "Are you sure they are under 18?"

He's noticed Sonny Walsh, Eastbourne's strong and quick striker, because he'll be the one marking him if the home side go through. He has picked the right man to keep an eye on. The young striker has turned out regularly for Eastbourne Town U18, U23, and the senior side this season. He has played 16 games for the first team, all appearances off the bench, and picked up his first senior goal when he slid home in the dying seconds against Saltdean United last month. For Town U23, he's found the net three times in 18 appearances, while for Town U18, it's 12 goals (including two in the FA Youth Cup) in 14 outings. Walsh doesn't score tonight, but Parkfield will still be facing the Eastbourne youngsters, who sneak past their neighbours 2-1 thanks to goals from Arthur Karapetyan and the ever-impressive defender Jack Hammond.

It's a rare goal for Hammond, who is Mr Consistent for this

side, but Parkfield will have plenty of regular scorers to worry about. There are goals aplenty from strikers Noah Titterton-Manos (nine so far this season), Flynn Sweeting (eight), and the hard-running Matthew Myall (five), plus useful contributions from midfielders Spencer Morley (four), Joseph Hill, and Leo Groombridge (three apiece) It's certainly a nice spread of goals for manager Ryan Reid to enjoy.

The Eastbourne Junior Cup is, as the name suggests, a cup for sides who play at a junior level, with the higher ranked sides in the Southern Combination putting out junior-age teams to even the playing field in the tournament.

The Junior Cup is a relative baby when it comes to the history of the Eastbourne FA — lifted first by Spartan FC in 1972–73. Other early winners include Old Grammarians, Wannock, Hartingdon, and Berwick. In recent years, the roll of honour has included some familiar contemporary names, such as Polegate Town, Eastbourne Rangers, Sovereign Saints, Herstmonceux, and Parkfield (the holders). In the past, however, wedged between triumphs for pub teams such as the Rose & Crown and Beach Tavern, came victory for a club with an even more resonant name: Langney Sports (now Eastbourne Borough). It's a reminder of what can happen in football's pyramid.

Eastbourne Town have won this cup only once, in 1999–2000. On their current goalscoring form, it may well be down to that Parkfield defender, to stop them doing it again.

• *For Eastbourne Town U18's next match, see Game 100 on page 195.*

Game 91: Saturday 20 April (2pm) at Shinewater Lane, Eastbourne
Sovereign Saints 4 Hurstpierpoint 1 (Mid Sussex Championship)
Weather: no wind and there's the odd burst of sun, but it's cold
MOM: Patrick Seymour. Comes off the bench and slots in two beautiful goals

Shinewater Lane has become a bit like El Dorado to me. I've tried to see a Saints fixture a couple of times during the past few weeks, but to no avail. I've checked the fixtures, checked online to see how to get to the venue, even sought out directions from various people along the way. But, alas, I haven't been able to find a match on. Bus 1A and 1X both go to Saints' home ground, according to the Apple map professor on my phone. But when I get there… where are the posts? …where are the players? Have I got the right place?

As it turns out, I have indeed been going to the correct ground. Well, it's usually the correct ground. Unfortunately, on the days of my previous visits, the fixtures had been shifted to Hampden Park due to the heavy rain. Still, I've had a lovely time wandering around Shinewater, exploring the park and poking my face through rusty fences in search of a bit of grass with white poles sticking out.

But today, as I nip up Lavender Close, past a man washing his car outside his suburban house, and emerge through the bushes, there is the glint of white goalposts and the movement of players in the yellow and black stripes of Sovereign Saints. The sun is shining. El Dorado does exist, after all. Sir Walter Raleigh would be proud of me.

Today is what the TV companies might dub 'Super Saturday' at Shinewater Park: the first team have a two o'clock kick-off and that is followed by the reserves' match at four. The facilities are pretty good, with a decent-size pitch, a white metal rail right around it and block-built dugouts on the Milfoil Road side of the ground. It's on this side that most of the spectators gather. It is a decent turnout for this level and there's a steady stream of people wandering backwards and forwards across the small children's pitch behind one of the goals to the clubhouse for refreshments.

I ask some young lads sitting behind the goal who Saints are playing. "Dad, who are the other team?" one of them shouts to the home goalkeeper. "I dunno, I just turn up and play," he replies, before rushing out to clear a through ball. The opposition are in fact Hurstpierpoint, a name most people from outside the area will recognise, if only because of the famous college that bears its name. It's an ancient and historic village, summed up succinctly in the Domesday Book of 1086 as: "Large; church; some Georgian houses."[40] There were fewer than two million people in England in those days, so the 51 households living on the Land of William of Warene remarkably put Hurstpierpoint in the top 20 per cent of largest settlements as recorded in the manuscript of the famous Great Survey.[41] You had to like peace and quiet back then.

The Hurstpierpoint football team of today are nestled comfortably in mid-table, with only a couple of games to play; not going up and not going down. A couple of the Saints subs play keepy-uppies on the edge of the pitch by the dugouts, and for a while there seems to be a similar kind of contest happening on the field itself. The Saints no. 4, Cameron Apted, immediately stands out. He's pretty skilful and likes his tricks. He twists one way, then swivels another, then tries a Cruyff turn. The opposition midfielders try to match him and for a while it becomes a bit of a trick competition in midfield. But finally, someone gets to grips with what is needed and bashes through a couple of players to power a header forward. No nonsense. It wakes everyone up and Saints summon what usually wins games at this level: determination and commitment. Even though they are 1-0 down at this stage to an early Kevin Budge goal, they start to find some rhythm, with some lovely deliveries from Joe Sambrook on the left in particular.

Then the pressure from Saints pays off. The ancient villagers can do nothing to stop Wayne Green latching onto a through ball. His chip is a beauty, and with a little assistance from the wind, it evades the keeper. Goals have been a bit thin on the ground for Saints this season, with Green (this is his eighth goal), Stephen Jackson (nine), and Jack Griffin (five), the only players to have scored more than twice.

Enter some new blood, at least as far as first-team scorers are concerned. Phillip Chandler and Patrick Seymour are chalk and cheese when it comes to footballing styles; Chandler is big, strong, and direct, Seymour is sleight, tricky, and plays with a languid Jack Grealish swagger. The combination works a treat. Chandler gives Saints the lead. Then Seymour springs into life. A jink and a dink after a cracking through ball and it's in. "Come on Paddy" someone shouts. The two substitutes are linking up well, and after another bit of dinking from Seymour, it's 4-1 and Saints are able to celebrate their first win since early November.

For the first ten years of their existence, Sovereign Saints ran junior-age teams, but in 2013 they launched their first men's side.

Initially, the plan was to form the team from the youngsters who had grown up and played with the club at youth level, but in the end only a handful of them wanted to move up, so some older players were recruited. The first match was played on 31 July 2013, when the new team came from behind to beat Punnett's Town 3-1. The scene was set for their first season, which was to be played in East Sussex Division 4.

They were immediately promoted after finishing second in the league. The next season they stormed Division 3, losing just two league games, and picked up the Eastbourne FA Junior Cup — one of their players, Steve Prodger, also collected the Bill Hide Memorial Cup for man of the match. It was some start, but after a string of retirements, they were forced to resign from Division 2 in November 2015.[42]

Back with a new team the next season, they rejoined Division 4, which they duly won by a whopping 13 points — some going in a league of just ten teams. The 2016–17 season was undoubtedly the zenith for the club, as they also won the Eastbourne FA Junior Cup again (Phil Broom picked up the Bill Hide Memorial Cup), and the Eastbourne FA Vice-President's Cup (Saints entered a team using a group of players who had played youth football at Eastbourne Borough to represent them in the latter).

The next season, having been promoted two divisions, Saints duly won Division 2, perhaps putting to bed the frustrations of their resignation year. They then moved across to the Mid Sussex League to try their luck against some different teams.

Give it a season or two and maybe their keeper will know which team he is facing.

• *For Sovereign Saints' next match, see Game 95 on page ?.*

Game 92: Saturday 20 April (4pm) at Shinewater Lane, Eastbourne
Sovereign Saints Reserves 2 Northiam 75 5 (East Sussex Division 2)
Weather: the sun gives up and it gets colder by the minute. Spring has not sprung
MOM: Bradley Najair. Gets a double as Northiam 75 make sure they secure a victory

Sovereign Saints were founded by Paul Garnell, their chairman, treasurer, secretary, fixture secretary and, from what I can see, general odd-job man. I'm half-wondering why he's not out there at right midfield as well this afternoon. He's pretty level-headed about the first team's excellent win — in fact he has to ask me how the game went (he was in the clubhouse working). "Very impressive," I tell him. He smiles, but he's used to the roller coaster of football. Teams win and teams lose. Clubs go up and clubs go down. The important thing is that they keep going.

Clubs at this level rely on people like Garnell. When you are a player, you don't realise just how important they are. You turn up for a match and grumble about having to hand over a few quid for your subs, despite the fact that someone else has had to confirm the fixture, sort out the referee, cut the grass, mark those white lines, and ensure that the kits are clean, the showers are hot, and the beers in the fridge are cold. It happens just like magic when you are a player. Strange that, eh?

"Sovereign is a name used a lot in Eastbourne — the harbour, the shopping centre, and at one time, a radio station," Garnell tells me. He felt "it just fitted" as a name for the club. For similar "it just felt right" reasons, Saints was added to the name, even though Sharks was briefly considered.

The Northiam 75 players amble towards the changing rooms to get kitted up for the game. One of them is carrying a silver trophy, another is rolling a cigarette, and a third is wearing a top that displays the sponsor's name: Will's Bakery and Cafe. They nod their hellos and are soon back out warming up on the large grass area behind the goal.

Saints' reserves and a few of those who were involved in the first-team game earlier, including scorers Phillip Chandler and Paddy Seymour, cluster around Garnell as names are read out for the starting line-up. One player, who is not selected, grabs his bag and heads home.

Northiam is a small village to the north of Hastings. Its main claim to fame is a toss-up between being the place where Queen Elizabeth I left her slippers after taking a rest under a tree, and it being the village where four prime ministers once visited on the same day. On 12 May 1944, Winston Churchill, Mackenzie King (Canada), Jan Smuts (South Africa), and Godfrey Huggins (Southern Rhodesia) all paid a visit to troops who were readying themselves for D-Day.[43]

It's 1-0 to the visitors almost immediately, then 2-0. Defender Carl Bamford is doing his best to hold things together at the back, but it's not looking positive. But then someone clatters Seymour — playing his second match in the same day — and it clearly inspires him because he curls in a beauty of a free kick and then finds another to put Saints back in the game. Unfortunately, he hobbles off with an injury at half-time and with him goes the reserves' chances. The visitors run out comfortable 5-2 winners, with two apiece for man of the match Bradley Najair and Rhys Warren (off the bench), plus one for Jan Bailey.

• *For Sovereign Saints Reserves' next match, see Game 102 on page 198.*

Game 93 and 94: Sunday 21 April (10.05am and 11.15am double header) at the Oval, Eastbourne
Men United East Sussex 1 BN3 United 1 (Sussex Sunday Junior Division 5)
Weather: some weak sun but it's chilly and a bit windy
MOM: Ryan Rankin.
and
Men United East Sussex 2 BN3 United 1 (Sussex Sunday Junior Division 5)
MOM: Sean Hardie

A book on local football wouldn't be complete without some proper Sunday morning football. And what better than a good old double header in the Sussex Sunday Football League Junior Division 5? Especially when the first game kicks off at just past ten o'clock. Lovely.

But more importantly, I am here because I've discovered a club founded to support a very admirable cause: Men United East Sussex are a club dedicated to raising awareness of men's mental health issues, with the players helping each other "via the beautiful game".[44]

The football club was born in January 2021, just as the nation was entering its third national Covid-19 lockdown within the space of the year.⁴⁵ The chairman of the club, Stephen Edwards, along with co-founder and friend Louie Welfare, recognised that many people were struggling with isolation and loneliness during that time and "wanted to offer and create an environment where men can do something they love in the company of others", he tells me. "With the lockdown restrictions, it was very hard to start a sports team as we were simply not allowed to meet one another in person, so our journey started with Zoom call meetings." Eventually, however, they were able to meet in person and start playing football, and today I am seeing the fruit of those early meetings. Zoom, it seems, did serve a useful purpose beyond those endless quizzes the rest of us went through.

This morning's opponents, BN3 (it's a postcode) United, are from Hove,⁴⁶ so I doubt if they are overjoyed by the early start in Eastbourne. However, the BN3 postcode is apparently the "most valuable in [the] country outside of London", according to *The Argus*⁴⁷ so they've probably all got nice, fast cars to get here quickly. Maybe they will get the beers in after the game? Kensington, Chelsea, BN3… who would have thought?

The Men United games are played at the Oval, Eastbourne United's ground. Early on this morning, the 'crowd' is sparse to say the least. Apart from myself, there is another man, who shouts "C'mon United" periodically, and seemingly without purpose, and the irrepressible Barry Winter — an Eastbourne United man through and through, but, as I've learnt over the past few months, one who loves football at all levels. It's chilly, but the weak sun shining through is making a bit of an effort to pretend it's warm. It certainly seems to have fooled a few people because the attendance more than trebles as the game goes on.

The team from the expensive postcode take the lead despite the best efforts of Men United's goalkeeper Lewis Cole, who has previously played futsal (football played on a hard court) at a high level, and is having a great game.

I meet a Zimbabwean guy, who asks me if he should pay to come in to watch. "*Ndiepi*" I offer as a greeting, mustering a bit of my rusty Shona from my days in Africa. He looks unimpressed. "So, I don't need to pay?" He's looking for a team to play for, but James Reynolds, the Men United captain, tells him that they are oversubscribed and have a waiting list already. Apparently, the club have enough players for a second team but the lack of volunteers — and inevitably funds — means they can't extend this initiative beyond the players who are currently involved. It's a pity for many reasons. Although the club have links with ManKind,[48] the Eastbourne-based support and listening group for men struggling with emotional and mental wellbeing, this is a group whose members also look out for each other. The first training session of each month starts without a ball; the players split up into small groups simply to talk. And now, thank goodness, it's without Zoom.

Reynolds is hobbling along the sidelines with a leg brace on, courtesy of a recent operation, but he's still getting involved as best he can, directing here and shouting there. It's not having the desired effect though, as BN3 are still 1-0 up courtesy of their Connor Amstead-Payne goal. But more worrying is the performance of a particularly skilful young player on the wing: Alfie Goble, who plays for Montpelier Villa in the Southern Combination Division 1. It's a few notches up from this level, so it doesn't augur well for the home side.

Double headers on Sunday can be a bit confusing for players because each game only lasts an hour. The first 30 minutes is just enough to clear the Saturday night hangover and then, just as players are warming to the task after the half-time orange slice, the referee blows up and tells them that they've got five minutes until the second game starts.

But Men United are certainly not afraid of a good battle and are challenging enthusiastically for everything, and with Rocky Tsang leading the robust challenges in midfield, they are forcing their way back into the game with some urgency. These 60-minute matches are not ones you ease into gradually. Tick-tock.

And it looks as if captain Harry Wood knows that time is running out, because with a few minutes remaining he launches a beauty of a long ball from the back into the path of Ryan Rankin. 1-1. Next game.

The players did fall and tumble,
Oh ref! They say to grumble,
They've played before,
Game two's in store,
Let's get ready to rumble

Soaring on the wings of poetry, I move over to the dugout side of the ground for the second game and chat to the BN3 manager, who's hobbling along the line in his socks with a flag in his hand after playing the first game. It's not easy running the line at the best of times. It certainly doesn't help when you've stiffened up but you've still got to direct affairs and make substitutions for your side while looking for offsides at the same time. Especially next to the opposition dugout. There are some 'disagreements', as is common in most Sunday morning matches, but the manager is certainly fair, flagging for a few attacks so that even his own players turn on him.

If you can keep your flag high when all about you
Are waving their arms and blaming it on you,
If you can keep your arm high when even your own boys doubt you
But remain fair for all their grumbling too,
Then — you'll be a linesman, my son!

My apologies for ruining Rudyard Kipling's famous poem. *If* only I could write like him. Young Goble is still being a menace along the left wing for the visitors and BN3 are 1-0 up for the second time in a morning, thanks to his goal. But I've already seen enough of this Eastbourne team in their striking purple kit to know that it won't be over till the final whistle blows. In the 60th minute.

And so it proves. Not content with settling for a late equaliser again, Men United time their comeback a bit better in this game. Sean Hardie puts them level in the 45th minute, and despite a red card for vice-captain David Larkin soon after that, they look the only likely winners. With just a couple of minutes left, Ryan Mansell tucks away a winning penalty after coming off the bench.

Glimpses of skill, comical tumbling after clumsy challenges, dramatic late comebacks, a sending-off, arguments, and a linesman in his socks making the substitutions. Then a few beers with the players and the post-match(es) analysis. It's Sunday football at its best. It's everything I've remembered. And more.

• *For Men United's season summary see page 218.*

Game 95: Monday 22 April (7.30pm) at the Saffrons, Eastbourne
Eastbourne Town U23 3 Sovereign Saints 1 (Eastbourne FA Challenge Cup SF)
Weather: still chilly but no wind
MOM: Matthew Myall. Some good hard running and disruptive challenging up front

The Challenge Cup is the jewel in the crown of the Eastbourne and District FA and was first contested in 1893–94. According to their records, Eastbourne Swifts (who went on to be one of the seven founder members of the East Sussex League in 1896) dominated for the first three years, followed by Eastbourne Hornets for two years, and then came three successive wins for Eastbourne Rovers from 1898–99.[49]

Thereafter, the list of winners up to the start of World War II reveals how historically many clubs were born from companies and organisations where most of the players would no doubt have worked: Post Office FC, Eastbourne Gas Company, Eastbourne Dairies, and Eastbourne Trade and Labour. If these organisations entered teams today, they would probably boast the designations Royal Mail Group Ltd (which a Czech billionaire is currently trying to buy), EDF Energy (owned by the French state), Supermarket United (the UK imported £3.6 billion of dairy products in 2023),[50] and the Eastbourne Labour Party (500 members).[51] Is it just me or did the names of old teams have a better ring to them?

Town U23 were knocked out of the Southern Combination U23 East Challenge Cup semi-final in their last outing, whereas Sovereign Saints are fresh off their uplifting 4-1 victory over Hurstpierpoint a couple of days ago, so Saints will be fancying their chances tonight.

But they almost don't even get an opportunity to topple their illustrious neighbours because there's an early injury, and for a while it looks as if the game might not happen at all. Town's physio, the referee, and some Saints officials cluster round the injured player as an ambulance is called. But after a considerable break, the player is able to hobble off, and the game resumes.

Paddy Seymour, who scored four goals on Saturday (two for the first team and two for the reserves) is starting tonight, and he's causing the Town side a few problems up the left. Saints hit the bar and look threatening, but the older head of Tom Cherryman (part of manager Shaun Lee's coaching staff) is looking pretty solid at the back for Town.

Matty Marsh finds the net after 20 minutes and then Ethan Howard smacks in a world-beater. 2-0 Town. Meanwhile Cameron Apted is working his trickery in midfield for Saints. But tonight, he has a worthy adversary in the trickery Olympics in the shape of Town's 'Gilly' (Anthony Gill). One prefers the classic turn, the other the feint and jink. "And that would be a solid nine from me!" (cue applause).

There's always a nagging doubt in every player's mind about letting things slip when their team are leading by two goals and cruising. It's comfortable but not comfortable enough. And so it proves tonight. Saints pull one back through Chester Havard — much to his own surprise judging by the look on his face.

But once you have pulled one back from being two down the psychology on the pitch changes. Now just a goal behind, the chasing team have real hope of a comeback and they will go hell for leather to draw level. That's when the gaps start to appear. And so it proves again. As Saints push hard for the equaliser, the young Town team score a third to finish it off as Sonny Walsh latches onto a through ball, nods it forward, and tucks it away. The Challenge Cup final awaits. It's 130 years of history right there.

- *For Eastbourne Town U23's season summary see page 213.*
- *For Sovereign Saints' season summary see page 219.*

Game 96: Tuesday 23 April (7.30pm) at the Beaconsfield, Hailsham
Welcroft Park Rangers 0 Jesters Town 1 (Eastbourne FA Vice-President's Cup SF)
Weather: dry with no wind and this winter's ever-lingering chill in the air
MOM: Sam Crabb. Quality in midfield

'Wellers', as everyone seems to call Chris Weller, is a busy man: he's chairman of both Hailsham Town, who were formed in 1885, and tonight's hosts Welcroft Park Rangers, whose history dates back only to 2018. Everyone knows him and he's constantly turning around to acknowledge shouts of "Wellers! Hello!" or return raised-hand greetings.

I first met Weller a couple of weeks ago when the Rangers reserves were playing Seaford Town U18 in the Eastbourne FA Junior Cup at the Saffrons. Everyone knew him there too.

The 'Wellers', as Rangers are nicknamed, romped to the Mid Sussex Division 4 (South) title last season, then added the Eastbourne FA Vice-President's Cup to complete a stellar season. It must have impressed the league officials, anyway, because they pushed the team up to Division 2 (South).

But despite the move, Rangers currently sit in third place and need just one win from their remaining two games to overhaul second-place Burgess Hill Rhinos, thanks to their superior goal difference. They have already secured the Sommerville Challenge Cup, the league cup for teams competing in divisions 2 and 3, after beating Portslade Athletic 2-1 in the final, with goals from Bill Coles and Cameron Offord. And tonight, with home advantage, they will be looking to add another cup final to their list of achievements.

Rangers share Hailsham Town's ground, so tonight is a home game for them. I'm with Chris, the Melbourne groundhopper I met recently, and we eventually work out that the access to the ground is through the Recreation Ground near the library. The pathway, if somehow you don't see the football ground, will take you past the back of the units on the Diplocks Way Industrial Estate before emerging among rows of houses. But it's unlikely that anyone could pass by the entrance.[52] It is a gem, with two turnstiles (not open tonight, so the entry is through the gate to the side), and is bright green, with the club's name painted in yellow. The Beaconsfield itself is an instantly likeable ground, mostly open and surrounded by trees, but with two small stands, one with a few seats to the right as you enter, the other a larger covered area for standing to the left. The large clubhouse is also to the left, behind the goal. According to the club's website, Hailsham were the first club in Sussex to install built-in floodlights, which were 'switched on' in January 1960[53] (the lights at Brighton & Hove Albion's Goldstone Ground went up a year later).[54]

Rangers' success is thanks in large part to having two prolific goalscorers: Bill Coles (28 last season and 19 so far this term) and Jamie Bundy (27 and 17). Coles is a classic no. 9: big, strong, and clearly a handful. He's causing a lot of trouble upfront tonight and, just before half-time, he has a shot cleared off the line.

The clubhouse is a good place to watch the game when it's cold — if you don't mind a bit of crisscross fencing in your view. The majority of the decent crowd of about a hundred seem happy to brave the weather, and after Coles's first-half performance they must be fancying a home win.

Jesters have played only once since their final home game at the start of the month — a 2-1 defeat to Northiam 75 in the Robertsbridge Junior Cup semi-final — and they are looking a bit rusty, the slick movements I've seen earlier in the season missing tonight. Their shooting is pretty wayward for a while, but slowly they warm to the task, and with about 20 minutes to go the Rangers keeper has to pull off two point-blank saves against what look to be 'must-score' chances. And in Sam Crabb, Jesters have some real quality in midfield — and he's showing it tonight. Fittingly, it is Crabb who delivers the only goal of the game to win it for Jesters, who celebrate victory for East Sussex against their Mid Sussex League neighbours.

On the way out, on the road at the back of the industrial units,

I pass a huge, white pick-up truck emblazoned with 'Jesters Sports & Music Bar' lit up by the streetlights. I've a feeling it will play host to some rowdy singing on the way back to the bar tonight.
• *For Jesters Town's season summary see page 218.*

Game 97: Friday 26 April (7.45pm) at the Pilot Field, Hastings
Parkfield 0 Catsfield 3 (East Sussex Challenge Cup — Divisions 3 and 4 — Final)
Weather: mostly dry with little wind but still cold
MOM: Craig Fullerton

The East Sussex Challenge Cup (Divisions 3 and 4) final is being played in Hastings, a town that is home to more than 90,000 people. Tourism is an important industry for the town, generating nearly £400 million a year and providing jobs for more than 7,000 people in the town.[55] Okay, the place might be a bit tatty around the edges, but aren't most British seaside towns in Britain these days? Granted, if you take your holidays in Cannes or St Barts, then Hastings' charms will probably pass you by. But I like it. It's got history by the bucketful, a busy town centre, a lovely old town, a castle, fresh fish, the sea, and, of course, the battle. Except the battle wasn't actually in Hastings but a few miles north-west of here (see game 69), so we won't dwell on that one. It also has friendly bus drivers, and it's thanks to a loud call from one of them that I know at which stop to get off for the Pilot Field, home of Hastings United, who are hosting tonight's final.

The ground is a gem. There is a huge stand, dating back to 1926, with seating for 800 fans.[56] To the southwest and alongside it is the tea hut and club shop in case you need a new Hastings United shirt or bobble hat. And opposite the main stand is a large area of grass banking. When this was closed down to spectators for health and safety reasons, it cut the capacity of the ground from 9,000 to less than half that number.

The site was at one time proposed as the location for Hastings Workhouse, but that idea fell through because local residents weren't too keen on having poor people live near them, so in 1920 football arrived instead. The Pilot Field was also used for rugby, cricket, cycling, and later speedway. Hastings Saxons speedway team used to attract crowds of 9,000 but their tenure was short-lived because — surprise, surprise — local residents complained about the noise. There is still evidence of the speedway track on the site today.[57]

The long clubhouse, with a bar and a function room, plus decking along the front, is behind the goal near the entrance on Elphinstone Road. It's a good place to wait before the game starts.

The young players from the girls' teams are bobbing around excitedly because tonight is their presentation evening, followed by karaoke. The karaoke DJ herds the spectators for the football final into the smaller bar area, admonishing those who've put their beers on top of his speakers, as the girls start to head in for their evening's entertainment. Applause starts to ring out and before long Cyndi Lauper's *Girls Just Want to Have Fun* booms loudly across the room.

If only the game was as much fun. It is stupidly cold for this time of year and Parkfield, who smashed Catsfield 7-1 in the league last month, have gone walkabout tonight. Maybe it's the big pitch at Hastings, maybe it's the big crowd, maybe they've put too much effort into winning the league. But whatever the reason, they just don't get going. And you know things are not going well when Parkfield's prolific scorer, James Graham (33 goals this season) can't find the net.

After 20 minutes, Parkfield's captain Craig Fullerton slices a cross into his own net and Catsfield have the lead. On the hour, a corner is headed onto the bar and the rebound is tucked in. 2-0. Add one more and last month's 7-1 win has become a distant memory and so has the dream of an East Sussex league and cup double for the Eastbourne side.

But if we ignore tonight's performance, Parkfield are a team on the up and up. After getting promoted from East Sussex Division 4 in 2021–22, and securing a decent fifth-place finish in Division 3 the following season, they have romped to the title this time around. They are also in two finals: tonight's fixture, followed by the Eastbourne FA Junior Cup at the Saffrons next week.

When manager Brian Chambers formed the Eastbourne club in 1970, he brought together a group of friends who couldn't get games elsewhere and wanted a club where they could play regularly. But with just a few days remaining for the registration papers to be submitted to the league, they were still without a name. The answer appeared, as with the history of many football clubs, in a pub. Chambers met some of the players in the Parkfield in Hampden Park, but it was not the pub that supplied the chosen designation, but the road it was in. With discussions going nowhere, one of the friends looked out of the window and saw 'Parkfield Avenue' on a sign. The name was nailed. The pub has now gone but the club lives on.

In the early years, Parkfield were in the Eastbourne & Hastings League, but by the 1990s they were playing the Eastbourne and District League, before joining the East Sussex League where they play today.

Mostly, they have bobbed around in the lower leagues, but they have enjoyed a few promotions in their time, once reaching the top tier of the Eastbourne & Hastings League — home of one Langney Sports (now Eastbourne Borough) for many seasons. In the late 1970s, Parkfield actually met the Sports in the final of the Eastbourne FA Challenge Cup at the Oval. They won the Bill Hide Memorial Cup in 1994–95, and also lifted the third Eastbourne FA Vice-President's Cup in 2014–15, beating Victoria Baptists at Shinewater Lane — now the home of Sovereign Saints, but at that time the ground used by Langney Wanderers. The next year they were crowned champions of East Sussex Division 5.

Last season, Parkfield lifted the Eastbourne FA Junior Cup, with one of their players, Ethan Gabriel, winning the Bill Hide Memorial Trophy for man of the match. But tonight is not the night for the club that was formed by Chambers all those years ago.

• *For Parkfield's next match, see Game 100 on page 195.*

Game 98: Saturday 27 April (3pm) at the Oval, Eastbourne
Eastbourne United 2 Lingfield 0 (Southern Combination Premier)
Weather: rainy and a bit of wind
MOM: Kobe Agbude. A quality defensive performance from the young man

If you are looking for an archetypal meaningless end-of-season fixture, then this is it. Win, lose, or draw, Lingfield will finish 11th. And barring the unlikely scenario of United losing, and Haywards Heath winning with a 16-goal swing, United will be sixth. It matters not to the 135 who have turned up to watch, however, most of whom are clustered in the covered standing area to the side of the halfway line. Rain. As usual this season.

It's the ideal match to give a few youngsters a bit of game time. Kobe Agbude, Baran Kartal, and Luke Leppard have all made a few appearances this season, but mostly off the bench. This afternoon, they all start. Alfie Gander, Mardy Ovenden, and T'yano Wilson await their chance in the dugout along with Mathew Rodriguez-Barbosa, a stalwart defender of more than 40 games this season.

The United youngsters are impressive and will be aiming high. They certainly have a reputation to live up to because the club has had some top players over the years.

Bob Humphries joined United in 1955 after a spell with Tottenham Hotspur as an amateur and the next year he signed for Sheffield United. Although he never made an appearance for the Yorkshire club, he went on to play more than 50 games for Brighton and Millwall. He later returned to the Sussex coast to play for Hastings United and Bognor Regis Town.

Pat Terry, who was part of United's youth set-up, was another notable player in the 1950s. He represented nine Football League clubs, making nearly 500 appearances in total, including 108 games for Gillingham, 99 for Reading, and 97 for Millwall.

Barry Salvage also represented Millwall, making 57 appearances in two spells for the club, as well as playing for Fulham, QPR, and Brentford. In addition, he enjoyed a spell in the USA with St Louis in 1977, a year when the North American Soccer League (NASL) was packed with stars like Pelé, Franz Beckenbauer, and

Carlos Alberto. Salvage was with United as a teenager from 1965 to 1967.

Another player to ply his trade in the NASL in 1977 was striker Tony Funnell, who made ten appearances for the Canadian side Vancouver Whitecaps. Born in Eastbourne, he made his name with United in the Athenian League before being sold to Southampton for £250 and went on to a distinguished career in the professional game with Gillingham, Brentford, and Bournemouth, as well as his loan spell in Canada.

And the early 2000s saw the arrival of Danish defender Henrik Jensen[58] at the Oval, a young man still in the early stages of his career who was here studying. He moved on from Eastbourne to play for Vejle Boldklub, one of the most successful clubs in Denmark with five league titles and six cup wins, before joining Charleston Battery in the USA and then returning to his home town of Gauerslund to take up a coaching position.[59]

Today is officially the last match on grass at the Oval. Well, sort of. Men United, the Sunday team that use the ground for their home games, have a match here tomorrow morning. There are a few of them here watching today, in fact. But to the United fans it's like a farewell to the stuff that grows and hello to 3G. Next season is a new beginning.

"It's all about passion and creating something special," promises club chairman Matt Thompson who, along with manager Anthony Storey, and Tom Parker of the well-known building suppliers, is behind the creation of the Oval Arena company that will run the FIFA-grade 3G venue.

Improvements at Eastbourne United's ground in the summer will also include refurbishment of the players' lounge, the officials' room, and the exteriors of the buildings, as well as work on the car park. The investment at the Oval is upwards of £1 million and, it is hoped, will attract more local clubs and community teams to use the facilities, as well as boost the fortunes of Eastbourne United. The club will finish sixth in the league this year, just outside the play-offs, but in 2021–22 and 2022–23, before the play-offs had been introduced, they finished fifth and fourth respectively. Could this investment be the final nudge towards Isthmian League football? In his playing days, Thompson turned out for Langney Sports (now Eastbourne Borough) and he will be hoping that United can replicate some of the success that his previous club enjoyed.

Alfie Gander comes on to a few cheers from the people who have already seen him play in United's younger sides. "He looks about 12," comes a comment from the back of the stand. Nobody repeats it once they've seen his skill and strength on the ball.

The youngsters, particularly Kobe Agbude, have impressed against a Lingfield side who also have a fairly youthful appearance. But there's no danger of anyone dropping their guard, even if this is a 'meaningless' fixture, because the old heads are keeping things steady, not least the determined, and hard-tackling Sam Cooper. A first-half goal from Mason Creese, and one after the break from Charlie Ball, seal the victory.

The regular league season is over. United finish sixth and Lingfield 11th. Meaningless? Far from it.

• *For Eastbourne United's season summary see page 215.*

Game 99: Tuesday 30 April (7.45pm) at the Saffrons, Eastbourne
Eastbourne Town 2 Hassocks 0 (Southern Combination Premier Play-off SF)
Weather: dry with no wind
MOM: James Hull. A constant thorn in the visitors' defence and provides some clinical finishing

It's crunch time at the top of the Southern Combination Premier, with the play-offs locked and loaded. Town have secured a home tie after winning their final league match at Crawley Down. Hassocks, meanwhile, have snuck into fifth place with a stunning 5-1 home win at Newhaven, despite playing with ten men for most of the match, a victory watched by a bumper crowd of 673.[60]

On the day of the play-off, Town repost a message from Oldham Athletic striker James Norwood[61] encouraging fans to get down to the Saffrons and support their team. Norwood, who has played for Exeter City, Tranmere Rovers, Ipswich Town, and Barnsley, was born in Eastbourne and attended St Bede's School in Hailsham. After a youth career with both Brighton and Crystal Palace, he played for Town senior team, scoring eight goals in 16 games for them in 2008–09.[62] That same season he was selected to play for England Schools, making his debut against Wales on 6 March[63] and going on to claim three more caps that season, with his final game at Wembley against France — the last that England Schools would play at the famous stadium. Norwood scored to put England 2-1 up,[64] and although they eventually lost 4-2, the last Wembley goal to be scored by England in a schoolboy international still belongs to an Eastbourne Town player.[65] He later went on to represent England C team seven times.[66] Despite his impressive CV, however, the profile on his X account simply reads: 'Eastbourne Town's U9's Players' Player of the Year.'[67]

And here's something else you probably didn't know: fans can actually praise a referee. Yes, I know, I didn't think it was possible either. Tonight's referee, Tazlim Alli, is quite exceptional — so much so that spectators are actually commenting on it. If he puts a foot, whistle, or pointed finger wrong, I certainly don't spot it. Shove this guy up a few notches instantly, please.

Meanwhile, something strange is happening at the Saffrons tonight. There is singing. The 'Eastbourne is wonderful, it's full of old people and seagulls' song is beating out across the terraces. The thud of a drum even makes an appearance. It feels odd for this usually sedate ground to be so alive. But something is stirring. The Town fans among the 604 supporters here tonight[68] ("actually 684 if you count the freebies", I'm told by one of the Town people) believe this is their moment.

And their optimism is rewarded. While the clinical James Hull is popping them in at one end — Town are 2-0 up at half-time — Toby Bull, the stand-in goalkeeper for the injured Chris Winterton, is keeping them out at the other. To be fair, a team couldn't wish for a better replacement between the posts than this superb young keeper who was with Brighton U23, has made several National League South appearances,[69] and represented Ireland U19.[70]

And it's Bull who has the final say in the affair, because in the second half Hassocks are awarded a penalty. He saves it, of course. A dab hand on social media with his goalkeeping tips, it'll be no surprise to see a special on how to save spot kicks @TobyGKBull on YouTube soon.

The Hassocks fans start drifting away and the singers are emboldened to try something new.

You're going home,
You're going home,
Hassocks fans, you're going home
(To the tune of *Three Lions* by David Baddiel and Frank Skinner)

One or two of them even raise a cheeky hand to wave the visiting fans goodbye. The Saffrons. Genteel? Not tonight apparently.
• *For Eastbourne Town's next match, see Game 103 on page 200.*

Game 100: Wednesday 1 May (7.30pm) at the Saffrons, Eastbourne
Eastbourne Town U18 8 Parkfield 0 (Eastbourne FA Junior Cup Final)
Weather: mild and dry
MOM: Sonny Walsh. Shows his class and bags a first-half hat-trick

Parkfield never got out of second gear in their final at Hastings a few days ago (see game 97). Tonight, they are stuck in reverse.

I'm not sure what the description is when a player 'skilfully' strikes a ball and it flies in off the other foot. Maybe the player who scores knows, because that is how the goal goes in. A few minutes later Sonny Walsh scores from the penalty spot. Then, on 18 minutes, Walsh smacks home again from an angle. Three minutes later there's another one. Then another. Parkfield are understandably shell shocked. I'm standing on the steps outside the clubhouse when Neil and Harry come out from behind the Saffrons' bar and poke their heads around the door.

"Anything happening?" they ask.

"Don't worry, you haven't missed much," I reply, shell shocked myself.

The rout continues in the second half, albeit at a less rapid pace. For the record it finishes 8-0, thanks to goals from Walsh with a hat-trick (he picks up the man of the match award), Joe Hill, Arthur Karapetyan, Frazer Price, Phoenix Ward-Gibbs, and Noah Titterton-Manos.

To his credit, the Parkfield goalkeeper, Marley Jesson — who is playing because regular goalkeeper, Liam Rowley, picked up an injury in the East Sussex League Challenge Cup final against Catsfield at Hastings — pats the trophy on the way up to collect his runners-up medal from Eastbourne FA Chairman Dave Rogers, and with resigned good humour and a smile, says: "That was ours last year."

• *For Eastbourne Town U18's season summary see page 213.*
• *For Parkfield's season summary see page 219.*

Game 101: Thursday 2 May (6.30pm) at the Little Common Recreation Ground
Little Common U23 2 Eastbourne United U23 2 (Southern Combination U23 East)
Weather: mild
MOM: Charlie Yeates. Dangerous wide man throughout and provides some excellent delivery

I like Little Common. It's a nice village and a friendly club. It was way back in August when I first visited. Tonight, it's a bit colder. Actually, it's a lot colder. By the entrance gate, as I am watching United attack the goal I'm standing behind, I chat to a man who tells me he's lived here for two years and thought it was about time he checked out his local club. He's a football man too, and reels off a list of pretty decent clubs (Dulwich Hamlet etc) he represented in his day. What's taken him so long? Little Common might be nice, but I'm not sure there is two years' worth of things to keep you occupied before you visit the football club.

A younger and, it has to be said, much more athletic man joins us for a chat as the Common keeper makes a good save. It turns out it's the club's senior team player-manager, Russell Eldridge. Not content with playing and managing since 2011, he is on duty to open the clubhouse when someone needs to use the toilet or order a drink from the bar. I'm half expecting him to put out some cones and do some shuttle runs if there is a spare moment between his other jobs. As a former Isthmian League player, he is ambitious to help progress the club as far as he can, but he is also acutely aware that finances and regulations play an increasingly important role in football. However, Little Common will have 22 teams of various ages next season, so they are obviously doing something right.

But tonight is about U23 football, and more specifically Eastbourne United U23. The whites from the Oval have already won the league after receiving three points in a walkover win last week, when their neighbours Eastbourne Town couldn't raise a team. So, it's effectively a crowning of the champions at the stroke of 6.30pm. Why so early? Well, according to the restrictions imposed when the floodlights were erected in 2011, they can only be used from September till the end of April to limit the light pollution for the neighbours. After all, if you buy a house next to a recreation ground, it's a bit of a nuisance if they actually play sport on it.

Matt Thompson, the United chairman, is here to cheer on his U23 side, and he greets the league official who's turned up with the trophy and the medals for the league winners. The official heads off to get a cup of something hot and I take a peek at the medals, which are stuffed in a fabric shopping bag for life and perched on a bar stool.

Little Common U23 are near the bottom of the league, having won only ten points all season, but they don't seem too keen on releasing the party poppers for the champions-elect from down the road just yet.

Charlie Yeates is supplying some great dead-ball deliveries and is driving United on with a great performance on the right. The visitors grab two goals — a fierce whipping shot in the 52nd minuted from Ollie Hull that leaves the keeper floundering, and another from Max Thompson in the second half. But United can't shake off Common, who strike with goals of their own from Archie Warmington and Frankie Manning. It's a draw, but it doesn't really matter to the United lads, who jump around with the cup in the half-light in front of a row of iPhones flashing away merrily. Floodlights anyone?

In the fading light
Strode the team in all white
In a Common of trees
They chant Champi-ow-nies
It's their league, tonight is their night

• *For Eastbourne United U23's season summary see page 216.*

Game 102: Saturday 4 May (2pm) at Shinewater Lane, Eastbourne
Sovereign Saints Reserves 0 Bexhill Rovers 9 (East Sussex Division 2)
Weather: sunny
MOM: Jay Tomlin. A hat-trick from Bexhill's prolific striker

Despite going a goal down early on to an Iain Steuart-Pownall goal, Saints look to be holding their own against the league leaders for a fair chunk of the first half. Then one of the Saints players heads the ball out of play needlessly after being wound up, Rovers score another by Bobby Bowles from the resulting throw-in, and Saints fall apart.

From there on, the goals fly past the Saints goalkeeper at regular intervals, with a hat-trick for Jay Tomlin, who averages more than a goal a game for Rovers this season, two for David Ammoun, and a goal each for Shane Friend and Jack Hobden. The Saints keeper has no protection at times, although young substitute Anderson Eze does put in a determined shift at the back when he comes on. When you are leaking goals it's difficult to get anything from a game at the best of times, but when your joint top scorers only have three goals apiece — Alfie Morris and Luke Maglennon — it's a near impossibility.

A 9-0 defeat for Saints Reserves. It's a disappointing and frustrating end to the season for them. They were moved up a division last season despite finishing fourth, some 14 points adrift of the league leaders. They end this season with just three wins and a goal difference of -50, so it probably wasn't the wisest decision by the league officials when they reorganised the divisions.

But today's comfortable victory for Bexhill Rovers means they secure the East Sussex Division 2 title and they are bouncing about celebrating.

"That was f-in embarrassing," mutters one of the Saints players, as he marches off to the clubhouse waving his arms theatrically. Clearly, it was someone else's fault. One or two others follow him in a huff of smoke, obviously not responsible either. The game had ended with a few handbags at dawn, more out of frustration and humiliation at the result than anything else. Nicholas Barden, the veteran striker who started on the bench, ensures the rest of the Saints team line up to applaud the visitors as they lift the trophy.

Later, at the entrance to the clubhouse, once things have cooled down, all the Saints players and officials shake the hands of the opposition players as they come in, waving their new silver cup, and singing badly.

"All a bit silly really," says Chris, the Melbourne groundhopper. "That's why I don't bring my sons. Too much swearing."

I smile.

"English park football. It's all in the heat of the moment. They will have a beer together now and laugh about it," I tell him.

At the end of every game at Shinewater Park, the flags, goalposts, even the seats from the dugout are brought into the fenced-off area around the clubhouse by the players to avoid the vandalism that plagues so many clubs at grassroots level. It's a shame it needs to happen, because the club are the trustees of the park and work to ensure its upkeep, so they obviously invest a lot of time in the area. The youngsters involved in the destruction would probably be welcomed by the club if they decided to swap smashing things needlessly for playing football. The clubhouse is neat and modern, and there are some of those wooden picnic tables of the pub garden variety on the grass outside (also in the fenced-off area) in case the sun should ever appear. The whole place has been upgraded recently following a £20,000 grant from the council. With the club approaching its 25th anniversary in a few years, it would be nice if it stayed this way.

Saints Reserves have been going for only six seasons — and two of those were disrupted by the lockdowns. They joined the East Sussex League in 2017–18 and were placed in Division 4. After a couple of seasons of consolidation,[71] followed by the lockdowns, they secured promotion with a second-place finish in 2021–22, as well as lifting the League Challenge Cup (Divisions 4 and 5). Last season's fourth-place finish in Division 3 and a place in the League Challenge Cup (Divisions 2 and 3) semi-final could have been a good foundation on which to build further. But from the look of the result today, it's pretty clear they were pushed up before they were ready.

• *For Sovereign Saints Reserves' season summary see page 220.*

Game 103: Sunday 5 May (3pm) at the Saffrons, Eastbourne
Eastbourne Town 2 Newhaven 0 (Southern Combination Premier Play-off Final)
Weather: apart from a few spits of rain, dry and mild
MOM: Tom Vickers. A masterclass from a man who looks determined to remind everyone exactly how good a player he is

I've never arrived at a non-league match more than an hour before kick-off. Certainly not at the Saffrons, where turning up 30 seconds prior to the start is usually plenty of time for settling in. When I arrive today, I am greeted by the hum of a food van's generator at the Meads Road end. Burgers and chips are always on offer at the club's Corner Flag cafe at the other end (for senior team games at least), but the new humming trailer has been brought in to meet the extra food demands from today's anticipated larger-than-usual turnout. The sleek, black trailer looks a bit like a spaceship and Mackenzie Whitehouse, the man who will be supplying

Town's X updates for the match, immediately recommends I try the wraps.

There are already about 150 people in the ground — about the size of the attendance at a regular match. A similar number of people are in the bar. Neil, Nicky, and Honey are already pulling pints and cracking open cans of Coke at a rate of knots, and judging by the steady stream of people heading in, it seems likely they'll be doing this non-stop for the next few hours.

The official attendance is 1,051,[72] although with the club and league officials who get in for free included, the actual crowd is more likely around 1,150. But as the teams kick off, you'd be forgiven for thinking that there were only ten people here. It's deathly silent, apart from the three o'clock chimes ringing out from the tower in the Town Hall, the building which provides a glorious backdrop to the ground.

"Is this a library?" asks Nigel, a regular at Eastbourne Borough matches, although I've seen him at United and Town as well as Priory Lane, so let's call him an Eastbourne football fan. In the hush, a small group of us start estimating the size of today's attendance, scanning the terraces as football fans do, as if we have some sort of sensory counting vision. I whisper my guess, as if frightened of breaking the incredible spell of nervousness that holds both sets of fans in its grip.

Richard Marsh, the club secretary, is walking around handing out team sheets. With Frankie Chappell out injured, Tom Vickers is playing in a withdrawn role at the back, while the ever-reliable Nathan Hover is patrolling the field for danger. Boom! At that moment Vickers steps forward and meets a goal kick from the Newhaven keeper with a crashing header. It's a statement of intent. The Newhaven player who challenged him for the ball staggers up, stunned that he never managed to get near it and wondering what's just hit him. I think he might have a sore back in the morning. When Vickers is on song he is one of the best players in the league, and Town need him to be at the top of his game today (spoiler alert: he is).

Newhaven have a couple of chances but Chris Winterton in the Town goal makes some good saves, ensuring that the tension of the deadlock remains at the break. With the queue snaking round outside the door at the Saffrons club, I head to the Bibendum pub for half-time victuals, where I meet two young men who appear to have had the same idea. Except that they were at the Brighton versus Aston Villa game today. "I watched till half-time, then they tried to rip me off by charging £7 for a beer, so I left," one of them tells me. He then hands over £5.50 for his Becks as if the 'huge' saving vindicates his decision to leave the Amex Stadium early.

"You lads should pop up to the Saffrons for the second half," I urge them, doing my best to boost the attendance by two.

Tesco, just outside the ground, is packed with people getting snacks; even with the extra food van, the queues for the football burgers are pretty long. When I get back for the second half, the Corner Flag cafe is shutting up shop. "They've run out of food," a young woman tells me. "She wants some chips," she adds, nodding down towards her little girl. "But I can't face making my way through that lot." She points to the packed open terraces along the bowls club side of the ground and under the Roger Addems stand. It's a pleasure to see.

Dave Shearing, the Town chairman, sartorially elegant as always in his Rupert-the-Bear trousers and long coat, is pacing up and down nervously as the clock ticks by. But the general nervousness in the ground is slowly lifted thanks to the efforts of Pier Pressure and the Beachy Head Ultras, groups of fans who have brought some colour to the ground in recent years. A drum beats away. Chants even.

Oh Eastbourne Town (is wonderful)
Boom! Boom!
Forza Eastbourne
Boom! Boom!

Nearby, a few of the older, regular fans stare at them as if they have never heard singing at a match before. Their usual relaxed afternoon out is disturbed. The hush is broken. A football match has broken out at last.

Don't be mistaken, don't be misled
Boom! Boom!
We are the bastards from Beachy Head!
Boom! Boom!

It looks to me as if only three or four people actually know the words to the songs, but gradually some of the more enthusiastic fans around them start shouting *Ole!* and clapping along. If it's going to penalties, then it will at least be with some atmosphere.

I've been chatting to Ollie Davies's dad, who tells me that this is the first home game he's been to watch (although he's been to a few away games). Apparently Davies thinks his dad brings him bad luck when he watches. Superstitions and football players, eh? But as the game drags on, I'm starting to think that Davies senior should leave after all. Davies junior, one of Town's most reliable players this season, has already got his feet in a tangle once, when a chance comes his way in the first half. Then, in the 78th minute, he does it again. Surely not. An absolute sitter. The no. 7 never normally misses chances like that. Dad, it really is time you left.

But he doesn't leave, and five minutes later the goal comes. Vickers, who's been taking every free kick and corner, as well as controlling the back line, is probing forward more now, and he swings in a cross. Davies heads it back across the goal and into the bottom corner of the net. Superstitions? I knew there was nothing in them all along. Inspired by the energy of the ultras and the rhythmic beat of the drum, the Saffrons erupts. Well, as much as a crowd with so many old people *can* erupt.

Two minutes later, substitute James Stone loops in another header, then charges off on one of those crazy, ecstatic celebration runs that is going nowhere in particular but is fuelled by pure adrenaline. Isthmian League? How do you pronounce that again?

Despite the cushion, however, Shearing is still looking nervous. And with good reason. Newhaven might appear defeated, but they are a quality side who were leading the league at the start of March.

But eventually the whistle is blown. Arms are raised, yellow and blue smoke fills the air as flares are released, and the players run and dive into the arms of the dancing, singing ultras. Anesu Sisimayi raises a flare and runs around as if he is holding the Olympic torch aloft. Jude McDonald's side have strung together a run of 17 unbeaten league games at just the right time.

Shearing shakes endless hands that are thrust towards him but looks stunned by the emotion of it all. I move out of the way of a man on a blue mobility scooter who wants to go home.

It's 3pm, the tower bells ring
Ding-ding, the play-off let's sing
But sounds of silence in the crowd of 1,000
Hush, hush it's nervous time

It's halfway, nothing to give
Here and there but prods and probes
The bar's a fluster
It's the midway time

Penalties loom
A goal, then two; who knew they would come?
Songs and flares
It is now Town's time

• *For Eastbourne Town's season summary see page 212.*

Spring

We've Got that Winning (and Losing) Feeling

Eastbourne Athletic
League: 3rd. **Sussex Junior Challenge Cup:** 2nd round. **Stratford Cup:** Semi-final. **Malins Cup:** 1st round
Most appearances: Oliver Albertella and Andy Ratcliffe (21 each)
Top goalscorers: Jake Lambert (7) and John Clarke (6)

It was a case of 'nearly but not quite' for Athletic after falling just short of promotion and a place in the Stratford Cup final. They finished third in the Mid Sussex Division 3 (South), albeit some eight points adrift of Cuckfield Rangers Development side, who were promoted in second place. Athletic walloped them 6-1 away from home in September. Ultimately, they'll be rueing dropped points against the bottom three sides — Nutley, Southwick, and Polegate Reserves.

Gray Hooper Holt LLP Mid Sussex Football League Division 3 (South)

		P	W	D	L	F	A	GD	Pts
1.	Ringmer AFC III	16	12	0	4	65	35	30	36
2.	Cuckfield Rangers Development	16	11	1	4	59	43	16	34
3.	**Eastbourne Athletic**	**16**	**8**	**2**	**6**	**39**	**33**	**6**	**26**
4.	Lancing United	16	6	1	9	36	44	-8	22*
5.	Peacehaven & Telscombe III	16	7	2	7	39	37	2	20*
6.	The View	16	6	3	7	41	39	2	18*
7.	Polegate Town Reserves	16	5	2	9	38	57	-19	17
8.	Southwick	16	3	7	6	28	45	-17	16
9.	Nutley	16	3	4	9	37	49	-12	13

* points adjusted

Eastbourne Borough

League: 19th. **FA Cup:** 2nd qualifying round. **FA Trophy:** 2nd round. **Sussex Transport Senior Cup:** Quarter-final
Most appearances: Decarrey Sheriff (46)
Top goalscorer: Fletcher Holman (10)

The great escape. There is no better way to describe Borough's season. An astonishing run at the end — six wins and four draws in their last 11 matches — kept the Sports in the National League South when it looked as if they were destined to return to the Isthmian League. Fletcher Holman was sold to Wolverhampton Wanderers and Leone Gravata was sold to York City.

Vanarama National League South

		P	W	D	L	F	A	GD	Pts
1.	Yeovil Town	46	29	8	9	81	45	36	95
2.	Chelmsford City	46	24	12	10	76	43	33	84
3.	Worthing	46	26	6	14	104	72	32	84
4.	Maidstone United	46	24	11	11	72	52	20	83
5.	Braintree Town	46	23	12	11	64	42	22	81
6.	Bath City	46	20	13	13	69	51	18	73
7.	Aveley	46	21	10	15	68	61	7	73
8.	Farnborough	46	20	12	14	76	67	9	72
9.	Hampton & Richmond	46	20	12	14	61	57	4	72
10.	Slough	46	18	14	14	81	69	12	68
11.	St Albans	46	20	8	18	77	67	10	68
12.	Chippenham Town	46	16	14	16	62	62	0	62
13.	Weston-Super-Mare	46	17	8	21	66	74	-8	59
14.	Tonbridge Angels	46	15	13	18	65	66	-1	58
15.	Weymouth	46	13	17	16	57	64	-7	56
16.	Truro City	46	15	10	21	58	67	-9	55
17.	Welling United	46	12	18	16	56	71	-15	54
18.	Torquay United	46	19	7	20	73	76	-3	53
19.	**Eastbourne Borough**	**46**	**14**	**10**	**22**	**53**	**74**	**-21**	**52**
20.	Hemel Hempstead	46	13	11	22	55	71	-16	50
21.	Dartford	46	12	10	24	56	75	-19	46
22.	Taunton	46	10	16	20	44	71	-27	46
23.	Havant and Waterlooville	46	10	7	29	52	92	-40	37
24.	Dover	46	4	15	27	40	77	-37	27

Eastbourne Borough U19 Academy

League: 8th
Most appearances: Charlie Collings and Stanley Ketchell (20 each)
Top goalscorer: Sonny Walsh (11)

Borough's Academy failed to impress in the league despite having a number of players with senior experience from other local clubs in their squad. They mostly whipped the lower-placed teams, including thrashing Whitstable Town 7-1, but they took some batterings as well, the worst being the 9-0 defeat at Tonbridge Angels, who finished fourth. They notably did the double over second-placed Ebbsfleet United to show what they can do when on form.

National League U19 Alliance Division B (bottom six)

		P	W	D	L	F	A	GD	Pts
7.	Dover Athletic	22	9	4	9	43	57	-14	31
8.	**Eastbourne Borough**	22	9	2	11	49	69	-20	29
9.	Margate	22	8	4	10	56	57	-1	28
10.	Maidstone United Reserves	22	5	0	17	40	97	-57	15
11.	Charlton Athletic Trust Kent	22	2	2	18	29	110	-81	8
12.	Whitstable Town	22	2	2	18	27	122	-95	8

Eastbourne Borough U18

League: 9th. **Sussex Dennis Probee Youth Cup:** 4th round. **Isthmian Youth League Cup:** 2nd round

It was a season to forget for Borough youngsters after finishing second bottom, only topping a hapless Horsham YMCA side. Their best wins were 8-1 at Mile Oak U18 Orange in the county cup and an impressive 5-1 at home against Whitehawk in the league.

Isthmian Youth Football League U18 South Division (bottom six)

		P	W	D	L	GD	Pts
5.	Whitehawk	18	7	2	9	-15	23
6.	Hastings United	18	7	1	10	-11	22
7.	Bognor Regis Town	17	6	4	7	4	22
8.	Three Bridges	18	6	4	8	-1	22
9.	**Eastbourne Borough**	18	3	4	11	-41	13
10.	Horsham YMCA	17	0	0	17	-67	0

Eastbourne Borough Women

League: 2nd. **Sussex Women's Challenge Trophy:** 1st round. **SCWGFL Challenge Cup:** Quarter-final.
Eastbourne FA Chairman's Cup: Final
Most appearances: Phoebe Cram and Erin Mai Todd (both 16)
Top goalscorers: Charlotte Gurr and Rebecca Simmons (both 14)

It was a season of two halves for Borough Women. They lost their opening four games, conceding 25 goals in the process, including a 7-1 defeat to local rivals, Eastbourne Town. The arrival of Billy Wood as manager after that defeat changed all that and they went on a great run in their remaining league games, including inflicting the only defeat on the all-conquering Saltdean DS, to finish runners-up.

Sussex County Women's and Girls' Football League Open Age Premier Division (top four)

		P	W	D	L	F	A	GD	Pts
1.	Saltdean United DS	14	13	0	1	52	10	42	39
2.	**Eastbourne Borough**	14	9	0	5	56	44	12	27
3.	Horsham	14	8	1	5	31	30	1	25
4.	Shoreham	14	8	0	6	48	34	14	24

Eastbourne Borough Women Development Squad

League: 3rd. **Sussex Women's Challenge Trophy:** Quarter-final. **SCWGFL Challenge Cup:** 2nd round.
Eastbourne FA Chairman's Cup: Quarter-final
Most appearances: Madalin Bowerman, Matilda Clowes, and Ruby Starkey (all 19)
Top goalscorers: Madison Norwood (17) and Abigail Tucker (14)

The Borough Development Squad had an impressive season, picking up 15 wins, including the scalp of title winners, Worthing Town. They were in pole position in mid-January after nine wins from ten games, but defeat in the return game against Worthing and too many draws against mid-table sides put paid to their own title hopes.

Sussex County Women's and Girls' Football League Open Age Division 1 (top four)

		P	W	D	L	F	A	GD	Pts
1.	Worthing Town	22	18	0	4	96	33	66	54
2.	East Preston	22	15	3	4	68	31	37	48
3.	**Eastbourne Borough DS**	22	15	3	4	77	50	27	48
4.	Brighton Seagals	22	14	1	7	75	43	32	43

Eastbourne Borough Women's Recreational Squad
League: 2nd

Borough's Recreational Squad certainly enjoyed themselves in the first season of the Sussex Flexi Ultra League, finishing second. They now move to a new home and will play their Friday night matches on the newly laid 3G surface at the Oval Arena. Going forward they will be the Eastbourne United Recreational Squad.

Sussex Women's Flex Ultra League (top five)

		P	W	D	L	Pts
1.	Burgess Hill Town Bobcats	10	8	2	0	26
2.	**Eastbourne Borough RS**	**10**	**6**	**1**	**3**	**19**
3.	Bexhill United Ladies Veterans	10	5	2	3	17
4.	Pevensey & Westham Junior	10	5	0	5	15
5.	Kingswood	10	4	1	5	13

Eastbourne Rangers
League: 2nd (promoted). **Sussex Junior Challenge Cup:** Quarter-final. **Edgar German Cup:** Semi-final
Most appearances: Martin Bell and Oscar Linzey (22 each)
Top goalscorers: Oscar Linzey (10) and Kyle Daines (9)

It was a return to intermediate football for Rangers, with their previous reserve side — who took on the mantle of being the club's top (and now, only) team after their first side folded — gaining promotion with some solid performances. Despite twice beating the champions, Reigate Priory Reserves, too many draws meant they lost out on the title, while a place in the Edgar German Cup final also slipped from their grasp after a disappointing game of missed chances against Crawley United from Division 2 (North).

Gray Hooper Holt LLP Mid Sussex Football League Division 1 (top five)

		P	W	D	L	F	A	GD	Pts
1.	Reigate Priory Reserves	18	12	1	5	49	29	20	37
2.	**Eastbourne Rangers**	**18**	**10**	**4**	**4**	**36**	**31**	**5**	**34**
3.	Crawley AFC	18	8	3	7	35	29	6	27
4.	Nutfield	18	8	1	9	39	45	-6	25
5.	Wivelsfield Green	18	7	3	8	41	37	4	24

Eastbourne Town

League: 2nd (promoted after winning the play-offs). **FA Cup:** Extra-preliminary round. **FA Vase:** 1st round.
Sussex Transport Senior Cup: 1st round. **Royal Ulster Rifles Charity Cup:** Semi-final.
Peter Bentley Challenge Cup: 2nd round
Most appearances: Harvey Greig (39), Ollie Davies (38), Nathan Hover (36), and Anesu Sismayi (35)
Top goalscorers: Ollie Davies (14) and James Hull (12)

After a ten-year absence, manager Jude McDonald led Town back to Isthmian League football after an astonishing end-of-season run that saw them pick up 16 wins and a draw in their last 17 league games (including the play-off matches). The most remarkable of those wins came in February, at the then league leaders, Newhaven, whom they beat 4-0 in a near-perfect display of quick passing and clinical finishing.

Southern Combination Football League Premier Division

	P	W	D	L	F	A	GD	Pts
1. Steyning Town Community	38	27	7	4	119	36	83	88
2. **Eastbourne Town**	38	26	4	8	71	31	40	82
3. Crowborough Athletic	38	25	6	7	81	36	45	81
4. Newhaven	38	23	10	5	99	55	44	79
5. Hassocks	38	24	6	8	87	42	45	78
6. Eastbourne United Association	38	20	12	6	67	40	27	72
7. Haywards Heath Town	38	23	6	9	90	45	45	69*
8. Peacehaven & Telscombe	38	18	7	13	62	42	20	61
9. Crawley Down Gatwick	38	19	3	16	86	63	23	60
10. Midhurst & Easebourne	38	17	8	13	75	74	1	59
11. Lingfield	38	13	8	17	57	65	-8	47
12. Little Common	38	14	4	20	63	82	-19	46
13. Pagham	38	11	11	16	59	64	-5	44
14. Horsham YMCA	38	11	9	18	48	69	-21	42
15. Shoreham	38	9	9	20	53	94	-41	36
16. Loxwood	38	7	9	22	46	87	-41	30
17. AFC Varndeanians	38	7	4	27	32	95	-63	25
18. Bexhill United	38	6	9	23	57	89	-32	24*
19. Saltdean United	38	6	5	27	44	94	-50	23
20. AFC Uckfield Town	38	3	5	30	34	127	-93	14

* points adjusted

Eastbourne Town U23

League: 5th. **Sussex U23 Challenge Cup:** Final. **Southern Combination U23 Challenge Cup:** Semi-final.
Eastbourne FA Challenge Cup: Final (to be played in the 2024–25 season)
Most appearances: Shay Hollobone (19), Mackenzie Stiles (18), and Mykee Worman (17)
Top goalscorers: Tyler Pearson (10), Leo Groombridge and Flynn Sweeting (both 6)

The high-intensity, attacking style of Town's U23 side certainly made them attractive to watch and provided matches with plenty of goals. Although they were inconsistent in the league, they thrived in the cup competitions, reaching two finals and one semi-final.

Southern Combination Football League U23 East (top five)

		P	W	D	L	F	A	GD	Pts
1.	Eastbourne United Association	16	11	4	1	39	23	16	37
2.	Peacehaven & Telscombe	16	11	2	3	45	26	19	35
3.	Saltdean United	16	9	3	4	41	29	12	30
4.	Newhaven	16	9	2	5	45	36	9	29
5.	**Eastbourne Town**	**16**	**8**	**0**	**8**	**39**	**31**	**8**	**24**

Eastbourne Town U18

League: 3rd. **FA Youth Cup:** 1st round. **Sussex Dennis Probee Youth Cup:** 2nd round.
Southern Combination Youth Challenge Cup: 2nd round. **Eastbourne FA Junior Cup:** Winners

Town U18 led the league for most of the season, but defeats to Little Common and Peacehaven & Telscombe meant they were overhauled by both of these sides and had to settle for third place. They lifted the Eastbourne FA Junior Cup for only the second time in the club's history after enjoying an emphatic 8-0 victory over Parkfield in the final.

Southern Combination Football League U18 East (top five)

		P	W	D	L	F	A	GD	Pts
1.	Little Common	14	11	2	1	44	21	23	35
2.	Peacehaven & Telscombe	14	10	2	2	54	13	41	32
3.	**Eastbourne Town**	**14**	**10**	**1**	**3**	**53**	**27**	**26**	**31**
4.	Eastbourne United Association	14	7	1	6	40	29	11	22
5.	Newhaven	14	7	1	6	42	35	7	22

Eastbourne Town Women

League: 6th. **Sussex Junior Challenge Trophy:** Final. **SCWGFL Challenge Cup:** Quarter-final
Most appearances: Hayley Chapman, Sarah Da Silva, Ali Das, and Lucia Law (all 13)
Top goalscorers: Geri Burt (13) and Danielle Parfitt (12)

It all started so well for Town after gaining promotion the previous season. They won four and drew one of their opening five games, banging in 32 goals in the process. They were top of the table towards the end of October, but apart from a couple of walkovers, they didn't win another match in the league, although they did have the consolation of reaching the county cup final.

Sussex County Women's and Girls' Football League Open Age Premier Division (bottom five)

		P	W	D	L	F	A	GD	Pts
4.	Shoreham	14	8	0	6	48	34	14	24
5.	Pagham	14	6	1	7	30	33	-3	19
6.	**Eastbourne Town**	**14**	**5**	**2**	**7**	**42**	**31**	**11**	**17**
7.	Horsham Sparrows	14	3	1	10	20	49	-29	10
8.	Whitehawk	14	1	1	12	10	58	-48	4

Eastbourne Town Women Development Squad

League: 12th. **SCWGFL Challenge Cup:** 1st Round
Most appearances: Lauren Hughes and Summer Mooney (both 14)
Top goalscorers: Lauren Hughes and Georgina Leonard (2 each)

It was backs-to-the-goal for the newly formed Town Development Squad, who lost 21 of their 22 league games (although five of those were walkovers). They picked up their only point of the season at home against Uckfield Town thanks to a goal from their substitute Georgina Leonard.

Sussex County Women's and Girls' Football League Open Age Division 1 (bottom five)

		P	W	D	L	F	A	GD	Pts
8.	Newhaven DS	22	8	1	13	45	54	-9	25
9.	Hawks	22	6	6	10	39	50	-11	24
10.	AFC Uckfield Town	22	6	2	14	35	41	-6	20
11.	Bognor Regis DS	22	4	1	17	19	86	-67	13
12.	**Eastbourne Town DS**	**22**	**0**	**1**	**21**	**8**	**93**	**-85**	**1**

Eastbourne United Association

League: 6th. **FA Cup:** 2nd qualifying round. **FA Vase:** 3rd round. **Sussex Transport Senior Cup:** Quarter-final.
Royal Ulster Rifles Charity Cup: Quarter-final. **Peter Bentley Challenge Cup:** 2nd round
Most appearances: Alfie Headland (36), James Broadbent (34), and Ed Ratcliffe (32)
Top goalscorers: Callum Barlow (24), Hayden Beaconsfield (8), and Max Thompson (7)

United started the season in rip-roaring style, losing just once in their first 15 matches and delighting their fans by reaching the FA Cup 2nd Qualifying Round (that was the match they lost). However, a lacklustre performance against Seaford Town in the Peter Bentley Cup led to a string of disappointing results, as points were dropped and they exited more cup competitions. With some great young talent, they remained entertaining to watch throughout, but just missed out on joining the play-off party.

Southern Combination Football League Premier Division

		P	W	D	L	F	A	GD	Pts
1.	Steyning Town Community	38	27	7	4	119	36	83	88
2.	Eastbourne Town	38	26	4	8	71	31	40	82
3.	Crowborough Athletic	38	25	6	7	81	36	45	81
4.	Newhaven	38	23	10	5	99	55	44	79
5.	Hassocks	38	24	6	8	87	42	45	78
6.	**Eastbourne United Association**	**38**	**20**	**12**	**6**	**67**	**40**	**27**	**72**
7.	Haywards Heath Town	38	23	6	9	90	45	45	69*
8.	Peacehaven & Telscombe	38	18	7	13	62	42	20	61
9.	Crawley Down Gatwick	38	19	3	16	86	63	23	60
10.	Midhurst & Easebourne	38	17	8	13	75	74	1	59
11.	Lingfield	38	13	8	17	57	65	-8	47
12.	Little Common	38	14	4	20	63	82	-19	46
13.	Pagham	38	11	11	16	59	64	-5	44
14.	Horsham YMCA	38	11	9	18	48	69	-21	42
15.	Shoreham	38	9	9	20	53	94	-41	36
16.	Loxwood	38	7	9	22	46	87	-41	30
17.	AFC Varndeanians	38	7	4	27	32	95	-63	25
18.	Bexhill United	38	6	9	23	57	89	-32	24*
19.	Saltdean United	38	6	5	27	44	94	-50	23
20.	AFC Uckfield Town	38	3	5	30	34	127	-93	14

* points adjusted

Eastbourne United Association Reserves

League: 2nd. **Sussex Intermediate Challenge Cup:** Quarter-final. **Mid Sussex Senior Charity Cup:** Final.
Eastbourne FA Challenge Cup: Final (to be played in the 2024–25 season)
Most appearances: Daniel Rogers (28), Zackary McEniry (27), and Charlie Yeates (25)
Top goalscorers: Paul Rogers and Daniel Tewksbury (both 13), and Nathan Crabb (11)

Despite topping the league by four points, United Reserves had to settle for the runners-up spot after they were deducted points for playing ineligible players. They also missed out on league cup silverware after losing 3-1 to Balcombe in the final. The reserves have now folded and their Eastbourne FA cup final will be played by United's U23 side.

Gray Hooper Holt LLP Mid Sussex Football League Premier Division (top five)

	P	W	D	L	F	A	GD	Pts
1. Ringmer AFC	26	17	3	6	74	37	37	54
2. Eastbourne United Association	26	18	4	4	61	27	34	52*
3. Reigate Priory	26	15	6	5	74	35	39	51
4. Oxted & District	26	15	5	6	64	42	22	50
5. Westfield	26	14	6	6	67	46	21	48

* points adjusted

Eastbourne United Association U23

League: Champions. **Sussex U23 Challenge Cup:** Winners. **Southern Combination U23 Challenge Cup:** Final.
Most appearances: Jordon Funnel (18), Jordan Pittam (17), Mackay Msezanes and Charlie Yeates (both 16)
Top goalscorers: Logan Copley (14), Jordan Pittman (6), and T'yano Wilson (5)

It was a masterclass of how to blend hard-working and skilful young players with quality overage players from manager Bailo Camara, as the United U23 side won the league and the county cup, and reached the final of the league cup.

Southern Combination Football League U23 East (top five)

	P	W	D	L	F	A	GD	Pts
1. Eastbourne United Association	16	11	4	1	39	23	16	37
2. Peacehaven & Telscombe	16	11	2	3	45	26	19	35
3. Saltdean United	16	9	3	4	41	29	12	30
4. Newhaven	16	9	2	5	45	36	9	29
5. Eastbourne Town	16	8	0	8	39	31	8	24

Eastbourne United Association U18

League: 4th. **FA Youth Cup:** 1st round. **Sussex Dennis Probee Youth Cup:** 3rd round.
Southern Combination Youth Challenge Cup: 1st round

In a solid, if unspectacular season, the United U18 side enjoyed some notable victories, including a 10-0 thrashing of Hangleton in the county cup and two 6-0 wins over Seaford Town. Their adventure in the FA Cup ended early at the hands of Jersey Bulls in a fixture played in Littlehampton.

Southern Combination Football League U18 East (top six)

		P	W	D	L	F	A	GD	Pts
1.	Little Common	14	11	2	1	44	21	23	35
2.	Peacehaven & Telscombe	14	10	2	2	54	13	41	32
3.	Eastbourne Town	14	10	1	3	53	27	26	31
4.	**Eastbourne United Association**	14	7	1	6	40	29	11	22
5.	Newhaven	14	7	1	6	42	35	7	22
6.	Bexhill United	14	4	2	8	12	44	-32	14

Eastbourne United Association Women

League: 8th. **Women's FA Cup:** 2nd Qualifying round. **L&SERWFL League Cup:** 2nd round.
L&SERWFL Trophy: 2nd round

Eastbourne United Women were certainly competitive in this decent league, with nine wins, but up against the top teams they struggled — especially Bromley, who beat them 8-0 and 6-0. A disappointing performance against Montpelier Villa saw them exit the Women's FA Cup early on. The United women's team has now folded.

London & South East Regional Women's Football League Division 1 (bottom five)

	P	W	D	L	GD	Pts
8. **Eastbourne United Association**	22	9	1	12	-17	28
9. Hastings United	22	9	1	12	-35	28
10. Bexhill United	22	6	4	12	-20	22
11. Steyning Town Community	22	5	3	14	-33	18
12. Hassocks	22	2	0	20	-40	3*

* points adjusted

Jesters Town

League: Champions (promoted). **Robertsbridge Charity Junior Cup:** Semi-final.
Eastbourne FA Vice-President's Cup: Final
Most appearances: Callum Baldwin and Harry Gutsell (both 15), Samuel Fielder and Travis Parks (both 14)
Top goalscorers: Travis Parks (12) and Musa Camara (9)

The lively Jesters Town ensured there were no slip ups in this small league of seven teams with some impressive performances, but they fell short in their important end-of-season cup fixtures after a long spell without action.

East Sussex Football League Division 1

		P	W	D	L	GD	Pts
1.	Jesters Town	12	10	0	2	31	30
2.	Ninfield	12	9	0	3	6	27
3.	Peche Hill	12	8	1	3	5	25
4.	Battle Town Reserves	12	3	1	8	-10	10
5.	Little Common Reserves	12	3	1	8	-13	10
6.	Herstmonceux	12	3	1	8	-14	10
7.	SC Pass Move Arrows	12	4	0	8	-5	9*

* points adjusted

Men United East Sussex

League: 4th. **SSFL Lower Invitation League Cup:** Final. **SSFL Aaron Clements Memorial Trophy:** 1st round.
SSFL Roy Terrington Challenge Trophy: 2nd Round
Most appearances: Stefan Rumary (30), Aidan Neale (29), John Jacobs (28), and Nathan Hartney (23)
Top goalscorers: Ryan Mansell (18), Mauro Lai (17), Ryan Rankin (12), and Sean Hardie (11)

In true Sunday morning football style, Men United dished out some whoopings and took a few beatings themselves. But they are an impressive side and move up to Division 4 after league reorganisation.

Sussex Sunday Football League Division 5 (top four)

		P	W	D	L	GD	Pts
1.	West Sussex Wanderers	22	18	2	2	56	54
2.	AFC Grinstead	22	15	4	3	42	49
3.	Worthing Brazilian Masters	22	14	4	4	27	46
4.	**Men United East Sussex**	22	14	3	5	28	45

Season Summaries

Parkfield

League: Champions (promoted). **ESFL Challenge Cup (Divisions 3/4):** Final.
Eastbourne FA Junior Cup: Final
Most appearances: Adam Smith (20), Craig Fullerton and James Graham (19)
Top goalscorers: James Graham (33) and Stuart Lewis (6)

It was certainly some way for manager Brian Chambers to celebrate his 54th season in charge of Parkfield: they were promoted as champions and reached the final of two cup competitions. And with a striker like James Graham, who grabbed an astonishing 33 goals, they've certainly got a chance of adding to that success.

East Sussex Football League Division 3 (top five)

		P	W	D	L	GD	Pts
1.	**Parkfield**	16	12	1	3	22	39*
2.	Bexhill AAC Reserves	16	9	4	3	34	31
3.	Castlefield	16	7	5	4	9	26
4.	Ticehurst	16	7	3	6	7	23*
5.	Westfield Thirds	16	6	4	6	0	22

*points adjusted

Sovereign Saints

League: 9th. **Mowatt Cup:** 2nd round. **Montgomery Cup:** 2nd round. **Eastbourne FA Challenge Cup:** Semi-final
Most appearances: Ben Murphy (17), Ciaran Hearne (16), and Wayne Green (15)
Top goalscorers: Stephen Jackson (9), Wayne Green (8), and Jack Griffin (5)

It was a disappointing season for Saints, but they'll be looking to draw on the experience of their campaign in the Championship — and notable triumphs such as the 4-1 win over Hurstpierpoint — as they take on another season in the same division.

Gray Hooper Holt LLP Mid Sussex Football League Championship (bottom five)

		P	W	D	L	F	A	GD	Pts
6.	Hurstpierpoint	18	6	3	9	32	53	-21	21
7.	Ringmer AFC Reserves	18	5	4	9	35	49	-14	19
8.	DCK	18	5	1	12	31	55	-24	16
9.	**Sovereign Saints**	18	5	0	13	30	48	-18	15
10.	West Hoathly	18	2	2	14	28	65	-37	8

Sovereign Saints Reserves

League: 9th. **ESFL Challenge Cup (Divisions 1/2):** 1st round. **Eastbourne FA Vice-President's Cup:** 1st round. **Eastbourne FA Junior Cup:** Semi-final

Most appearances: Luke Maglennon (16), Nicholas Barden, Jamie Price, and Joe Sambrook (all 13)

Top goalscorers: Luke Maglennon and Alfie Morris (both 3)

The Saints were pushed up to Division 2 despite finishing only fourth in Division 3 in 2022–23 and they found the going too tough at the higher grade. They picked up only three wins and amassed a goal difference they'd probably prefer not to look at, although they just missed out on a place in the final of the Eastbourne FA Junior Cup after losing on penalties in the semi-final.

East Sussex Football League Division 2

		P	W	D	L	GD	Pts
1.	Bexhill Rovers	18	13	3	2	42	42
2.	Rye Town Reserves	18	13	2	3	33	41
3.	Crowhurst Reserves	18	11	2	5	21	35
4.	Northiam 75	18	10	4	4	21	34
5.	Hooe	18	10	2	6	12	32
6.	Sedlescombe Rangers Reserves	18	8	0	10	1	24
7.	Victoria Baptists	18	5	5	8	-18	20
8.	Wadhurst United	18	4	3	11	-17	12*
9.	**Sovereign Saints Reserves**	**18**	**3**	**1**	**14**	**-50**	**9***
10.	Robertsbridge United	18	2	0	16	-44	5*

*points adjusted

Notes

Introduction
1. wikipedia.org/wiki/Meads Retrieved 12 September 2023.
2. Marples, Morris (1954). *A History of Football*, Secker and Warburg.
3. The match is not recognised by FIFA as a full international because the Scottish team was selected only from London-based players.

Summer
1. Triallist F for Aldershot Town was Lorient Tolaj. theshots.co.uk/match-report-eastbourne-borough/ Retrieved 4 June 2024. Tolaj, who has represented Switzerland at U17, U18, and U19 levels, was subsequently signed by Aldershot and scored 19 goals in 44 appearances in the 2023–24 season for them.
2. slattersportsconstruction.com/case-studies/eastbourne-borough-fc/ Retrieved 1 February 2024.
3. theshots.co.uk/match-report-eastbourne-borough/ Retrieved 11 February 2024.
4. breakingcharacter.com/youll-never-walk-alone/ and creativereview.co.uk/no-one-likes-us-we-dont-care/ and ltlf.co.uk/2012/07/anthemic-origins-football-songs/ Retrieved 18 June 2024.
5. wikipedia.org/wiki/Maidstone_United_F.C._(1897) Retrieved 18 June 2024.
6. wikipedia.org/wiki/Gretna_F.C. Retrieved 18 June 2024. Gretna 2008, formed from the ashes of Gretna FC, now play in the Scottish Lowland League.
7. Thanks to Adam Smith from the Hastings United media team.
8. wikipedia.org/wiki/Haywards_Heath_Town_F.C. Retrieved 18 June 2024.
9. Unless otherwise stated, all information and statistics on leagues and players in this book are from https://fulltime.thefa.com/home/index.html
10. @eastbourneunitedafc on X. Posted 29 July 2023.
11. sussexlive.co.uk/news/sussex-news/crowborough-hidden-celebrity-hotspotin-sussex-4881432 Retrieved 18 June 2024.
12. Id and dirkbogarde.co.uk/icon/house-and-home/ and wikipedia.org/wiki/Kim_Philby Retrieved 18 June 2024.
13. espncricinfo.com/cricket-grounds/the-saffrons-eastbourne-56966 Retrieved 7 July 2024.
14. wikipedia.org/wiki/The_Saffrons Retrieved 7 July 2024.
15. stats.acscricket.com/Records/First_Class/Overall/Batting/Double_Hundreds_by_Score.html Retrieved 7 July 2024.
16. cricbuzz.com/cricket-series/4863/womens-world-cup-1973/matches *Wisden* and cricketcountry.com/articles/archie-maclarens-amateurs-fell-warwick-armstrongs-mighty-australians-in-one-of-crickets-greatest-fairytales-181521/ Retrieved 7 July 2024.
17. rugbyworld.com/tournaments/rugby-world-cup/sin-bin-rugby-99236 Retrieved 18 June 2024.
18. idiomation.wordpress.com/2013/10/30/sin-bin/ Retrieved 18 June 2024.
19. wikipedia.org/wiki/Penalty_box and rugbyworld.com/tournaments/rugby-world-cup/sin-bin-rugby-99236 Retrieved 18 June 2024.
20. theguardian.com/football/2023/nov/28/sin-bins-football-trial-ifab-referees-abuse Retrieved 18 June 2024.

21. Another league by the name of the Kent County League is a feeder to the Southern Counties Eastern Football League.
22. eventspace.thefa.com/FA/event/the_fa_cup_the_fa_trophy_the_fa_vase_and_the_fa_youth_cup_competitions_season_2023-24_08022023#init Retrieved 18 June 2024.
23. the-emirates-fa-cup---prize-fund-1.pdf and mirror.co.uk/sport/football/saudi-pro-league-highest-wages-30582363 Retrieved 18 June 2024.
24. Jonathan Wilson (2008) *Inverting the Pyramid*, London, Orion Publishing Co.
25. There is a famous story about Brian Clough and dribbling, in which he asked his winger John Robertson to run down to the halfway line with the ball and then repeat the run without it. He asked him which he found easier. "Without the ball, of course," Robertson answered, to which Clough responded: "Well, learn to pass the ball then." Or words to that effect.
26. Jonathan Wilson (2008) *Inverting the Pyramid*, London, Orion Publishing Co. Wrexham used this formation in the Welsh Cup final in 1878 when they played Druids.
27. Jonathan Wilson (2008) *Inverting the Pyramid*, London, Orion Publishing Co. *Football Manager* (various editions), wikipedia.org/wiki/Formation_(association_football) and wikipedia.org/wiki/Football_Manager Retrieved 19 June 2024. For those not familiar with formations, the first number refers to the number of the defenders, the second the number of midfielders, and the third the number of attackers.
28. topendsports.com/events/worldcupsoccer/firsts.htm Some sources say the player sent off was Mario de las Casas. Retrieved 19 June 2024.
29. Cris Freddi (2002) *The Complete Book of the World Cup 2002*, London, HarperCollins Publishers.
30. wikipedia.org/wiki/Argentina%E2%80%93England_football_rivalry#1966_World_Cup Retrieved 21 June 2024.
31. bbc.co.uk/news/uk-england-23634720 Retrieved 21 June 2024.
32. cultkits.com/blogs/news/untold-stories-the-life-and-innovations-of-ken-aston Retrieved 21 June 2024.
33. statbunker.com/competitions/TopYellowCards?comp_id=317 and Chile's Carlos Caszely was shown a red card against Germany in the World Cup finals of 1974. wikipedia.org/wiki/List_of_FIFA_World_Cup_red_cards Retrieved 21 June 2024.
34. eastbournetown.com/an-interview-with-dave-shearing/ and wikipedia.org/wiki/Eastbourne_United_A.F.C. and sussexexpress.co.uk/sport/football/hailsham-town-0-brighton-3-shearing-so-proud-of-stringers-despite-cup-exit-1181723 and theargus.co.uk/sport/sportsnews/1929775.town-boss-is-not-being-forced-out/
35. eastbournetown.com/an-interview-with-dave-shearing/ Retrieved 6 July 2024.
36. Josh Gould came on a substitute for Littlehampton in their Isthmian League South East match v Beckenham on 13 August 2024. footballwebpages.co.uk/match/2023-2024/isthmian-football-league-south-east-division/littlehampton-town/beckenham-town/473302 Retrieved 21 June 2024.
37. dailymail.co.uk/sport/football/article-4135702/Ryman-s-20-year-sponsorship-deal-Isthmian-League-ends.html Retrieved 21 June 2024.
38. wikipedia.org/wiki/Sidemen Retrieved 6 July 2024.
39. thesun.co.uk/sport/21065997/buy-prime-hydration-farnham-town/ Retrieved 21 June 2024.
40. A number of people repeated this to me during the season, although I didn't contact every club in the Southern Combination to confirm it. After all, how would

you respond if someone rang you up and asked how much you pay your staff?

41. wikipedia.org/wiki/2009_UEFA_European_Under-21_Championship Retrieved 21 June 2024.

42. transfermarkt.co.uk/james-milner/profil/spieler/3333 Retrieved 6 July 2024.

43. fifa.com/fifaplus/en/articles/dino-zoff-the-enduring-legacy-of-italys-mr-dependable and wikipedia.org/wiki/Dino_Zoff

44. eloratings.net/Eastern_Samoa Retrieved 6 July 2024.

45. eastbournetownfc.clabautdfc.co.uk/about/ Retrieved 13 June 2024.

46. *Eastbourne Chronicle*, 13 November 1880, p5.

47. Id.

48. 'Gaol' was the preferred spelling of 'jail' in British English between 1730 and 1960. wiktionary.org/wiki/gaol

49. *Eastbourne Chronicle*, 13 November 1880.

50. Id.

51. Id.

52. In the early days of rugby, if a team touched the ball down between the posts, they didn't get any points but instead gained the right to have a 'try at goal'. Gradually some teams started making up their own scoring system and a touchdown was awarded a rouge (or minor point). To confuse matters more, Cheltenham College called all points 'rouges'. Luckily, this only lasted until 1886 when everyone accepted the scoring system that exists in rugby union today. More or less, anyway. rugbyfootballhistory.com/scoring.htm

53. *Eastbourne Chronicle*, 20 November 1880, p5

54. *Eastbourne Chronicle*, 4 December 1880.

55. In the first international match in 1872, England used a 1-1-8 formation while Scotland chose 2-2-6. Although there were a lot of strikers, the game ended 0-0, so which formation was the best certainly wasn't decided that day. wikipedia.org/wiki/Formation_(association_football) Retrieved 13 June 2024.

56. eastbournetownfc.clabautdfc.co.uk/about/ and lta.org.uk/fan-zone/international/rothesay-international-eastbourne/ Retrieved 13 June 2024.

57. eastbournetown.com/history/ Retrieved 13 June 2024.

58. imdb.com/title/tt0385002/ Retrieved 6 July 2024.

59. thenonleaguefootballpaper.com/latest-news/415278/common-return-to-home/ Retrieved 11 July 2021.

60. littlecommonfc.co.uk/ Retrieved 11 July 2024.

61. hastingsfootballhistory.co.uk/clubs/ Retrieved 11 July 2024.

62. littlecommonfc.co.uk/news/common-manager-celebrates-his-ten-year-anniversary Retrieved 21 May 2024.

63. littlecommonfc.co.uk/ClubContacts.aspx Retrieved 11 July 2024.

64. sussexexpress.co.uk/sport/football/couple-honoured-at-buckingham-palace-2321374 Retrieved 11 July 2024.

65. thenonleaguefootballpaper.com/latest-news/415278/common-return-to-home/ Retrieved 11 July 2024.

Autumn

1. fchd.info/eastbouu.htm Retrieved 17 June 2024.

2. eastbourneunitedafc.com/a/history-17344.html?page=2 Retrieved 17 June 2024.

3. wikipedia.org/wiki/Sussex_Senior_Challenge_Cup Retrieved 6 July 2024.

4. wikipedia.org/wiki/The_Saffrons Retrieved 7 July 2024.
5. sussexexpress.co.uk/news/end-of-an-era-as-eastbourne-magic-shop-to-disappear-forever-1128918 Retrieved 2 July 2024. Sabrina Cooper was murdered at her home in Eastbourne in 2022.
6. visiteastbourne.com/things-to-do/tommy-cooper-magician-memorial-p1235221 Retrieved 2 July 2024 and the framed information on Tommy Cooper displayed in the London & County pub, Eastbourne.
7. Eastbourne Borough programme 16 September 2023.
8. wikipedia.org/wiki/2023%E2%80%9324_FA_Youth_Cup Retrieved 7 July 2024.
9. wikipedia.org/wiki/FA_Youth_Cup_Finals_of_the_1990s Retrieved 7 July 2024.
10. pitchero.com/clubs/vcdathleticfc/a/a-history-of-vcd-athletic-fc-43847.html Retrieved 7 July 2024.
11. fchd.info/cups/favasesummary.htm Retrieved 7 July 2024.
12. s3-eu-west-1.amazonaws.com/files.pitchero.com%2Fclubs%2F28339%2FSeafordTownFC.pdf Retrieved 4 July 2024.
13. wikipedia.org/wiki/Seaford,_East_Sussex#Freedom_of_the_Town Retrieved 4 July 2024.
14. s3-eu-west-1.amazonaws.com/files.pitchero.com%2Fclubs%2F28339%2FSeafordTownFC.pdf Retrieved 4 July 2024.
15. budgetshippingcontainers.co.uk/info/40ft-hc-stadium-seating-container-for-fc-hartlepool/ Retrieved 26 July 2024 and @officialAPFC on X on 12 August 2024.
16. grayhooperholt.co.uk/ Retrieved 18 July 2024.
17. midsussexfl.co.uk/cms-data/depot/hipwig/MSFL-History.pdf Retrieved 18 July 2024.
18. midsussexfl.co.uk/cups/ Retrieved 18 July 2024.
19. 92club.co.uk/ Retrieved 8 July 2024.
20. guinnessworldrecords.com/world-records/fastest-time-to-visit-all-english-football-league-stadiums Retrieved 8 July 2024.
21. futbology.app/ Retrieved 8 July 2024.
22. thefa.com/competitions/the-womens-fa-cup/prize-fund Retrieved 4 July 2024.
23. wfahistory.wordpress.com/wfa-cup/ Retrieved 4 July 2024.
24. The FA banned their member clubs from using their grounds for women's matches. theguardian.com/football/2022/jun/13/how-the-fa-banned-womens-football-in-1921-and-tried-to-justify-it Retrieved 4 July 2024.
25. wikipedia.org/wiki/2023%E2%80%9324_Women%27s_FA_Cup#Final Retrieved 4 July 2024.
26. wikipedia.org/wiki/James_Tilley_(footballer) Retrieved 5 July 2024.
27. northcliffecollection.co.uk/famous-faces/actress-diana-dors-home-farmhouse-billinghurst-19145092.html Retrieved 5 July 2024.
28. greatbritishlife.co.uk/magazines/sussex/22608264.billingshurst-battler---edward-enfield/ Retrieved 5 July 2024.
29. billingshurstfc.co.uk/news/1002 Retrieved 5 July 2024.
30. wikipedia.org/wiki/Shoreham_F.C. Retrieved 8 July 2024.
31. shorehamfc.co.uk/clubinfo/About%20Us Retrieved 8 July 2024.
32. shorehamfc.co.uk/news/club-announcement--manager-appointed?id=433657 Retrieved 10 February 2024.
33. shorehamfc.co.uk/news/captain-is-back Retrieved 8 July 2024.
34. The attendance for Shoreham v Brighton on 10 September 2023 was 655.
35. eastbourneunitedafc.com/a/history-17344.html?page=2 Retrieved 1 July 2024.

Notes

36. Courtesy of the framed biographies in both the Cornfield Garage and the London & County pubs, both in Eastbourne. Thanks to Robert Renak, who researches local history for Wetherspoon pubs (*WetherspoonNews* Summer/Autumn 2024).
37. wikipedia.org/wiki/George_III Retrieved 28 July 2024.
38. 2024-Somerville-Cup-Final-Programme.pdf
39. 2024-Somerville-Cup-Final-Programme.pdf and information supplied by Richard Marsh at Eastbourne FA. All information on the Eastbourne FA in this book is courtesy of Marsh unless otherwise stated.
40. youtube.com/@PitchSidePod/videos As of 8 July 2024. Retrieved 8 July 2024.
41. statista.com/statistics/1450156/the-times-newspaper-subscribers/ Retrieved 8 July 2024.
42. thepersonpedia.com/en/person/theo-baker Retrieved 8 July 2024.
43. youtube.fandom.com/wiki/Theo_Baker#cite_note-8 Retrieved 26 May 2024.
44. thepersonpedia.com/en/person/theo-baker Retrieved 8 July 2024.
45. Subscribers and followers were as of 8 July 2024.
46. Information supplied by Eastbourne Rangers' club secretary Nick Stephenson.
47. ebfc.co.uk/2023/06/a-new-era-begins/ Retrieved 6 February 2024.
48. sussexexpress.co.uk/sport/football/lets-behave-like-a-football-league-club-league-two-spot-is-aim-for-new-eastbourne-borough-owner-4192935 Retrieved 6 February 2024.
49. bbc.co.uk/news/uk-england-sussex-67485713 Retrieved 6 February 2024.
50. theargus.co.uk/sport/sportsnews/2268902.boroughs-rise-is-the-stuff-of-dreams/ Retrieved 6 February 2024.
51. Id.
52. wikipedia.org/wiki/Eastbourne_Borough_F.C. Retrieved 5 July 2024.
53. ebfc.co.uk/club/history/ Retrieved 6 February 2024.
54. The National League was then known as the Conference Premier.
55. thefa.com/-/media/files/pdf/fa-competitions-archive/fa-competitions-1415/9386-fa-state-of-the-game-final-apr15.ashx?la=en Retrieved 6 February 2024.
56. wikipedia.org/wiki/Joe_Marler Retrieved 9 July 2021
57. Eastbourne beat East Grinstead 26-24 in the rugby on 18 November 2023.
58. investindover.co.uk/Key-Locations/Port-of-Dover.aspx Retrieved 5 February 2024.
59. Detailed towns data 2009–2022, from visitbritain.org/research-insights/inbound-visits-and-spend-trends-uk-town Retrieved 5 February 2024.
60. kentonline.co.uk/dover/news/new-marina-finally-opens-as-part-of-250m-docks-revival-286076/ Retrieved 5 February 2024.
61. wikipedia.org/wiki/Crabble_Athletic_Ground#cite_note-crabble-6 Retrieved 5 February 2024.
62. doverhistorian.com/2014/01/07/crabble-athletic-ground-and-county-cricket/ Retrieved 5 February 2024.
63. 90min.com/posts/first-ever-official-football-match Retrieved 5 February 2024.
64. fifamuseum.com/en/blog-stories/blog/scotland-v-england-150-years-of-international-football/ Retrieved 5 February 2024.
65. scottishsporthistory.com/england-v-scotland-1870.html Retrieved 5 February 2024.
66. wikipedia.org/wiki/1888%E2%80%9389_Football_League. Retrieved 5 February 2024.
67. football-stadiums.co.uk/articles/first-ever-football-matches/ Retrieved 5 February 2024.
68. powermag.com/national-grids-evolution-branching-out-from-deep-roots/ Retrieved 5 February 2024

69. footballsite.co.uk/History/Sunday%20Football.htm Retrieved 5 February 2024.
70. premierleague.com/history/origins Retrieved 5 February 2024.
71. wikipedia.org/wiki/Monday_Night_Football_(British_TV_programme) Retrieved 5 February 2024.
72. theguardian.com/media/2014/dec/12/premier-league-friday-live-football-matches-tv Retrieved 5 February 2024.
73. citypopulation.de/en/uk/southeastengland/admin/chichester/E04009914__loxwood/ Retrieved 10 July 2024.
74. mirror.co.uk/news/uk-news/tiny-village-declares-independence-united-16238251?int_source=amp_continue_reading&int_medium=amp&int_campaign=continue_reading_button#amp-readmore-target Retrieved 10 July 2024.
75. loxwoodfc.co.uk/our-history 10 July 2024.
76. peakd.com/hive-101690/@wolfgangsport/smallest-premier-league-clubs-in-history-2023-edition 10 July 2024.
77. citypopulation.de/en/uk/northwestengland/lancashire/E63000800__burnley/ 10 July 2024.
78. citypopulation.de/en/uk/southwestengland/gloucestershire/E63004612__nailsworth/ 10 July 2024.
79. refchat.co.uk/threads/leaving-the-vicinity-after-a-red-card-team-official.16948/ Retrieved 4 February 2024.
80. thefa.com/football-rules-governance/lawsandrules/laws/football-11-11/law-12---fouls-and-misconduct Retrieved 4 February 2024.
81. The Eastbourne United burger is hereby declared the winner of the Eastbourne Football Cheeseburger Challenge. See @FishChipsFooty on X for the scores.

Winter
1. wiktionary.org/wiki/isthmian Retrieved 4 February 2024.
2. ancientolympics.arts.kuleuven.be/eng/tb003en.html Retrieved 4 February 2024.
3. treatment-of-injuries-guidance.pdf from fa.com Retrieved 1 February 2024.
4. ebfc.co.uk/2023/12/report-the-sport-0-yeovil-town-1/ Retrieved 1 February 2024.
5. ytfc.net/match-report-eastbourne-borough-0-1-yeovil-town/ Retrieved 1 February 2024.
6. gloverscast.co.uk/match-report-eastbourne-borough-0-1-yeovil-town-1/ Retrieved 1 February 2024.
7. somersetlive.co.uk/news/history/remembering-yeovil-towns-famous-old-8284567. Retrieved 1 February 2024
8. Plymouth Argyle and Forest Green in the Football League. Yeovil Town in the National League South. Farsley Celtic and Blyth Spartans in the National League North.
9. @nonleaguecrowd on X. Retrieved 26 December 2023.
10. eu-football.info/_match.php?id=4406 Retrieved 12 June 2024.
11. famousfix.com/list/eastbourne-town-f-c-players and wikipedia.org/wiki/Category:Eastbourne_Town_F.C._players Retrieved 12 June 2024.
12 Id and famousfix.com/list/eastbourne-town-f-c-players.
13. wikipedia.org/wiki/Category:Eastbourne_Town_F.C._players Retrieved 12 June 2024.
14. ons.gov.uk/peoplepopulationandcommunity/housing/articles/townsandcitiescharacteristicsofbuiltupareasenglandandwales/census2021#built-up-areas Retrieved 2 July 2024.
15. thegeographist.com/uk-cities-population-1000/ Retrieved 2 July 2024.
16. eastbournelive.org.uk/6.html Retrieved 2 July 2024.
17. Id and the display board in the London & County pub.

Notes

18. groundhopuk.wordpress.com/
19. ebfc.co.uk/2023/10/borough-women-add-two/ Retrieved 31 January 2024.
20. Id.
21. thefa.com/womens-girls-football/heritage/kicking-down-barriers Retrieved 13 July 2024.
22. The Free Dictionary by Farlex. Meaning number 3. thefreedictionary.com/flexible Retrieved 29 July 2024.
23. *The FA Handbook 2017–18* p467. thefa.com/football-rules-governance/lawsandrules/fa-archive-handbooks Retrieved 13 July 2024.
24. thefa.com/football-rules-governance/lawsandrules/fa-handbook Retrieved 29 July 2024.
25. surreyfa.com/news/2018/nov/12/surrey-fa-launches-first-ever-female-flexible-league Retrieved 13 July 2024.
26. sussexfa.com/players/women/recreational-football
27. With thanks to Karen Parsons of the (now named) Eastbourne United Recreational Team for information used in this section.
28. skysports.com/football/brighton-vs-man-city/teams/4692 Retrieved 13 July 2024.
29. skysports.com/football/brighton-and-hove-albion-vs-leeds-united/teams/112699 Retrieved 3 February 2024.
30. espn.co.uk/football/match/_/gameId/671256/crystal-palace-brighton-hove-albion Retrieved 15 July 2024.
31. mybrightonandhove.org.uk/places/placesport/withdean-stadium/withdean-stadium-2. Retrieved 3 February 2024.
32. mybrightonandhove.org.uk/people/peopsport/steve-ovett/steve-ovett Retrieved 17 July 2024.
33. brightonandhovealbion.com/club/history/club-history/the-withdean-years. Retrieved 3 February 2024.
34. mybrightonandhove.org.uk/places/placesport/withdean-stadium/withdean-stadium-2. From *Brighton and Hove in Pictures* by Brighton and Hove City Council. Retrieved 3 February 2024.
35. theguardian.com/football/blog/2014/jun/11/world-cup-stunning-moments-johan-cruyff-turn-1974 Retrieved 17 July 2024.
36. wikipedia.org/wiki/Category:Eastbourne_Borough_F.C._players Retrieved 22 June 2024.
37. wikipedia.org/wiki/Hampden_Park_railway_station Retrieved 10 February 2024.
38. sporteastbourne.co.uk/eastbourne-sports-park/ Retrieved 10 February 2024.
39. @eastbourneatfc on X. Posted 17 February 2024.
40. citypopulation.de/en/uk/southeastengland/east_sussex/E63006607__newhaven/ Retrieved 17 February 2024.
41. web.archive.org/web/20061012222038/http://www.nomad-online.co.uk/html/newhaven.html Retrieved 17 July 2024.
42. wikipedia.org/wiki/Battle,_East_Sussex Retrieved 26 March 2024.
43. english-heritage.org.uk/visit/places/1066-battle-of-hastings-abbey-and-battlefield/history-and-stories/what-happened-battle-hastings/
44. saxonhistory.co.uk/Battle_of_Hastings_1066AD_Senlac.php Retrieved 22 July 2024.
45. *The History of the Norman Conquest* (published in six volumes 1869–79) and wikipedia.org/wiki/Edward_Augustus_Freeman Retrieved 22 July 2024.
46. wikipedia.org/wiki/Battle,_East_Sussex Retrieved 26 March 2024.

47. harveys.org.uk/pub/grenadier Retrieved 26 March 2024.
48. Thanks to Brian Shacklock, Sussex County FA Stadium Supervisor.
49. lancingfc.co.uk/club-information/facility/ Retrieved 28 March 2024.
50. wikipedia.org/wiki/Lancing_F.C. Retrieved 26 March 2024.
51. sussexfa.com/news/2021/jul/12/40-years-at-culver-road Retrieved 28 March 2024.
52. sussexfa.com/news/2024/mar/04/superb-saltdean-lift-womens-trophy Retrieved 17 July 2024.
53. sussexexpress.co.uk/sport/football/beard-sacked-by-eastbourne-borough-after-worthing-inflict-latest-defeat-4462494 Retrieved 5 July 2024.
54. wikipedia.org/wiki/Derby_County_F.C. Retrieved 5 July 2024.
55. espn.co.uk/football/story/_/id/37387878/sir-alex-ferguson-numbers Retrieved 22 June 2024.
56. eastbournetownfc.clabautdfc.co.uk/about/ Retrieved 24 March 2024.
57. athletic-club.eus/en/news/2024/03/19/eastbourne-town-fc-non-league-day-2024/ Retrieved 24 March 2024.
58. rsssf.org/tablesp/paris-tourn.html Retrieved 1 July 2024.
59. rsssf.org/tablesc/challenge-int-nord.html 1 July 2024.
60. nonleagueday.co.uk/basque-non-league-day/ Retrieved 24 March 2024.
61. theguardian.com/football/copa90/2016/jan/15/athletic-club-bilbao-loyalty-spain-liga-basque Retrieved 24 March 2024.
62. fabrikbrands.com/kappa-logo-history-symbol-meaning-and-evolution/ Retrieved 22 April 2024.
63. thefa.com/competitions/thefacup/prize-fund Retrieved 24 April 2024.
64. myfootballfacts.com/trivia/which-eight-clubs-outside-the-top-flight-won-fa-cup-finals-from-1888-89-onward/ Retrieved 24 April 2024.
65. thefa.com/competitions/thefacup/prize-fund Retrieved 24 April 2024.
66. midsussexfl.co.uk/cups/ Retrieved 18 July 2024.
67. midsussexfl.co.uk/cms-data/depot/hipwig/2023-24-Challenge-Cup-Rules.pdf Retrieved 24 April 2024.
68. shop.treasuryofbritishcomics.com/catalogue/RCA-R4001D Retrieved 24 April 2024.
69. comicvine.gamespot.com/hot-shot-hamish/4005-83434/ Retrieved 24 April 2024.
70. Thanks to Barrie Tomlinson, Editor of *Tiger* 1969–76.

Spring

1. eastbournetown.com/the-eastbourne-derby/ Retrieved 24 April 2024. And the Eastbourne Town v Eastbourne United programme 1 April 2024.
2. pitchero.com/clubs/ringmerfc/teams/6428/player/anthonystorey-1344009 Retrieved 29 April 2024
3. Id.
4. Eastbourne United programme 27 April 2024.
5. hassocksfc.net/2023/03/tuesday-night-take-two-with-eastbourne-united/ Retrieved 6 June 2024.
6. wikipedia.org/wiki/Ron_Greenwood Retrieved 6 June 2024.
7. theguardian.com/news/2006/feb/10/guardianobituaries.football Retrieved 6 June 2024.
8. whufc.com/news/articles/2021/november/11-november/remembering-ron-greenwood-west-ham-uniteds-legendary-cup Retrieved 6 June 2024.
9. wikipedia.org/wiki/George_Smith_(footballer,_born_1915) Retrieved 6 June 2024.
10. *Inside United*, Barry Winter (2021) PlanAhead.

Notes

11. wikipedia.org/wiki/Gordon_Jago and https://en.wikipedia.org/wiki/Tampa_Bay_Rowdies_(1975%E2%80%931993) Retrieved 6 June 2024.
12. *Inside United*, Barry Winter (2021) PlanAhead and wikipedia.org/wiki/Micky_French#citerefcroxfordlanewaterman2011 Retrieved 6 June 2024.
13. whufc.com/news/articles/2008/december/20-december/bill-lansdowne Retrieved 19 July 2024.
14. *Inside United*, Barry Winter (2021) PlanAhead.
15 Id.
16. The match was subsequently moved to 15 May and the opponents changed to Eastbourne Town when their semi-final defeat against East Grinstead was overturned and Town were awarded a 'walkover' due to an ineligible player being played by East Grinstead. United won the final on penalties.
17. eastbournetown.com/history/ and David Bauckham via wikipedia.org/wiki/The_Saffrons Retrieved 13 June 2024.
18. wikipedia.org/wiki/The_Saffrons Retrieved 13 June 2024.
19. sussexexpress.co.uk/sport/football/roger-addems-was-one-of-those-few-local-sports-legends-about-whom-nobody-would-have-a-bad-word-ken-mcewan-580363 Retrieved 13 June 2024.
20. eastbournetown.com/club-records/ Retrieved 13 June 2024.
21. Melton (Taffy) Jones was manager of Eastbourne Town from 14 May 1968 until 22 April 1972, and from 4 July 1978 until 23 May 1979. eastbournetownfc.clabautdfc.co.uk/management-history/ Retrieved 13 June 2024.
22. bexhillsussex.uk/directory/activities/football-clubs/listing/the-polegrove/ Retrieved 18 May 2024.
23. alamy.com/1980s-architecture-the-west-parade-flats-bexhill-tn39-by-lionel-heather-evenden-image355210916.html?imageid=D14E42EC-C4A7-4072-A8E1-5E035DF93F8D&p=1401910&pn=1&searchId=092e96ba1e2c76af1d68c7ddc5b359de&searchtype=0 Retrieved 18 May 2024.
24. bexhillmuseum.org.uk/access-centre/museum-exhibitions-displays/sporting-bexhill/bexhills-sporting-time-line/ Retrieved 18 May 2024.
25. bbc.co.uk/sport/africa/54510898 Retrieved 22 May 2024.
26. cray-wanderers.com/cray-wanderers-squad-update-yahya-bamba-joins-eastbourne-borough-on-dual-registration/ Retrieved 22 May 2024.
27. wikipedia.org/wiki/Pierce_Bird Retrieved 22 May 2024.
28. wikipedia.org/wiki/Moussa_Diarra_(footballer,_born_1990) Retrieved 22 May 2024.
29. chippenhamtown.com/match-report-eastbourne-borough-3-0-chippenham-town-national-league-south-saturday-13th-april-2024/ Retrieved 22 May 2024.
30. wikipedia.org/wiki/Ovenden%27s_Mill,_Polegate#cite_note-About-2 Retrieved 18 April 2024.
31. historicengland.org.uk/listing/the-list/list-entry/1043086 Retrieved 26 May 2024.
32. citypopulation.de/en/uk/southeastengland/admin/wealden/E04003860__polegate/ Retrieved 18 April 2024.
33. theweald.org/P2.asp?PId=Hm.Beerh Retrieved 18 April 2024.
34. wikipedia.org/wiki/Polegate Retrieved 30 June 2024.
35. polegatetowncouncil.gov.uk/about/ Retrieved 30 June 2024.
36. wikipedia.org/wiki/Beeching_cuts Retrieved 21 July 2024.
37. polegatecommunityassociation.org.uk/history/ Retrieved 30 June 2024.
38. sussexfa.com/news/2023/oct/26/100-year-club-award-polegate-town and

hastingsfootballhistory.co.uk/comps/eastsussex/1990s.html#1996 Retrieved 30 June 2024.

39. wikipedia.org/wiki/Polegate and https://www.sussexfa.com/news/2023/oct/26/100-year-club-award-polegate-town and hastingsfootballhistory.co.uk/comps/eastsussexcup/ Retrieved 21 July 2024.

40. domesdaybook.co.uk/sussex2.html#hurstpierpoint Retrieved 27 May 2024.

41. opendomesday.org/place/TQ2716/hurstpierpoint/ Retrieved 27 May 2024.

42. With thanks to Paul Garnell, chairman of Sovereign Saints, for the information supplied.

43. wikipedia.org/wiki/Northiam Retrieved 28 May 2024.

44. menunitedeastsussex.co.uk/ Retrieved 28 May 2024.

45. gds.blog.gov.uk/2022/07/25/2-years-of-covid-19-on-gov-uk/ Retrieved 28 May 2024.

46. wikipedia.org/wiki/BN_postcode_area Retrieved 30 May 2024.

47. theargus.co.uk/homes/property/news/19505448.hoves-bn3-postcode-valuable-country-outside-london/ Retrieved 29 May 2024.

48. mankindcic.co.uk/ Retrieved 17 June 2024. Not to be confused with Menkind, the gift and gadget retailer.

49. According to the Eastbourne Town website, a team by the name of Eastbourne Rovers merged with Eastbourne FC on 29 October 1880 to form what was to become Eastbourne Town. eastbournetownfc.clabautdfc.co.uk/about/ Retrieved 4 June 2024. The merger is also reported in the *Eastbourne Chronicle*, 13 November 1880, p5.

50. farmersguardian.com/news/4204583/opportunities-uk-dairy-exports Retrieved 30 May 2024.

51. eastbournelabour.org/ Retrieved 30 May 2024.

52. hailshamtownfc.org.uk/club.html Retrieved 3 June 2024.

53. Id.

54. sussexlive.co.uk/news/sussex-news/goldstone-ground-demolished-hove-football-5386416 Retrieved 3 June 2024.

55. ons.gov.uk/visualisations/censuspopulationchange/E07000062/ and ryenews.org.uk/opinions/letters/tourists-are-important Retrieved 22 July 2024.

56. wikipedia.org/wiki/The_Pilot_Field Retrieved 4 June 2024.

57. Id.

58. Not to be confused with the Henrik Jensen who was appointed assistant manager of Burnley in June 2024.

59. famousfix.com/list/eastbourne-united-f-c-players Retrieved 3 July 2024.

60. @NonLeagueCrowd on X. Posted 29 April 2024.

61. @jnorwood_10 on X. Posted 29 April 2024.

62. wikipedia.org/wiki/James_Norwood#Honours Retrieved 9 June 2024.

63. esfa.co.uk/news/?2009/03/06/132233/u18-carnegie-centenary-shield-england-3-0-wales Retrieved 9 June 2024.

64. esfa.co.uk/news/?2009/06/15/105853/fallenhero-trophy-england-2-4-france Retrieved 9 June 2024.

65. theguardian.com/football/2020/jul/02/the-strange-tale-of-the-england-schoolboys-football-team Retrieved 9 June 2024.

66. wikipedia.org/wiki/James_Norwood#Honours Retrieved 9 June 2024.

67. @jnorwood_10 on X. Posted 29 April 2024.

68. @eastbournetfc on X. Posted 30 April 2024.

Notes

69. transfermarkt.co.uk/toby-bull/profil/spieler/654166 Retrieved 9 June 2024.
70. worthingfc.com/2024/03/reds-land-toby-bull/ Retrieved 9 June 2024.
71. fchd.info/lghist/esuss2019.htm Retrieved 4 June 2024.
72. @eastbournetfc on X. Posted 6 May 2024.

Author

Daniel Ford has been a football writer for more than 30 years and has written about the game in England, Argentina, Bermuda, Hong Kong, and numerous countries in Europe and Africa. He covered the 2010 World Cup in South Africa and the CECAFA Cup, the oldest cup competition in Africa, in Zanzibar in 2002.

His first football book, *Football Grounds Then and Now* (Dial Press) was published in 1994. *A Fan's Guide to Football in Europe* (New Holland) was released in 2009 and has subsequently been translated and published in various countries, including China, Indonesia, Russia, Poland, Belgium, and the Netherlands. He has been involved in more than 100 books as author, editor, or publisher, many of them about football or other sports such as rugby, cricket, running, swimming, cycling, and triathlon.

He loves non-league football and supports Aldershot Town.

The author would like to thank everyone bought an advance copy of *Fish, Chips & Football*... Mark Shave, Tim Shave, Craig Gladwell, Ram Paudal, Garry Cole, Barry Winter, Matt Barnes, Adam Hathaway, Alan Thompsett, Alasdair Ross, Neil Crowley, David Connelly, Dunstan Harris, Dave Shearing, Chris Ludlow, Andrew Campbell, Susan Dow, Steve Sharman, Neal Weekes, Matthew Thompson, Josh Claxton, Daniel Jenkins, Emma Storey, Evan Warren, Carol Tipping, Keith Tipping, André Siebert, Dillon Siebert, Kelly Headland, Bill Norton, William Garfield, Eastbourne United Supporters, Daniel Eldridge, Mark Shuff, Peter Shuff, Paul Garnell, Sovereign Saints, Chris Dixon, Mark Barker, Paul Reynolds, Charlotte Reynolds, James Reynolds, Daniel Smith, Jan and Ken Weller.